⚓ ⚓ ⚓
TROUT
STRATEGIES

TROUT

ERNEST SCHWIEBERT

Illustrated by the author

STRATEGIES

E. P. DUTTON, INC.   NEW YORK

Trout Strategies, *first published by E. P. Dutton, Inc.*
in 1983 is drawn from Ernest Schwiebert's two-volume Trout, *published*
by E. P. Dutton, Inc. in 1978.

Copyright © 1978, 1983 by Ernest Schwiebert

Published in the United States by E. P. Dutton, Inc.,
2 Park Avenue, New York, N.Y. 10016

Library of Congress Catalog Card Number: 82-74471

ISBN: 0-525-48052-8

Published simultaneously in Canada by Clarke, Irwin & Company
Limited, Toronto and Vancouver

10 9 8 7 6 5 4 3 2 1

First Edition

CONTENTS

PREFACE

The twelve chapters in *Trout Strategies* are the material found in Book Six of my book, *Trout,* which was published in a two-volume set in 1978. The original work includes sixteen color plates, more than one thousand black-and-white drawings and diagrams, and 1,745 pages.

Trout Strategies is intended as the first in a series of paperbacks.

It is hoped that such paperbacks will make the scope of the two-volume *Trout* available to a wider fishing audience. Our purpose in publishing *Trout* in paperback volumes is quite simple: to make the work available to a wider audience.

Like the earlier work, the paperback *Trout Strategies* offers a dozen chapters on trout fishing techniques and tactics. Each chapter explores a basic fishing method through its history and evolution, and each describes our modern variations on older themes. There is extensive material on wet-fly fishing, dry-fly tactics, bucktails and streamers, nymphs, terrestrials, the magic of small streams, fishing in lakes and reservoirs, tailwater, fisheries below dams, high-altitude ponds, western fishing, studies in matching the hatch, and observations on ethics and philosophy astream.

I hope you enjoy these pages.

ERNEST SCHWIEBERT
Princeton, New Jersey
March, 1983

PUBLISHER'S NOTE

One thing Ernest Schwiebert neglected to mention in the preface is the monumental nature of his classic study, *Trout*. Not only does it consider trout fishing from the earliest times to the present, it covers every subject—from anatomy and physiology to rod selection and fly presentation—of interest to the fisherman. And, to the astonishment of most readers, each of the book's one thousand plus illustrations is the work of Mr. Schwiebert.

Lee Eisenberg wrote the following assessment of Ernest Schwiebert's work soon after the book's publication:

"*Trout* is a prodigious landmark in the literature of angling. It is more than a book about fishing. It is *the* book about fishing for *trout,* which means it is about poetry and the weather, about insects and rocks, about rivers and fine bamboo. It is about good fellowship, sturdy adventures, and a hundred other experiences that make time worth wasting. It is about how life evolves, sustains, and ends—and it is about how life may be craftsman-copied through delicate creations of marabou, mallard, and hare.

"*Trout* does not mark the arrival of Ernest Schwiebert: it seals his place in the fisherman's pantheon. It retires his fly rod. For it is hard to imagine a more rigorous and loving examination of why something happens—or doesn't—when a man throws a calculation of feathers at a fish."

What is special about the present book, *Trout Strategies,* is the essential "how to" nature of the work. The reader is invited to fish at the master's side, literally to match the hatch at streamside and find out why on a particular stream one moring a Light Cahill was rejected in favor of a hatching nymph of the Hendrickson persuasion.

J. M. III

⌄⌄⌄

TROUT
STRATEGIES

1. The Ancient Art of the Wet Fly

The rivers were superb, their swift currents flowing over straw-colored gravel, and we fished them all in those early Michigan summers. There was the legendary Au Sable, with its lazy day-floats and large fish hiding in the cedar sweepers, and the sombre flow of the Big Manistee. We fished the pale deadfall tangles on the lower Boardman in mayfly time, and counted foraging whitetail deer in the meadows at twilight on the Little Manistee. There were many happy brook-trout mornings on the tumbling reaches of the Pine and the tea-colored currents of the Black, its moody character enshrined in the early stories of Ernest Hemingway.

The wet-fly was common on the Michigan rivers in those days. It was the method for teaching a boy about trout, and it is still perhaps the best manner in which to start fly-fishing. It was my introduction to trout water and trout problems. There were strangely peaceful tree-frog summers in those first years of the Second World War, with twilight whippoorwills and swamp-peepers. Those summers were spent on the beautiful, smooth-flowing rivers of lower Michigan, thousands of miles from the fighting. Both their swift gravel-bottom riffles, and the shy trout lying in their tangled deadfalls, first taught me about the wet-fly method.

There are many memories of those years.

Spring mornings were often clear and cold, with cedars and skeletal branches sheltering sun-washed riffles, although an April river was sometimes pewter-colored in the rain. There were cowslips and pulpit flowers and violets, mixed with bloodroot and skunk cabbage, and the nights were surprisingly cold in a sleeping bag. Later, there were shadbush and flowering dogwoods, with May apples carpeting the forest floor. June

I

was always bright with delicate new leaves in the Michigan trout country. The summer rivers flowed smooth and clear, and there were fine fly hatches. Columbines and summer buttercups were blooming in the June river bottoms then, and the late summer meadows ripened into a time of gentians and swamp lilies and pye-weed.

My first wet-fly trout came on the Pere Marquette.

It took a small Cahill fished in a deep shadow of willows, about a mile below the Forks Pool. It was unquestionably taken with a fly, but my technique was a little like worming. I simply trailed the fly downstream in the current, working my rod back and forth, and the fish hooked itself. It measured barely ten inches, but it seemed like a sailfish in my eyes. It had followed my swinging Cahill from the willows into the sunlight, and the praise of my father and his friends was exhilarating as we celebrated on the stream. With that first fly-caught trout in my wicker creel, it seemed that I had truly entered their world. It was a morning baptized by my first cup of coffee, freshly brewed over a gravel-bar fire, while they celebrated with the stronger catalyst of sour-mash whiskey in their fishing-vest cups. After that morning I never fished bait again.

Such wet-fly tactics are deeply rooted in fly-fishing history. Modern anglers are often preoccupied with the more fashionable dry-fly method or wrestle with the little understood complexities of nymph fishing, but there are still many times when the river belongs to a skilled wet-fly fisherman, and modern developments in leaders and fly lines and other tackle have opened up a whole new spectrum of wet-fly techniques.

Despite extensive research here and abroad precise origins of the wet-fly method are unknown. However, recent evidence indicates that it dates back more than 2,300 years to the Chou Dynasty in China. It is clear that the wet-fly method reigned without challenge from the rivers of Macedonia to the Scottish Highlands, until the birth of dry-fly fishing in England slightly more than a century ago. Although many modern fishermen seem to have forgotten its secrets in their dry-fly myopia, the qualities that made it effective for literally thousands of years still exist on our rivers today. Anglers once began fishing wet flies and then graduated to the dry-fly and nymph methods as their skills increased. Everyone had some boyhood familiarity with wet flies in the past, but with the gradual spread of the dry-fly mystique, more and more fishermen now start fishing with floating patterns. The result is a generation of anglers whose training lacks the primary skills of the wet-fly method. Men who lack these skills are ignoring a singularly effective technique, and none of the fly-fishing innovations of the last century has made the wet fly obsolete.

Since fly-fishing was limited to sunk patterns for thousands of years, perhaps a fresh definition of the wet-fly method is needed. It should probably be based on the firm relationship between wet flies and our growing knowledge of American trout-stream entomology. Most anglers understand the clear relationship between dry flies and the imitation of various types of floating insects. Standard dry-fly patterns imitate a galaxy of adult mayflies, stoneflies, caddis, and various terrestrial insects like ants and grasshoppers and beetles. So-called fancy patterns are suggestive of any number of insect forms. Before the evolution of nymphs and disciplined nymph-fishing tactics early in this century, wet flies like the traditional Blue Dun and Greenwell's Glory and Hare's Ear were most effective as imitations of hatching nymphs.

Modern wet-fly fishermen are again becoming aware that their sunk patterns are often the best imitations of certain insect types. Patterns like the Hare's Ear are perfect imitations of species that emerge into the winged state below the surface, unfolding their diaphanous wings before they reach the atmosphere. Wet flies also suggest drowned aquatic insects. Cold-weather showers and high water often drown significant numbers of hatching flies before their wings have fully dried and they can escape the surface film to fly off. Fast water drowns large numbers of stream insects all season long. Many aquatic insects are blown into the water and drown while laying their eggs, and after their mating swarms have finished, large numbers of spent flies fall into the river and are submerged in rough currents. Some species of mayflies actually migrate below the surface to lay their eggs and few return to the atmosphere. Certain species of caddisflies flutter down to the water, pierce the surface film, fold their wings, and swim to the bottom to lay their eggs on stones and deadfalls. During this oviposition, the flies are enveloped in a glittering cloak of tiny bubbles, which explains the success of many tinsel-ribbed patterns. Such caddis flies are swept away along the bottom when their egg laying is completed. Hot windy weather also blows many terrestrials into the water, drowning large numbers of ants and grasshoppers and beetles. Although many fly-fishermen scoff at two- and three-fly snells these days, these methods have their valuable moments—since a skittering dropper fly is still perhaps the best method we have for suggesting the erratic, fluttering hopscotch of some egg-laying flies.

Wet flies are still the best patterns with which to begin fly-fishing. The basic principles are certainly the easiest for a neophyte to master and catch some trout in the bargain. Common downstream tactics do not demand the precise casting and fly manipulation typically required in other methods, and many fish will take a wet fly and hook themselves. Like bait fishing, exploring a stream with the wet-fly is an excellent way for the beginner to learn its secrets and to read its changing moods.

Wet-fly tackle has changed considerably in the past few years. Traditional wet-fly rods were soft and slow in action, in part because of the technical limitations in past years, and because a slower casting rhythm kept the flies and leaders moist enough to sink readily. Lines were silk and leaders were usually silkworm gut. Both have a higher specific gravity than water and sink quickly without line dressing. Undressed silk lines sank well to moderate depths, much like the modern sink-tip taper.

Modern fly rods for fishing the wet fly are avilable in compound tapers that flex well into the cork grip, and with calibrations at the tip guide designed to fish the delicate modern leaders. Such rods are usually described as parabolic or semi-parabolic, and usually balance with one line size smaller than comparable fast-action rods of similar length and weight. Such parabolic-type tapers will fish a longer line and finer tippet, with somewhat less casting effort, than fast-action rods of similar size. Their casting rhythms are complex and more demanding to master. They combine slow-action power with casting rhythms that retain maximum moisture in both leaders and flies, like the soft wet-fly actions fashionable on American streams in the past century.

Relatively small rivers mean a seven- to seven-and-a-half-foot rod weighing from three to three and three-quarters ounces. The well-equipped wet-fly man will carry reels or extra reel spools equipped with a matching DT5F floating line, DT5ST sinking-tip line, and DT5S full-sinking design. Such double-taper lines cast and fall softly enough for the skittish fish of small rivers. Their floating and sinking qualities are all valuable. The floating five-weight is singularly useful in fishing shallow runs or for suggesting emerging insects. Sinking-tip lines are needed to present the fly at intermediate depths of water. Full-sinking lines are required to work very fast currents and relatively deep places. Such precise control of fly-swing depth was impossible before the comparatively recent development of synthetic lines of dacron—and polyvinyl chloride lines having a higher specific gravity than water.

Proper tackle for fishing medium-size rivers requires bigger rods and heavier forward-taper lines. Eight-foot rods weighing from four to four and a half ounces, matched with six- and seven-weight lines, are fine all-around tools for most wet-fly work. My own experience favors double-taper designs in the floating line and weight-forward tapers in the sink-tip and full-sinking types. Medium-size rivers having unusually deep pools or swift currents may also make a fast-sinking synthetic line useful to the fully equipped angler.

Big water is the world of sinking lines and weight-forward tapers designed for distance work. Since most of our big trout rivers lie in the western states and western rivers also introduce the factor of high winds, such conditions demand rods of eight and a half to nine feet, weighing from four and a half to five and a half ounces. Lines matching these rods have eight- and nine-weight specifications. Although double-taper floating lines are sometimes useful in greased line wet-fly tactics during a hatch on the biggest rivers, their character usually requires a forward-taper line. Really big rivers mean distance casting and fishing deep, and the modern weight-forward sinking lines do both. Such recent technology represents perhaps the single most important breakthrough in wet-fly tackle since the evolution of fly-dressing itself, allowing us to fish heavy currents and water depths totally impossible fifteen years ago.

Effective wet-fly fishing for trout demands such varied manipulation of the fly that the fashionable midge-sized rods, weighing from two to two-and-three-quarters ounces are not really effective. Wet flies can be fished with them, but they lack the power to handle a sinking line, and they lack the length to modify and control fly swing. Such rods are also limited to relatively small flies, and although they will cast a long line in calm weather, they lack the power and control to punch out long casts into a big-water wind.

The reasons for fishing the deep runs and undercut banks with sinking lines lie in current-speed dynamics and their relationship to trout holding lies. The average stream at a five-foot depth has a current of about one foot per second at the surface, slightly more than a foot per second one to two feet deeper, and a bottom cushion of flow caused by hydraulic friction, its speed reduced to a third of the surface currents.

Bank friction has similar lateral effects on current speed. Surface currents five feet from a bank will average as much as one and a half feet per second, while bank speed is about one-quarter of a foot per second. Bottom currents at an undercut bank are even slower, and it is little wonder the fish like these places.

Bottom currents are approximately three times slower than surface levels of water in open-stream, and current speed deep in an undercut bank is typically four times less than main current tongues only a few feet away. Food carried in the primary current tongues moves too swiftly for a fish to capture it easily, and holding in such current speeds forces a trout to expend energy faster than it generates calories from the food ingested. Therefore, the fish lie in quieter flows waiting for their food to drift deeper, where it can be taken easily without exposure to the dangers found at shallower depths and in open currents. Such hydraulic factors are essential to reading and understanding a river and help explain the advantages of modern sinking lines—the only tackle which will successfully present a wet-fly in these bottom currents.

Technically speaking, wet flies are fished under the surface of the water and include all types of streamers, bucktails, and nymphs. However, these are special types of flies that are fished underwater. Streamers and bucktails imitate baitfish; nymphs suggest subaquatic forms of stream insects, some types of hatching flies, and many small crustaceans.

Dry flies are not only presented floating on the surface, their basic techniques of manipulation are also less complex. The dry-fly method typically involves a natural float, completely free of current drag in most cases. Some cross-stream and downstream techniques with the dry fly involve twitching and skating the imitation to suggest the surface fluttering of craneflies or caddis. But wet flies are usually fished either with current tension, conscious rhythms of retrieve, or precise control of fly-speed—although some dead-drift techniques are also useful at times.

Since quick-sinking flies and a swimming retrieve are basic criteria in wet-fly design, most patterns are dressed on heavy hooks with a configuration designed to fish smoothly under the surface. Materials should include body dubbing, floss, and crewel wools that readily absorb water. Most wet flies are hackled with soft hen feathers or body hackles from birds like grouse and woodcock. Such soft feathers work and move in a current or during a teasing retrieve in still water, giving a fly an added suggestion of life. However, some experts who dress wet flies for particularly swift rivers argue for hackles stiff enough to work in the heaviest chutes and rapids. Such theories are found in the work of English writers like W. H. Lawrie, with his *Book of the Rough Stream Nymph*, and are also important in the hair-hackle concepts developed by men like Franz Pott and George Grant in Montana. Generally speaking, however, wet-fly wings and hackles should pulse along the hook in response to the flow of the current.

There are literally thousands of wet-fly patterns. Most group themselves into two basic categories: brightly colored flies with a glitter of tinsel, dressings that function primarily as lures; and darker patterns conceived as imitations of trout-stream insects. The gaudy traditional flies often have their origins in sea-trout fishing and the Scottish loch patterns popular in Europe, and with the foolish brook trout that thrived in our northeastern wilderness early in the nineteenth century—flies like the Tomah Jo and Parmachene Belle and Belgrade.

Modern fishing has seen the gradual decline of these bright-feathered dressings in favor of more imitative patterns, even on wilderness waters of the Labrador. Some years ago I fished the River of the Martens less than a mile from its subarctic estuary on Ungava Bay, and we found that the modern imitative flies outfished the gaudy brook-trout confections of the past.

However, a river in spate or freshly stocked with hatchery fish in early season sometimes calls for a tinsel body. These days I dress a dark traditional like a March Brown or Grey Partridge with a body of silver tinsel to attract fish under such conditions. There are also times when tinsel-body flies match a hatching or egg-laying insect in its glittering sheath of bubbles. Many experienced wet-fly men believe their tinsel-bodied patterns are also sometimes taken for tiny baitfish. Certainly such tinsel-wrapped flies are more easily visible in cloudy water and at greater distances than the darker dressings. Tinsel is not the only source of highlights in a wet-fly pattern. Its feathers and body dubbing often entrain air bubbles that catch the light dramatically, and its bulk and hook-point often stream a trail of similar bubbles. Cavitation can also coat a swimming wet fly with entrained air, since the separation of flow layers that the fly causes in a river often results in a series of tiny vacuums. Such light patterns are frequently the secret of wet-fly success, and a gold or silver ribbing of tinsel is sometimes the difference between failure and taking fish consistently.

The wet-fly fishing that Claudius Aelianus described in the third century worked with a line of fixed length, and was more like dapping or bushing than actual casting. Such fixed-line tackle was still in use when Dame Juliana Berners wrote the first English book on fly-fishing in the fifteenth century; and although Barker and Walton knew of the fishing reel at the middle of the seventeenth century, it was not recommended in their discussions of fly tackle for trout. In 1653 Izaak Walton described such fishing in *The Compleat Angler*:

But I promised to tell you more of fly-fishing for a trout, which I may have time enough to do, for you see it rains May-butter across our meadow, and its silvery streams; and let me tell you again, that you keep as far from the water as you possibly can, and fish down the stream: and when you fish with the fly, if it be possible, let no part of your line touch the water, or casting it into the water, you yourself being also almost always moving down the stream.

These lines unmistakably describe the rudiments of the wet-fly method. There are a number of other ancient truths, like making as few false casts as possible to keep the leader and flies wet. Cast as little as possible, leaving the fly in the water as much as possible. Many surprisingly experienced anglers are so compulsive about casting properly that they will pick up a poor cast immediately, even though the slash of the pickup may occur right over the holding lies of the fish. Such bad habits frighten the trout long before they can observe the fly.

Some years ago there was a well-known tournament caster fishing on a river in arctic Norway. It was a river famous for its impressive catches of big fish, yet his boat came in night after night with surprisingly few salmon. His casting was superb, double hauling faultlessly at considerable distance; but such distance work demanded a lot of false casting, and the boat gillies usually hold an angler only fifty or sixty feet from the fish. Long casts were unnecessary on most pools, and we asked the riverkeeper about his poor luck.

His casting is beautiful. The old man paused and lit his pipe. *But he casts well beyond the fish.*

Too much casting in the air, said a boatman.

That's a double haul, I said.

Yes, smiled the old riverkeeper, *but the fish are only found in the river—there are no fish in the air!*

You're right! I smiled.

There are a number of variations on the basic downstream theme of traditional wet-fly angling. Some are the result of modern developments in tackle, particularly in leader nylons and sinking-type lines. Others result from a new understanding of fly hatches, and still others are borrowed from salmon fishing or from the revival in traditional wet-fly methods that had died with the generation that fished them. It is all part of an exciting renaissance in wet-fly tactics, and there are fifteen basic variations in the technique.

1. The Simple Wet-Fly Swing

This is the closest modern application of the fixed-line method found in the time of Berners and Walton. It is perhaps the best technique to teach a beginner, since it involves only rudimentary manipulation of the fly and fly tackle. It is the kind of fly-fishing that I first learned on the small

willow-choked streams of Michigan, where we waded slowly and sound-
lessly downstream, roll casting a fixed length of line to the undercut alders
across the current.

The fly is simply allowed to swim in a quarter-circle against the
tension of the current, without manipulation of the rod or fly line. It is
fished without movement except for the life imparted by the current, and
the fly swing should be followed around with the rod tip. Such tactics
suggest a drowned insect or emerging aquatic species that cannot swim
directly against the flow of the current.

The simple fixed-line swing can also suggest insect forms capable of
limited subaquatic motion. The fisherman makes his cast directly across the
stream in relatively quiet currents, to increase the fly speed of the swing,
and quartering downstream in faster water. The swing is then followed
around with the rod tip pointed directly at the fly, and the rod is raised and
lowered with a slow, teasing rhythm geared to the current speed. Since the
line length remains unchanged, and the line is held between the index
finger and the rod grip, no manipulation of the line with the left hand is
involved. Such basic wet-fly tactics should also include directly downstream
presentation, with the angler holding and working a fly almost like bait. It
is the way that I started fly-fishing and caught that first trout on a wet fly
years ago, allowing a downstream fly to probe along a willow-hung bank
and under fallen trees.

2. The Hand-Twist Retrieve

This technique introduces line manipulation with the left hand. It is fished
to create a wide variation of teasing, half-swimming rhythms to imitate
different types of subaquatic trout foods. Its applications are best using slow
to moderate rhythms of retrieve, and it was a favorite sunk-fly method
described by Bergman in *Trout*—particularly in stillwaters and brook-trout
bogans and in deep, slow-flowing pools.

It is slightly more complicated than a simple fixed-line swing, but it is
still a relatively simple technique. The cast is made and allowed to sink,
and the retrieve is manipulated by weaving the line around the left hand or
through its fingers. This weaving rhythm is accomplished with a rolling
motion of the left wrist, either wrapping the line around the palm at the
base of the fingers, or lacing it through the fingers in a rhythmic
figure-eight. It is perfect for imitating all types of diet forms that swim
slowly in the water, like scuds and egg-laying caddis and hatching
duns—stream life that swims in almost imperceptible rhythms.

The hand-twist retrieve is absolutely basic. Since most slow-swimming
insects are found in relatively quiet currents, or in beaver ponds and other
impoundments, it is a primary technique for quiet water. When the fly is
allowed to sink deep in a pool or flat, fishing it back along the bottom can
be deadly. Sometimes I let a wet fly ride down a long current-tongue,
perhaps into water too deep to reach by wading, and then retrieve it slowly
the full length of the line.

It is a method that once produced a deep-bodied five-pound brown on the pastoral Grundbach in Germany. The fish was rising to a hatch of tiny *Paraleptophlebia* flies at the head of a deep bend in the river. The alders on its sheltering bank prevented an upstream cast from that side of the current. Similar alders and a thick stand of conifers across the stream made a presentation from the opposite side equally impossible. There was a meadow bank below, across from the fish and a fruitless two hundred feet away, so a downstream presentation was the only possible strategy.

It was raining softly and the fish was feeding often. It seemed to be taking a myriad of fluttering little duns, drowned hatching flies, and tiny emerging nymphs without discrimination. Only its unreachable position in the river seemed to protect it, since its feeding was hardly selective. It was finally caught with a simple method.

Fishing it with a downstream dry fly in such quiet water would have allowed only one cast, since the fly would ultimately drag in the current and put down the trout. But the wet-fly would not frighten the fish when it reached the end of the cast; in fact, its teasing in the current might entice the big brown into taking. There was a small wet-fly imitation in my fly-book, and I clinched it to my tippet.

It was an infantry problem to get within range. The high bank above the fish was bounded by open meadow, and I had to crawl very slowly to reach a casting station within reach of its feeding lie. It was a little like stalking an *Auerhahn* in the European forests, the huge black grouse that closes its eyes while cackling. The hunter must stalk the bird only during its calling, when it cannot see his movements, or this wariest of game birds will simply melt into the trees. Any stalk of the fish was limited to the brief period of its rise forms, when I hoped it was preoccupied enough to miss my approach. It seemed to work and the fish kept working steadily.

The cast dropped out into the smooth current, checked well away from the fish with the rod, and I paid out just enough line to reach its station and slightly more. The tiny wet fly was submerged with a twitch and worked around slowly until it hung slightly below the trout. The fish did not stop feeding, apparently failing to notice the leader nylon trailing past its position in the current. After a few moments, I started an imperceptible hand-twist retrieve, and the fish took the fly without hesitation when it reached its holding lie.

3. The Hand-Strip Retrieve

This technique is a method of suggesting both a more rapid retrieve of slightly longer swimming motions than are possible with a hand-twist rhythm. It is achieved by holding the line between the index finger and the rod-grip, and stripping back short lengths of line with the other hand.

These stripping lengths can vary from about six inches, about the maximum retrieve possible when winding hand-twist retrieve around the fingers, to a free arm-pull of two to three feet. Such stripping rhythms are useful for imitating trout foods that move with steady, pulsing movements in the water, and the faster pulls are especially exciting to wilderness fish and also to hatchery trout fresh from the stocking trucks.

4. The Rod-and-Line Strip

Although this method is similar to the hand-strip retrieve, it introduces a teasing movement of the rod between left-hand strips of the line. The fly action is erratic and contrapuntal in its rhythms. It consists of a compound pattern of strip, and rod-tip pulse and strip, that can suggest erratic swimming behavior. Such rhythms are typical of tiny baitfish and some species of hatching and egg-laying flies. It is valuable as a change of pace; and like the fast hand-strip retrieve, it often excites back-country and freshly-stocked trout. Its stripping and rod-tip rhythms are slightly more complicated to handle than the more basic wet-fly methods, but they are soon mastered with practice.

5. The Cast-and-Strip Method

This is a technique for getting greater fly depth with a sinking line in heavy currents and still waters and lakes. It involves making a relatively long cast, stripping line out from the reel, and shaking it out through the guides onto the water with a side-to-side flexing of the rod. Such abrupt paying-out of a sinking line will allow the fly time to reach considerably more depth than the actual cast length. The fly can then be given life with any of the basic fly swings or retrieves. It is a singularly effective method of fishing very deep reaches of water, and I have used it to take trout on big western rivers and high-altitude lakes, as well as in ledgerock pools in the Catskills.

Several years ago I was fishing the Barn Pool on the Brodheads with Philip Nash. It was a bright morning in May, and the current flowed smooth and strong into a pool as still as a millpond. There was a jumble of big boulders in the main holding depths of the pool, and I fished it from the shade of its swinging footbridge.

There had been two weeks of fine *Rhyacophila* hatches, and a few of these little green-bodied caddis were laying their eggs. There were no rises anywhere, and the spreading flat below the barn was like a mirror. It was unseasonably hot and I waded over to the rocks where the current chuted into the shelving depths of the pool. Caddisflies were fluttering over the surface, and suddenly I noticed several scuttling about on the boulders near my waders. They scurried nervously at the water line, and then I realized that a fly occasionally slipped below the surface, wriggling deep along the underwater currents. It disappeared into the dark eddies in the throat of the pool as I watched another caddis migrate into the swirling currents downstream.

Suddenly it disappeared in the flash of a trout, catching the light deep in the current. *Maybe the fish are taking those egg-laying caddis,* I thought excitedly. *Maybe a sinking line and a small Greenwell's Glory.*

I always carry a second reel fitted with a sinking line in my rain-jacket pouch, and I quickly switched it and strung the rod. There were a few

HAND-STRIP RETRIEVE STROKES

size-fourteen Greenwells in my fly book and I fastened one to the tippet. I let it soak with the leader in a backwater while I watched a number of other flies slip underwater on a deadfall to lay their eggs.

Finally it was ready and I worked a sixty-foot cast straight down the pool. When it dropped and started sinking, I stripped another ten feet off the reel, and shook it out through the guides. It rode still deeper into the throat of the pool, and when it finally swam taut and began trailing in the current, I started to work it back upstream with a patient hand-twist retrieve.

It had teased back a half-dozen turns when there was a strong pull and a sixteen-inch fish bounced out wildly, its threshing splashes disturbing the smooth currents. *That's the ticket!* I thought happily. *They're taking these egg-laying caddisflies!*

It was the secret of fishing the Barn Pool on the Brodheads that morning, and the cast-and-strip method quickly produced two dozen fat browns and rainbows, all taken with a little Greenwell fished slowly along the bottom.

6. The Upstream Dead-Drift

Its origins lie in the innovations of W. C. Stewart on the rivers of the Scottish Lowlands, which were outlined in his book *The Practical Angler*. It appeared in 1857, and its pages are the codification of the upstream method. The upstream dead-drift presentation of the wet fly was a major breakthrough in fly-fishing tactics, and it was also the prelude to the basic dry-fly technique.

Fishing a wet fly upstream has several basic applications: it works on skittish trout in shallow water, where such fish are easily frightened by an angler wading down; it is perfect for suggesting a drowned aquatic or terrestrial insect drifting with the current; it is equally effective for fishing a hatch of emerging insects that cannot swim and that reach the surface film by riding the current tongues, rising with the gases generated inside their loosening skins; it is also a valuable method of working a fly really deep into heavy currents and deep pools.

Fishing the upstream dead-drift wet is particularly effective in the *Epeorus* mayfly hatches on eastern rivers, especially the famous Gordon Quill flies that come off in April. These mayflies begin to unfold their wings as soon as their nymphs let go from the bottom to emerge. The *Ephemerella* mayflies reach the winged stage just before they reach the surface, wriggling and unfolding their wings a few inches below the film. There are many species on American waters from the Dennys in Maine to the swift Deschutes in Oregon, including the eastern Gordon Quills and Hendricksons, and equally famous western hatches like the Pale Morning Olives and Leadwing Olive Drakes. These hatching duns ride some distance, fully winged and wriggling impatiently to hatch just under the surface, and are perfect for imitation with wet flies fished upstream. Stoneflies are another diet form that can be imitated with a dead-drift wet fly. These Plecoptera hatch from the swiftest riffles and pocket water, and fishing an upstream wet-fly method in the holding places is quite effective.

Although the upstream dead-drift is one of the most deadly methods of wet-fly presentation, it is also perhaps the most difficult technique to master. Most downstream wet-fly fishing is relatively easy, in terms of observing a taking fish and hooking it. Many fish hook themselves on a downstream wet fly. But wet flies fished upstream are a subtle problem of sensing a strike from a number of ephemeral, half-seen clues. Experienced wet-fly men often tighten into a taking fish on a dead-drift technique without being able to tell you exactly what they saw or sensed that made them strike: an imperceptible bulge or variation in the current, the upstream pause or darting twitch of the leader, little more than a subtle difference between the drift of the current and the floating line, or the partially glimpsed flash as the trout turned deep at the fly and its bright flanks caught the light.

It is a subtly honed skill that seems almost extrasensory to less gifted fishermen. The beginner can modify his tackle to help, and we have recently evolved better tackle than the dry-fly bobber that Bergman recommended in *Trout* almost forty years ago. He watched the bobber's movements on the surface when a fish took, but the bobber was difficult to keep floating and awkward to cast. Modern wet-fly men like Dave Whitlock recommend a tiny fluorescent tube attached to the line at its leader butt, or a leader knot brightly lacquered with fluorescent paint. Bright yellow or orange with an intense chroma are readily visible in the most tumbling current tongues—and a modern fisherman can watch such strike indicators twitch or pause when a fish takes as easily as Bergman watched his snelled dry-fly bobber.

7. The Cast-and-Countdown Method

This technique is necessary for fishing a wet-fly right on the bottom in relatively deep water, perhaps to suggest a drowned mayfly or caddis of the species that migrate to the bottom for egg laying. Sometimes it is perfect for imitating freshwater scuds and shrimps. Such bottom scratching is often necessary in early season, when the water is still extremely cold and the trout are sluggish and lying deep.

It is an uncomplicated method requiring only patience and a little self-discipline. It consists of making a cast and counting while the line and fly sink toward the bottom. Counts are added to the sink rate until the fisherman can actually feel the line touch bottom on the fly swing or the retrieve. The countdown is then reduced a count or two on subsequent casts to work the fly just above the bottom, fishing it back either with a simple swing or with various retrieves.

8. Multiple Wet-Fly Method

Fishing more than one wet fly on a single cast is undoubtedly as old as fly fishing itself, and was certainly in use in the fifteenth century on the trout streams of Europe. It was widely practiced on the north-country rivers of England when Charles Cotton wrote *Being Instructions How to Fish for a Trout or Grayling in a Clear Stream* in 1676, and further codified in the later work of Bowlker. It was a standard method on our brook-trout waters during the nineteenth century, and it is still found on western rivers in the hands of old-timers who grew up in the cutthroat years that followed the opening of the frontier. It is surprisingly effective in swift water.

Casting a multiple-fly rig is awkward unless the leader is properly designed and tied. Its nylon cannot be too limp or light and, instead of the snell loops popular in the past, dropper strands are required. The dropper strands will tangle in casting if they are too fine in diameter. There should be extensions left when the blood knots are formed to assemble the leader taper itself. For example, if the tippet is about .007 or 4x, the first dropper strand should be attached about twenty inches above, where the tippet is joined with a length of .008 nylon. The dropper strand should consist of about six inches of this heavier 3x leader material.

The method has been neglected on our eastern brown-trout rivers in recent years. Certainly the old looped leaders and snelled wet flies are too clumsy and too visible on our heavily fished waters. However, the modern angler can make up his own leaders to provide short lengths of dropper strands at mid-leader for attaching a second or third wet fly. It is a method that still has its uses, not only on western and northern brook-trout rivers, but also on the difficult fish of the Catskills.

Past generations of wet-fly experts like John Pope and Herman Christian fished those same Catskill rivers in their wet-fly years. They sometimes fished as many as four flies, skittering them back across the current to excite the fatally-curious native brook trout. But, as we have seen, the lumbering and the acid-bark industry ended the reign of the brook trout on our eastern rivers; once the pines and hemlocks were cut, every springhead in the region ran several degrees warmer, and the primeval cold-water biosystem of the brookies was doomed.

The European brown trout could stand warmer temperatures as well as increased angling pressure, and it quickly and handsomely filled the vacuum left with the decline of the brook trout. These new fish were harder to catch. The gaudy brook-trout patterns did not fool them, and American fishermen began to study the theories of British fishing writers to understand the much warier browns. It led to the first American flies designed to imitate our hatches—classic patterns like the Hendrickson and Gordon Quill and Cahill.

Anglers also refined their techniques to cast a single fly to a fish that was feeding, in the manner of Marryat and Halford and Skues, or to cover a likely looking pocket in the current. The years that followed saw an angling generation evolve that had forgotten the simple three-fly tricks that had regularly filled their wicker creels before 1900.

Past experience seems to argue that the reasons for the success of a multiple-fly cast are twofold. Sometimes a number of flies working in the current prove an irresistible attraction to the fish. Certainly the professional fishermen who still fish as many as eight to ten wet flies to supply hotel kitchens in the British Isles and the south of France are aware of this truth. However, there are also times when so many naturals are available below the surface—heavy caddis hatches or mating swarms of flies that lay their eggs underwater or mayfly species that exhibit schooling behavior among their nymphs—that fishing two or three imitations is quite effective.

9. The Fluttering-Dropper Technique

This method is more difficult to master than I first expected when I saw it used skillfully on the Frying Pan in Colorado twenty-five years ago. It was the technique of a grizzled fly-fisherman who had once supplied trout from the Frying Pan to a buyer from the Colorado & Midland Railroad—fish that ultimately were poached in court bouillon or broiled *meuniere* in the halcyon days of the Brown Palace in Denver, and the storied Antlers Hotel in Colorado Springs.

The old man usually fished three flies. His choices were almost always the Gray Hackle, Rio Grande King, and partridge-hackled March Brown. One evening I watched him on a swift reach of the Frying Pan about a half mile above its still water at Seven Castles. Caddisflies were egg laying, fluttering, and hopscotching over the broken current tongues. The old man was fishing his three-fly cast, using the two lowest patterns as a kind of sea anchor, raising his rod high and stripping in line and working the rod tip to bounce the small March Brown on the surface. It hopscotched down the current like a natural and the hungry trout took it eagerly with splashy rises. The old man soon changed both droppers to little March Browns, and I watched him quickly take a brace of fat Frying Pan rainbows on a single cast. The tumbling run readily surrendered another double, and I eagerly studied his manipulation of both rod and flies. Although I later caught some fish with a similar bouncing dropper, it was not as easy as it looked. It works on sophisticated brown trout too, and there is nothing else in our bag of tricks quite like a fluttering dropper—particularly to imitate the erratic flight of many egg-laying flies in their hopping half-clumsy contact with the current.

10. The Riffling-Hitch Method

This is primarily a salmon-fishing technique from Newfoundland, but it has also proved extremely effective during fly hatches that skim and scuttle across the surface film. The common British caddis called the Caperer, and various western species of our still-water Trichoptera, are typical species that scamper rapidly in the surface film. Although such insect behavior can be imitated without attaching the fly with a riffling hitch, it is perhaps the best method of suggesting an insect that runs across the surface.

It is accomplished with a pair of half-hitch knots seated tightly around the wings and hackles, slightly behind the eye of the hook. Fishing it across a main current tongue lying downstream to the left, the leader must come out under the half-hitches at the left of the fly. Fishing from the opposite side of the current, the angler reverses his half-hitch loops to have the leader ride out on the right side of the fly. The leader must be exactly seated or the fly will not swim properly in the surface, cutting a perceptible V-shaped wake in the water. It works best with fly sizes above ten or twelve. The fly speed is critical, lying just between the speed of a roughly dragging fly and a speed too slow to keep the fly from actually sinking, bringing it around just under the surface.

The fly must skim just in the surface film, and the riffling-hitch knot is not the only factor affecting this behavior. Manipulation of the rod and the line held in the left hand also play a major role. The rod is worked the moment the fly touches the water, raised higher and higher to keep it from sinking and start its swimming wake. Both rod arm and left arm are smoothly extended in unison as the fly-swing progresses, until the rod is held straight up at full arm's length, and the left hand is extended full length against the body, holding the line against the hip. This simultaneous manipulation of fly swing, rod arm, and left hand requires practice, but it can be executed perfectly, and will skim the fly in the surface at optimum speed. It is a valuable secret on many rivers, particularly after dark.

11. Diving and Bobbing

This method involves both single- and multiple-fly casts, and apparently has its tactical origins in the trout lakes of Ireland and Scotland. It is most useful in lake fishing on wilderness fish, both in the brook-trout ponds of the Labrador and the high-altitude cutthroat lakes of our western mountains. It is surprisingly effective under dead-calm conditions, and involves dressing the flies with silicone. The flies will float half-submerged in the film, and a sharp pull with the rod will duck them under, although the silicone quickly buoys them up again. This diving-and-bobbing retrieve will often induce a rise when more conventional techniques fail.

12. Dapping and Bushing

The conceptual roots of these techniques are found in writings that date back to Aelianus in the third century, who first described bouncing the fly over the fish with a fixed length of line. Lowering the fly directly over a fish has been called dapping since its first mention in fifteenth-century Britain, and bushing is a variation in which the fly is dapped over a bush or other vegetation to fish the fly on the unseen current.

Cross-country casts are also a variation on bushing. They are used when the river is clearly visible, and the angler would be too exposed to the fish should he come too close. Crouching or kneeling on the grassy bank is necessary, and part of the cast must lie on either the bank, or sometimes across a weedbed in the shallows. Although the strike must be slightly harder than normal, to overcome the friction of the weeds or grass, it is not unlike a normal wet-fly presentation.

13. The Greased Line and Crosfield Pull

The greased-line method was conceived and perfected on the Cairnton salmon beat of the Dee, by the late Arthur H. E. Wood. It utilized a carefully dressed silk line, and was designed to control fly speed under low-water conditions for salmon. It involves casting almost directly across stream, which tends to increase line bellying and the speed of the fly swing. The floating line is then mended upstream as the fly approaches optimal speed halfway through its swing. The upstream mend dampens the drag of the current on the bellying line, increasing the distance of the fly speed at its optimal behavior by as much as fifty percent in skilled hands. It also increases the likelihood of enticing a fish to rise.

The greased line has a corollary technique intended to increase fly speed, which involves a downstream mend of the floating line. Making a line mend downstream increases the pull of the current on the line, accelerating the speed of a fly that is coming around lifelessly on its current-swing. Both techniques are valuable on trout.

The Crosfield pull was developed to increase fly speed when a sinking line makes the mending technique impossible. It was developed by the late Ernest Crosfield, fishing salmon on the Herefordshire Wye and the Laxamyri in Iceland. Crosfield held the line under his index finger, and made a smooth pull of a length and speed designed to make his fly accelerate and swim properly.

Crosfield also developed a line-strip designed to decrease the speed of a sinking-line swing. It simply involves paying out small increments of line into the fly swing to slow its speed at the *moment critique,* like a teasing slow ball gets a batter to swing. Both the Crosfield pull and the Crosfield strip are common practice on the Laxá in Pingeyjarsysla of northern Iceland. The Laxá is a smooth-flowing river with deep pools perfectly suited to the sinking lines, and Crosfield taught the ghillies there to fish his methods more than half a century ago. Although the present-day ghillies are unaware of the origins of their favorite tactics, their highly skilled knowledge of manipulating fly speed originally derived from Crosfield.

14. The Leisenring Lift

This effective method of suggesting a hatching fly was developed by the late James Leisenring on the Brodheads in Pennsylvania. It was Leisenring who first adapted the subtle lessons of British writers like Skues and Cutcliffe and Pritt to American wet-fly problems, just as Gordon and La Branche further modified the dry-fly theories of the British chalkstreams to our swifter rivers.

Leisenring studied and understood the dynamics of his fly swing, both in its horizontal patterns of coverage across a pool, and in its profile of sinking and swimming at maximum depth and starting back toward the surface. Experienced fishermen have come to understand how their cast across the current first begins to sink, then starts to ride in a crosscurrent

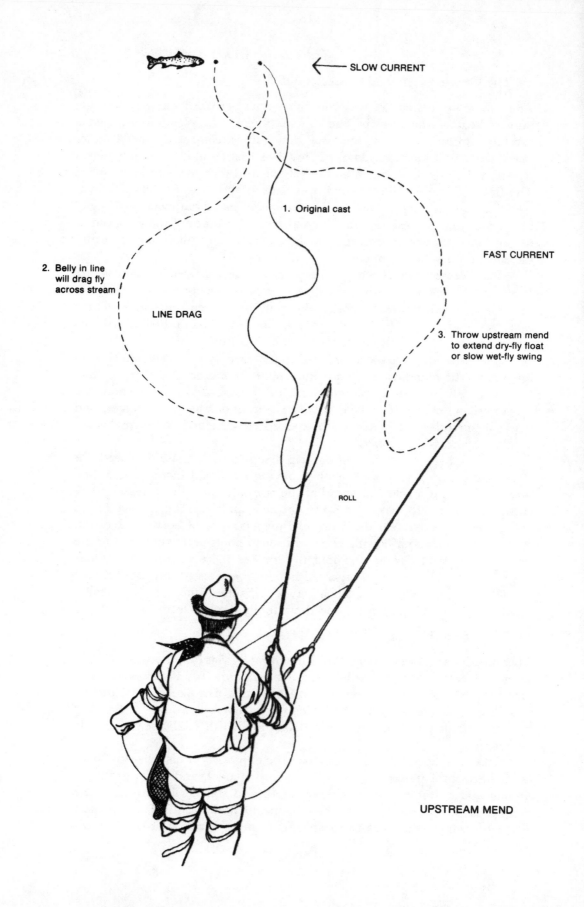

SLOW CURRENT

1. Original cast

FAST CURRENT

2. Belly in line
   will drag fly
   across stream

LINE DRAG

3. Throw upstream mend
   to extend dry-fly float
   or slow wet-fly swing

ROLL

UPSTREAM MEND

swing at maximum depth, and ultimately climbs back toward the surface with the velocity of the current. The so-called hot spot usually occurs at the time the fly has reached its maximum depth and has started to both swing and rise toward the surface.

The Leisenring lift recognizes that a fly working back toward the surface clearly imitates a hatching insect or nymph. Leisenring evolved his lift technique to suggest that movement, and make it even more attractive to a feeding trout. The result was a multiple retrieve. The cast was made across or even slightly upstream and allowed to settle dead-drift on the current. The dead-drift sink allowed the fly to reach maximum depth. When the fly had reached its depth and started to rise toward the surface on its crosscurrent swing, Leisenring began to raise his rod to accentuate the illusion of a hatching fly, working it with tip rhythm or just letting it swing, depending on the behavior of the naturals.

15. The Poacher's Retrieve

The origins of this ancient technique are unknown. Its name may be derived from the minimal amount of casting as well as the stealth involved, since both are important in concealing a poacher's craft. It is particularly valuable in the deep, quiet reaches of water where the trout cruise on the bottom, and too many casts will scatter them like frightened quail.

The poacher's retrieve is the solution. With it the leader and flies must be thoroughly soaked to sink quickly. The modern sinking lines are perfect for a technique that allows the fly to sink quickly to the bottom. It requires patience to wait while the trout forget the initial disturbance of the cast, although an occasional bold fish sometimes will dart back and take the fly while it settles slowly toward the bottom.

Most fish, however, will scatter and drift back cautiously when the fly and leader have stopped sinking. One or two may investigate the fly with considerable curiosity. Watching the fish at such times is a great advantage, although the technique can be used effectively without actually seeing the bottom. When the slow hand-twist retrieve starts the fly ascending toward the surface, after the fish have returned to the area, the man skilled in executing a poacher's retrieve will almost always raise a fish.

It was Henryville Charlie Ross, perhaps the most notorious market-hunter and poacher in the Poconos years ago, who demonstrated a poacher's retrieve to me along the Brodheads. It was deadly in his hands. Henryville Charlie ended his days on the paths of righteousness as a warden along its famous Henryville water. It was a role filled with an irony that his market-hunting cronies would have relished—and the old man could fish a skilled poacher's retrive until he had passed ninety.

Many years ago, my trout fishing began on a small meadow stream in Michigan. Getting the grasshoppers for bait was sport in itself, and we gathered them early in the wet morning grass. They were sluggish in the cold just after daylight, and we crisscrossed the meadows with our fruit jars, picking grasshoppers like brown-mottled berries.

The fishing began on the headwaters of the creek. Its meadows were willow-lined, its spring-fed origins deep in a cedar swamp. It was dark with alders and conifers there, and the bogs were filled with rust-colored seepages. Some places the springheads flowed through quivering swamps of sand and marl, and finally a small brook collected in the bog above the logging pond. The shallows were filled with stumps and deadfalls, and the beaver house stood just below the inlet. It was a beautiful place in the early morning.

Brook trout lay in its deepening emerald green channel, cruising and feeding in nervous schools. They were bright with color in these swamp-cold waters, but they usually cruised beyond the limited range of my boyhood casting. The fish almost always broke and scattered whenever my grasshopper plopped on the still surface of the logging pond.

It was a frustrating place. There were countless summer mornings when I crouched on the log-cribbing dam, trying to outwit these trout, but it usually ended in failure. There are still mornings when I remember those clear, cloud-scudding days of boyhood, and when I think about the skittish brook trout in that Michigan logging pond, it is always with the thought that a poacher's retrieve might have fooled them.

2. Modern Dry-Fly
Theory and Practice

Downstream from the brooding hemlock ledges on a river in Pennsylvania, the murky currents flowed smoothly over the dark winter-scoured stones, and the April sunlight danced weakly on the riffles. It had been a dour, almost bitter spring. There were still few buds on the trees except for the bright reddish swamp maples, and even the willows had only the faintest olive cast. There were no flies hatching, although the sunlight reached the riffle gravel, stirring its ripening early-season nymphs.

The cool wind eddied in the rattling branches, and there was little warmth in the midday sun. The swift current was cold around my waders. The stream thermometer read only forty-six degrees, and it seemed unlikely that such half-hearted sunlight could warm the river enough to trigger a decent hatch of flies.

The season was already several days old, but our fishing logs still recorded no fly hatches on the water. Early-season hatches usually emerge at midday and continue sporadically into early afternoon. The dark little stoneflies and *Paraleptophlebias* are late-morning species, and the April mayfly hatches come off the riffles between one-thirty and five o'clock. Although it seemed improbable that a good hatch might emerge with the river so cold, we stopped fishing before noon, hoping to finish our lunch well before any fly hatch could begin.

No sign of a hatch, I said unhappily and accepted a glass of Beaujolais. *We should have seen a few flies coming off before lunch.*

Since dry-fly fishing depends on insects hatching from the river bottom in early season, and on terrestrial insects falling into the river when warm weather begins, we were hoping for a hatch to generate a rise of trout.

Aquatic insects trigger surface feeding both when they hatch and when they lay their eggs, and midsummer trout rise eagerly to terrestrials like ants and leafhoppers and beetles. The surface-feeding trout is perhaps the apogee of our sport, because his rises are clearly visible, and our presentation with a floating imitation has a classic beauty.

Such poetry comes with a good hatch of aquatic flies.

Henryville Charlie Ross was the riverkeeper on our Brodheads water in those years, and he stopped his rounds to talk where we were eating thick onion soup and beef sandwiches above the Ledge Pool.

It's been a right hard winter, Ross squinted out across the eddying currents below the hemlock-sheltered ledge. *Ain't seen no sign of hatches!*

Seems too cold today, I said.

Maybe, the old man shook his head. *It's the best weather we've had—but we might see some flies later on!*

Hope you're right, I smiled.

The old riverkeeper nodded, and wandered on down through the river willows to study the pool. The sun slipped behind a cloud and we stood shivering in the April wind. The hot soup and sandwiches and coffee had helped, and the feeling had finally returned to my river-chilled body.

Still no sign of them flies, Henryville Charlie grumbled when he came back up through the thickly-grown willows along the river. *Could still get a hatch this afternoon.*

Hendricksons? I asked.

April Grays, the old man answered. *Always called them hatches April Grays in the old days, but you city boys got new names for everything nowadays.*

Times change, I laughed.

The river was several degrees warmer after lunch. The thermometer was bright, glittering among the stones in the tumbling shallows above the Ledge Pool. It lay there on the bottom for five minutes before I retrieved it.

Just over fifty! I yelled.

Fifty degrees, David Rose laughed. *That's a little too cold for me, but maybe it means something to a trout!*

It means even more to a mayfly, I grinned.

You mean we might get a hatch of Hendricksons with the stream temperature over fifty? he asked.

Gordon Quills are more likely, I said.

Our famous eastern rivers typically get good hatches of *Epeorus* flies a week or two before the heavier hatches of Hendricksons. When those rivers reach about fifty degrees each spring, both fly hatches and surface feeding trout soon follow. Sometimes these factors happily combine to produce good dry-fly fishing quite early in the season.

The shallow flat above the riffles that feed the pool looked almost inviting now, where the sunlight glittered on the currents. The whole afternoon seemed brighter in spite of the rattling branches. There were still no flies hatching, and I stood watching the current in the back-eddy shallows for nymphal shucks.

The warming sun reached deep into the murky depths, where the riffling currents shelved off into the deepening throat of the pool. The river tumbled and flowed swiftly there. Its bottom betrayed no signs of life, except for the black water mosses and tiny turquoise-colored tufts of *Cladophora* and brown winter algae on the stones. Its seemingly lifeless face was a deception, since the bottom of any fertile trout stream teems all winter with myriad forms of life.

Riffling currents are the principal larders of our rivers, since their oxygen-charged waters are life-giving and rich. Their life forms are organisms that swim with great agility, clamber along the bottom, or cling firmly among the stones. Others attach themselves to the bottom. The currents are so compelling that they both polish and shape the stones, forcing them into a series of shinglelike layers, until even a dry summer streambed shows clearly which direction its April currents flowed.

When there is sufficient current, such stones shelter a richly complex web of life. The stones themselves are slippery with the films of diatomaceous organisms. The crevices are filled with algae and water mosses. There are a few swift-water fishes like fingerling trout and creek darters, and sometimes the stones conceal an agile salamander. There are leeches and planarians, and the larger stones occasionally hide a crayfish. Our northeastern streams are not alkaline enough for large numbers of smaller crustaceans. Tiny fast-water *Planorbis* snails are found here feeding on the detritus between the stones. There are minute zooplankton and rotifers too, along with threadworms and other tiny nematodes. The quiet bottom eddies also support colonies of moss animalcules and hydras, and virtually all of these minute organisms sustain themselves on microscopic forms of aquatic life.

There are subaquatic insects too. Swift-water larvae of the two-winged Diptera are perhaps the most numerous species. There are predatory beetle larvae hunting other insects among the bottom debris and leaf drift. Water pennies adhere to the smooth bedrock ledges and current-polished stones. Some riffle bottoms are greenish black with *Simulium* larvae clinging to the gravel. Some crevices between the stones are the hunting grounds of stonefly nymphs, and there are the food-collecting net shelters of the free-ranging caddis worms. Other crevices are richly encrusted with colonies of case-building Trichoptera, their patchwork castles constructed of tiny bits of shell and vegetable matter and sand, until they are often the patchwork color of the river bottom.

Mayflies are the most elegant creatures inhabiting this subaquatic society. There are the swiftly-moving, swimming nymphs of the *Isonychia* flies, each crouched like a diminutive praying mantis on the stones with its fringed forelegs collecting minute food from the tumbling currents. There are clinging forms too, like the nymphs of the March Browns and Cahills that hatch much later in the year, and hiding between the larger stones are the fat three-tailed Hendrickson nymphs that would hatch and generate fine rises of trout before the April weather was finished.

But that April afternoon the most active mayfly nymphs in these riffles were the two-tailed *Epeorus* flies, since the gradually warming waters would soon encourage them to start their emergence. It was nearly one-thirty when the cool wind stopped and the afternoon seemed almost warm, and in the eddying shallows beside the riffles I finally saw a fresh nymphal skin drifting in the slack current. There were several others in the next half hour, and their presence in the river seemed to suggest the prelude to a coming hatch of flies.

The restless nymphs were losing their caution now, working out from under their hiding places and exposing themselves to the fish. The sunlight filtered through the water, warming the bottom currents. The nymphs clambered into position along the underwater sides of the stones, clinging with their tiny claws to the smooth surfaces. Working their bodies and gill plates carefully, they create a partial vacuum that fastens them firmly to the bottom. Emergence occurs there, with the thoracic structure splitting along the wing cases, and partially along the axis of the tergite surfaces. The wings struggle free of the nymphal skin, and then the legs work themselves loose. The hatching nymph sometimes pauses momentarily, and finally draws its writhing body and speckled tails from its nymphal shuck. The surprising vacuum created by the gill plates and legs is broken once the emerging mayfly has struggled free, and the loose nymphal skin drifts off with the current, while the freshly hatched insect wriggles and works toward the surface.

Mayfly hatches all begin with the hatching duns or nymphs migrating up through the water, beyond the tumbling surface of the river. The fish begin seeing and taking occasional nymphs when they first become restless; it is this prehatching restlessness that forces the normally shy nymphs to expose themselves more recklessly before emergence.

The rhythm of hatching quickens after midday with the *Epeorus* flies, until more and more nymphs split their nymphal skins, and their wriggling mayflies struggle toward the surface. Their folded wings help buoy them upward, their smoky veins and diaphanous structures alive with tiny air bubbles generated within the skins of the nymphs themselves. The fish respond to their increasing availability by taking the hatching flies as they wriggle past, and as the numbers of insects working toward the surface steadily grows larger, the hungry trout soon follow them. Finally the majority of the hatching flies are wriggling just under the surface film and riding the current itself. The fish have usually followed them up from the bottom currents, taking the hapless insects where they find them, until finally the trout hang poised just under the surface ready to feed extensively on the floating mayflies.

Dry-fly fishing has its origins in these ancient rhythms of aquatic entomology and the hatch; and the cycles disprove one of the classic myths of American dry-fly theory. George La Branche fervently believed that a skilled caster could create the illusion of a fly hatch for a nonfeeding trout by presenting his fly again and again to its feeding currents. La Branche argued that the parade of drifting dry flies created by his successive casts could trick the fish into thinking a hatch had started. *The Dry Fly and Fast Water* outlines the hypothesis of creating a hatch forged by the high priest of American presentation. Except for terrestrial insects or a fall of mayfly spinners after mating, La Branche was clearly mistaken, and neither of these latter happenings is actually a hatch. No trout could mistake his parade of perfectly cast flies for a genuine hatch of aquatic insects, since the fish would not previously have observed and fed on the first quickening rhythms of the emerging nymphs, as they lost their caution and drifted toward the surface.

That April afternoon on the Brodheads, the number of nymphal skins drifting past me in the smooth current was increasing steadily, and an occasional mayfly actually came fluttering off the riffles upstream. The sunlight caught another dun flying toward the trees, and a third came sailboating and hopscotching down the riffles on the cool wind. There were suddenly several in the air, and a hungry phoebe darted out from the alders to capture one just as it escaped the water. The agile little flycatcher wheeled back in midflight, its rapier-quick bill whiskered with the freshly hatched insect.

The current was quickly covered with flies now, riding the water like a regatta of minuscule sailboats, and close against the hemlock ledges across the current, the first trout rose and took one. It was the first dry-fly hatch of the season. Trout began rising regularly now, taking the flies just below the riffles where they were hatching, along the deep hemlock ledges in the upper pool, down the eddying hundred-foot spine below the outcroppings, and in the gathering currents of the tail shallows where they flowed against the sheltering willows.

Although I was relatively sure of their species, I did not select an imitation until I had collected one or two. Insects look quite pale in the air, flying from the river to shelter in the streamside bushes, and they appear even paler riding the current than when they are held in the hand. I waded out into a strong current tongue and collected two or three specimens, placing them in a small open-throat collecting bottle. Their wings were dark grayish and there were two tails. Their bodies were grayish olive, delicately ringed with brown. Their legs were amber, with strong brown mottlings on each femur, and these characteristics clearly identified the hatching insects as the early *Epeorus* mayflies common on eastern rivers like the Brodheads.

Gordon Quills should work, I thought.

It was one of those afternoons when the trout eagerly cooperated, and our dry-fly imitations worked perfectly. There was a good fish feeding in the tail currents. It was lying tight under the willows in a slightly slower current tongue, which made a carefully executed hook cast necessary to prevent the fly from dragging. The cast sliced out sideways into the soft wind, and I checked its final shoot gently to drop the slack-line hook above the fish. The upstream slack in the cast would buy a few seconds of drag-free float, long enough for a natural drift over the trout, and it took the fly without hesitation. When I tightened to set the hook, it threshed angrily along the willows and stripped line from my delicate reel. Several times it forced itself deep along the bottom gravel, and once its gyrations raked the fragile 6X tippet against a stone. Finally it surrendered to the waiting net, and I admired its brightly spotted sixteen inches before gently releasing it in the shallows.

It was typical of the dry-fly method.

History does not tell us precisely where or when the dry-fly method was born, which is rather surprising, considering its relatively recent origins. The literature of fly-fishing first mentions dry-fly tactics almost 150 years ago, and there is quite unmistakable evidence that the dry fly began somewhere on the chalkstreams of England.

There are many British rivers that have played a role in the evolution of the dry-fly method. Perhaps the best known are the silken Test at villages like Stockbridge and Whitchurch and Chilbolton, and the Itchen a few miles above Winchester, where Viscount Grey of Fallodon regularly fished almost a century ago. There is the pastoral Frome where George Selwyn Marryat first learned his fly-fishing, years before his famous collaboration with Halford in the development of the dry-fly technique on the Houghton water of the Test. There are the storied Kennet, famed throughout England for its blizzardlike mayfly hatches, and its delightful limestone tributary, the gentle Lambourne. Certainly there are also historic roots in the Wandle, where Halford himself first observed the dry-fly method, and the willow-lined Bourne, where Plunket-Greene fished at Hurstbourne Priors. The Coln at Fairford also has its own measure of history and fame. The gentle Avon is another classic chalkstream, winding through the water meadows below Salisbury Cathedral, and there are beats with poetic beauty along the little Wylye at charming Wiltshire villages like Fisherton-de-la-Mere.

Popular legend ascribes the dry fly and its origins to the Itchen, although its birth in angling literature lies still farther toward the west, on the little rivers fished by George Pulman. His famous *Vade Mecum of Fly-Fishing for Trout* appeared in 1841, and contains the first unmistakable description of the dry-fly method. Pulman was a tackle seller from Axminster in the rolling Devonshire hills, and his home rivers were moorland streams like the Barle and the Exe, and the classic beats of the Axe that he loved for so many seasons.

Frederic Halford is considered the father of the dry-fly method, as we explained at length in earlier chapters, although he did not fully originate its theory and practice. Halford was the historian of its early evolution, and codified the innovations of both his predecessors and his contemporaries on the smooth-flowing Hampshire and Wiltshire streams below London. Halford owed much of his philosophy and technique to the celebrated George Selwyn Marryat, who died tragically without publishing a fishing book himself. Marryat polished his fishing along the Coln in Dorsetshire, and Halford tells us in his memoirs that his baptism in the dry-fly method occurred on the willow-lined beats of the Wandle at Carshalton.

Yet his principal river became the world-famous Test at Stockbridge, and it is curious that our historical knowledge of that unique stream is less than two centuries old. It must have been fished in the centuries before Berners and Walton, since it has bountiful fly hatches and has always boasted incredible populations of fish, conspicuously lying over the mottled gravel among its beds of trailing weed.

It is strange that fly-fishing literature does not mention the Test until the threshold of the nineteenth century, with the meticulous diary of Colonel Peter Hawker, who fished its beautiful Longparish water. Hawker recorded his experiences along the upper Test from 1802 until 1853, and his chronicles are augmented by the diary of the Reverend Richard Durnford, who fished the Chilbolton water downstream from 1809 until 1819.

The historical records of the Houghton Club on the Test were finally compiled by Sir Herbert Maxwell in 1908, and they form an unbroken record of fly-fishing on the Test for more than eighty-five seasons. Canon Charles Kingsley described the river in his *Chalkstream Studies* in 1857, two decades before Frederic Halford emerged as its principal philosopher and historian. There were other writers who found inspiration in the crystalline reaches of the Test, men like Viscount Grey of Fallodon, Francis Francis, and George Edward MacKenzie Skues. Andrew Lang once held a beat on the Whitchurch water. John Waller Hills became its writer-in-residence with his poetic *A Summer on the Test* in 1924, and both Edward Ringwood Hewitt and George La Branche fished it in those same years. Our knowledge of the Test and its role in the evolution of the dry-fly method weaves a continuous written fabric reaching back more than 170 years to Hawker and Durnford.

Its character and the quality of its sport attracted a remarkable parade of famous men. There was Sir Francis Chantrey, the famous sculptor who was a founder of the Houghton Club; Chantrey was joined by J. M. W. Turner, perhaps the finest landscape painter in the history of European art. His drawings are still found in the journals of the Houghton Club. Sir Humphrey Davy also loved the Test and its fishing. Disraeli and Lord Nelson and the Duke of Wellington were all occasional fly-fishing pilgrims on the Test and its sister rivers. Disraeli even owned the beautiful Testcombe estate at Chilbolton. Thomas Phelps also fished the river and described it in *Fishing Dreams*, and his companion along the upper Test was J. C. Mottram, considered the finest British surgeon of his time. Lord Palmerston lived and fished beside the lower river at Broadlands, which later became the Hampshire estate of Lord Louis Mountbatten. It is a fishing tradition that is old and rich, reaching back to William of Wykeham and Izaak Walton himself, who lived along the Test at Norington Farme almost until his death. It is the Test and its difficult trout that polished the dry-fly method to its modern degree of refinement, and we owe a monumental debt to the men who have fished it over the past century, from its still Mayfly reaches at Stockbridge to the gravelly beats of the upper river at Longparish and Hurstbourne Priors and Whitchurch.

Such men worked out the basic topologies between dry flies and various species of floating insects. The rich phosphates of the chalkstreams sustained immense hatches of mayflies and caddis, and these orders were their first prototypes for fly patterns. Since their pioneering efforts, anglers have developed workable imitations for a whole galaxy of insect forms. Modern dry flies are dressed to imitate the adult or egg-laying stages of insects like mayflies, caddis, stoneflies, ants, leafhoppers, grasshoppers, craneflies, midges, and beetles. Such insects riding or floating pinioned in the surface film are the catalysts for the dry-fly method, and the trout greedily take them there with clearly visible rise forms.

Both the techniques of fly dressing and the fishing tackle worked out by these pioneers on the Test in the late nineteenth century have passed through a considerable evolution in the past one hundred years. Technology has continued to evolve so rapidly that virtually nothing, from popular fly patterns to our tapered lines and leader materials and the calibrations of the rods themselves, remains quite the same as it existed when Bergman first published *Trout* in 1938.

Edward Ringwood Hewitt initially followed the British modes in stiff rods capable of vigorous false casting to dry his flies, and his influence resulted in a whole generation of stiff-butt and relatively soft-tip calibrations in rods. Hewitt ultimately abandoned his stiff-butt theories, and in some classic film footage shot years ago along the Neversink by my good friend Martin Bovey, both Hewitt and La Branche are using supple, slow-action rods of more contemporary design. It seems doubtful, according to conversations with men like John Alden Knight and the late Guy Jenkins, that Hewitt ever really fished extensively with the fast-action tapers he often recommended.

Bergman advocated similar tapers in *Trout,* although his favorite rods had an action that flexed well down the butt section toward the grip. His preferences in rod design ran to models of seven and a half feet in a time when most trout rods ran from eight to nine feet. Several of my first split-cane rods were nine feet long, although they were delicate enough for a six-weight English line. The first was a darkly stained Heddon and the second was a South Bend from the skilled hands of Wes Jordan. Bergman advocated delicacy in his rods, combined with a supple feeling of power. Since he was the senior salesman at the old William Mills & Son shop in lower Manhattan, selling the original Leonard rods, Bergman was familiar with rod actions that had extremely fine tip calibrations combined with a taper that worked well down into the grip. His chapter in *Trout* devoted to dry-fly fundamentals and tackle made the following observations thirty-five years ago:

> First, for delicacy in casting it is best not to have a rod which is too heavy and stiff. Usually, better **grade** rods ranging from 7½ to

nine feet in length and from 3½ to 5½ ounces in weight will fill the bill in the matter of weight, but it is a good idea to be quite particular, as some rods of identical length and weight may have actions as different as night and day.

For instance, I have one 7½-foot rod of 3¾ ounces which is like a poker, and as far as I am concerned fit only for spinner or bait fishing, but I have several others of the same length and weight which are stiff and powerful without being pokers.

It's all in the feel, with power and stiffness being combined with resilience and suppleness. Some rods have this and others do not. Now this right feel is an elusive thing. It is indescribable, that is to the extent that you cannot possibly pick out a rod from the description. The nearest I can come to giving you an impression of it is that you feel the rod live and breathe right down to the grip. The action is distributed with a decreasing, even power from the hand grasp to the tip top.

Recent years have witnessed a trend toward rods under four ounces and eight feet in length, since increased fishing pressure and the sophisticated brown trout found in public water today require extremely delicate tackle. Short rods are surprisingly fashionable.

Generally speaking, rods that demand lines heavier than six- or seven-weight tapers are too heavy for modern dry-fly fishing, since they drop too hard on the current for the sensibilities of a sophisticated trout. Some rodmakers have pursued the concept of extremely short rods weighing from one to two and a half ounces, but some of these rods are really not designed for fishing over shy trout in smooth currents. Weight-forward lines on such small rods may make them impressive casting tools, tempting their owners into believing that their casting skills have been radically improved by the equipment, but such line tapers land too hard for a skittish fish in a smooth flat. Rods taking a six- and seven-weight line, while weighing only two to two and a half ounces, are too muscular in their tip calibrations to fish the delicate limp-nylon tippet diameters common on public waters. Such rods have become extremely fashionable in recent years, but I do not believe they are viable for difficult fishing. They are impressive in their line-handling qualities, shooting eighty to ninety feet in the hands of a skilled caster, but their torpedo tapers deliver harshly and their relatively thick tip calibrations are much too crude for .003 to .005 nylon.

Such short rods are also a problem in other aspects of dry-fly fishing, and wading a deep flat makes fishing a short fly rod difficult. Their length is ideal for fishing brushy streams that are densely shrouded in willows and alders, with overhanging trees. However, in bank fishing along some western spring creeks and the Pennsylvania limestone streams, sufficient rod length is critical to keeping the backcast out of the weeds and grass. Several times I have watched skilled casters brought to the threshold of total frustration on such rivers; and watching an American fish his so-called midge rods on the Hampshire chalkstreams, or limestone water meadows like the Liffey and the Maigue in Ireland, is another exercise in sympathy—since backcast after backcast inevitably hangs up in the waist-high grasses.

There are a number of superb midge-type rods available, however, that are valuable tools for fine work. These rods are consciously designed to fish flies under size sixteen, cast seventy to eighty feet in skilled hands, and hook a good fish without shearing delicate modern tippets measuring in .003 to .005 diameters. Such tackle is critical to success in fishing midge-sized imitations and tiny terrestrials on difficult rivers from Silver Creek in Idaho to limestone streams like Falling Springs or the famous Letort Spring Run in Pennsylvania.

Since the introduction of modern silicone fly dressing, it is no longer necessary to dry our flies with as much false casting, and stiffness is less important in a dry-fly rod design. Such fly oil was unknown thirty-five years ago, and Bergman recommended a relatively crude mixture consisting of two ounces of shaved paraffin dissolved in a pint of gasoline or carbon tetrachloride. Such mixtures often damaged silkworm-gut tippets, and when the temperature dropped below sixty degrees, the paraffin often congealed unless it was carried in inside pockets. Our modern silicones in plastic bottles or small spray cans are a considerable improvement over the old fly-dressing mixtures.

Modern fly lines are also exceptional. The British silk lines that I fished in boyhood were almost poetic in their suppleness and casting qualities, working in unmatched harmony with a silkworm-gut leader. Yet silk lines had their shortcomings. Their finishes became tacky and, unless they were regularly dried, silk lines tended to rot and lose their strength. Proper care demanded that silk lines be dried each night, and a well-equipped angler usually carried two lines for use on alternate days. Silk lines were also slightly heavier than water, and became easily waterlogged in the course of a day's fishing. This required daily applications of various line dressings like the well-known Mucilin paste from Britain. These problems have been largely solved with the development of nylon plastic-coated lines.

Fishing brooks and feeder streams with the dry-fly method can mean using delicate little rods from six to seven feet, weighing from two to three ounces and taking three- to five-weight lines. Double-taper designs are almost mandatory for such waters to avoid spooking the small-stream trout, and the ideal floating lines vary from DT3F and DT4F tapers for the smallest rods to the DT5F that will match most light-tackle rods. These are optimal late-summer rods as well, since they will cast delicately and fish the cobweb-fine leaders necessary for covering a gin-clear flat on many of our late-summer streams.

Proper dry-fly tackle for medium-size rivers demands somewhat bigger rods and heavier gear. Seven-and-a-half to eight-foot rods are in order now, weighing from two and three quarters to four ounces, depending on their design specifications. Deep wading requires the longer rods necessary to hold the backcasts high enough. Such rods will balance with five- and six-weight lines, and although double tapers were mandatory in the past, there are new long-belly types of forward tapers that deliver a cast softly enough for dry-fly tactics over smooth currents and selective fish. This past spring on the Dunraven Castle water of the Maigue in Ireland, such a six-weight taper proved itself remarkably effective in presenting tiny Iron Blues at distances beyond eighty feet—turning over a delicate twelve-foot stiff butt leader and settling the cast on the smooth currents without frightening its wary fish.

Big river dry-fly tactics can require equipment with still more muscle. Eight- to nine-foot rods are necessary to punch out a wind-resistant dry fly like a big Wulff or Hewitt Skater at eighty to ninety feet. Such rods will best function with lines of six- to eight-weight tapers, and the long-belly design is perhaps the best tool we have for long-range dry-fly work. The modern hard-plastic finishes possible with synthetic lines also permit a skilled fisherman to shoot a long dry-fly presentation.

Typical dry-fly presentation consists of casting from across and below a visibly rising trout, and the line is manipulated to provide a dragless float over the fish with a floating imitation of its food. Basic theory requires as natural a float over the rising trout as possible, completely free of any drag across its current tongues on the bellying leader.

British dogmatics from the Halford period ignored the skittering technique that men like William Lunn on the Test and Roger Foster on the Maigue in Ireland have always used to suggest a hatching or egg-laying sedge. Their methods are subtle, almost inducing a rise to the floating imitation in the way that nymph experts like Frank Sawyer and Oliver Kite perfected on the Wiltshire rivers at Salisbury. Hewitt also developed his Neversink Skaters to imitate the erratic hopscotch of egg-laying craneflies; and these induced-drag techniques are contrary to conventional dry-fly wisdom, often involving downstream casts.

Leonard Wright again outlined such variations on traditional dry-fly themes in his recent *Fishing the Dry Fly as a Living Insect*, which adapted these techniques of skittering a dry-fly with intentional drag to imitate the American caddisflies. However, basic dry-fly tactics imitating most of the fly hatches and terrestrial insects along trout water still demand the conventional dragless float.

Such dragless presentations are usually achieved in six basic types of dry-fly casts. Each technique involves a free drift over the trout, in which the floating imitation reaches the fish before it sees the leader tippet. The cast from directly downstream does not achieve this stratagem, although with the delicate and less visible modern nylons, it has become a somewhat more useful tactic. The direct upstream presentation is perhaps the easiest method of achieving a dragless float, since fly and leader and line all lie in current tongues of closely related direction and speed. Such methodology is a frequent theme in the books of Bergman, both the early *Just Fishing* and the later *Trout*; and his tactical anecdotes often involved crossing the main currents to fish a pool from its less-travelled bank—always finding the problems thwarting a drag-free drift were easier from there.

The leader-free presentations are considerably more difficult to master under field conditions. Each of these methods is used for fish lying to the right or left of the angler and rising steadily with the faster currents lying between. The right and left hook casts are both designed to fall above the fish with an exaggerated semicircle of upstream slack. These casts are useful when the current tongues between the angler and the trout are relatively swift. Particularly easy currents call for a less exaggerated hook-cast presentation, in which the hook is little more than a gentle curve. Placing the tippet only slightly above the rising fly-shy trout in a shallow flat may require a variation on this tactic, which places the fly slightly short of the fish, so that neither the leader nor the imitation falls too close to its position. The final leader-free presentations are the crosscurrent and downstream casts to right or left, and a directly downstream cast checked in flight to partially abort the cast and create a series of slack-line loops.

Before discussing the basic methods of dry-fly presentation, perhaps an admonition about sinking and floating leaders is in order. Unlike the other forms of fly-fishing, the dry-fly leader is usually required to float in order to insure a ready strike when a fish rises to the fly. Yet a floating leader can prove itself a serious liability in smooth currents, since its patterns in the surface film can cast surprisingly large shadows along the bottom. Such shadows can easily spook a crowd-skittish trout. However, sinking the leader to eliminate these surface-film shadows is not so easy with modern nylons, and is not always the solution in all cases. It is sometimes important on smooth pools and flats, but on broken currents a sinking leader will result in missed fish, and the leader should be lightly oiled so that its sunken drag and slack cannot slow our striking reflex.

There are fifteen basic techniques and primary variations of the dry-fly method as practiced on American waters, and they involve both drag-free and controlled-drag tactics. Our present philosophy of dry-fly fishing is a considerable departure from the drag-free dogma and rigid upstream rules first codified on the chalkstreams by men like Halford and Marryat.

1. Left-Hook Presentation

The left hook is a difficult cast for a right-handed angler, but it is a common tactical situation for a pool with its primary holding currents on the left bank of the stream. There are two basic methods of making the left hook work: the first involves turning the wrist inward in the final delivery of the cast, until the back of the hand faces left; and the second involves making a normal sidearm delivery until the final second of the cast, shooting loose slack, and then breaking the wrist sharply at the final moment to snap a crisp left hook into the leader.

No river is without pools or runs or eddying backwaters where the left-hook cast is critical to success. The trout lie across the primary current tongues from the angler, motionless under the willows or tight against the roots of the sheltering buttonwoods, and a direct cast is caught almost instantly by the flow. The bellying leader and line drag the dry fly across the suspicious fish almost as quickly as it touches the water. It is a familiar problem to any fly-fisherman.

The solution is a delicately thrown left-hook cast which drops the dry fly a few inches above the fish, driving the leader tippet farther upstream to fall in a slack loop of nylon when we shoot two or three feet of extra line and snub the cast at the final moment. Properly delivered, such a cast will provide a few inches of drag-free float until the current draws the cushion of slack from the upstream loop. The fish will have just enough time to rise to the drag-free imitation.

Both hook casts are difficult to execute well, since there is little margin for error in the size of the slack loop in the leader, the possible duration of the float in terms of current speed between the angler and the fish, and the initial arrival of the cast on the water. Experience is necessary to master these several variables, but the left-hand hook is not beyond a caster of moderate skills, and it is a primary tactic on trout water.

2. Right-Hook Presentation

The right-hook cast is a corollary to the left-hook cast. It involves a fish working along the right bank of the stream, and lying on the far side of the current tongue. Again the direct cast will almost immediately result in a dragging fly, unless the fisherman can throw enough upstream slack to achieve a drag-free float. Such a natural drift is possible with a well-placed right-hook cast.

It is easier for a right-handed angler to execute, since it is merely an incomplete cast with a slight shooting of left-hand slack. The cast is delivered in a sidearm or three-quarter position and is worked out over the fish, checked before it is dropped to the water by halting the normal wrist follow-through, and allowed to settle on the current with a soft upstream hook in the leader. Practice and experience will help you judge how to deliver and check your cast while the line loop is still unrolling to drop the leader in a perfect right-hook cast. Seasoned anglers also know how to use a downstream wind to their advantage rather than disadvantage, working the line from angles that help force the leader into a controlled downstream loop that presents the fly to the trout first and gains several seconds of drag-free drift.

This cast is less difficult than a left-hook presentation, and was the first difficult dry-fly tactic that I learned in my youth on the rivers of lower Michigan. Thinking back about those years, when my casting skills were rudimentary at best, the simple right-hook technique was a revelation. In those summers spent along the brushy tree-hung reaches of the Little South Pere Marquette, the growing ability to place a hook cast under the overhanging branches quickly multiplied my daily catches.

The right-hook cast is surprisingly easy to learn, more than several

other advanced techniques, and no fly-fisherman can master his journey-
man skills without it.

3. Upstream Check Cast

This is a basic dry-fly presentation used on shy fish when both fly and
leader must settle on the surface like thistledown. It is a simple procedure
once it is fully understood. The fisherman is perhaps thigh-deep in a glassy
flat known for its selective trout. The fly and leader must land softly
without frightening them, or they will stop rising altogether. It is a familiar
problem on hard-fished pools and flats from the Allagash in Maine to the
Nimpkish in British Columbia, and it is a primary tool of skilled dry-fly
technique.

Several days ago I watched two anglers fish the Hewitt Flat on my
home water of the Brodheads. It was bright and still, and the silken currents
of the pool shelved off into the waist-deep water below the bridge where
Edward Ringwood Hewitt tells us that he first tried the dry-fly method. It is
a fine pool with a good population of free-rising fish. Good hatches come off
the bridge pocket water above the pool, and its trout are well known for
their free-rising selectivity.

The first angler fished the pool in the classic American style, his
stiff-action rod working in a quick flick-flick rhythm of false casting. His
fishing was almost nervous and brusque. The casting rhythms were
rapierlike in character, and each final cast came with a driving follow-
through with the rod low above the current. His flies were thoroughly dried
and cocked high, coming down crisply above each rising trout. The casting
was accurate but much too hard, and from my vantage point on the bridge,
I watched him frighten a number of fish that either stopped feeding
altogether or bolted away in panic. Other than delivering the fly too hard,
his presentation was perfectly executed.

Can't understand it! he yelled upstream to the bridge. *There were at least a
dozen fish working!*

The mayflies were still hatching from the swift reach of water above
the bridge, but now they fluttered down the main currents of the pool
unmolested. The old dry-fly man waded slowly from the pool, and almost
immediately several fish began drifting back into feeding position. Another
fisherman slipped into the gathering currents in the tail shallows, and as we
watched for several minutes, the first trout rose again.

With this hatch, the second man laughed, *you'd think more fish would be
feeding in the Hewitt.*

There were, I said.

Somebody just fish through it? he asked.

Put them all down! I smiled.

There were several more rises now, and a number of other fish had
taken feeding stations again. Gradually they drifted higher in the current
until they hovered just under the glassy surface, and soon these trout were
feeding steadily too.

What're you using? I asked.

Red Quill seems to work just fine today, he said. *What was the other fisherman using over these fish?*

Red Quill, I laughed.

The second man nodded and eased slowly into casting position, where several trout were greedily working to the hatch of dark *Ephemerella* flies. His fishing style was radically different from the first man's: his casting rhythms were surprisingly relaxed; and his rod working almost lazily in its false casting. There was a good fish rising forty feet above him, and he took it on his second cast. It was a fine performance, and he coaxed the struggling fish carefully downstream from the other rising trout.

That fish was no accident! I thought.

The fisherman released the trout gently, washed the slime from his fly, and sprayed it with silicone dressing. He dried the fly with a few tantalizing slow false casts, and moved slowly into position for the second fish.

His cast worked out above its feeding station, travelling a few feet longer than necessary, and he delivered it like a false cast. The line and leader and fly unrolled and straightened about three feet above the surface, and at the final moment the fisherman drew back his casting hand slightly. It broke his follow-through, checked the cast in midair well above the glassy surface, and allowed it to settle softly. The fly cocked and fell virtually without disturbing the current above the rising trout, and when the fly reached its station, another fish rose confidently.

That makes two, I smiled.

It was a vivid episode that clearly proved the viability of the upstream check-cast technique on difficult fish in smooth water, and the second angler took nine fish from the pool, with the same fly that had been used half an hour earlier. Both fly pattern and terminal tackle diameter had been the same, but the driving follow-through used by the first angler had frightened the trout, while the gentle check cast had taken them.

4. Slack S-Cast

This is a clever variation on the check cast that is designed to throw enough slack across erratic surface currents to buy a few moments of drag-free float before the fly reaches a feeding trout. Sometimes a pool is a series of crosscurrents and eddies, making conventional hook casts useless.

The solution is often a well-executed slack S-cast that distributes a series of serpentine loops across the surface. The technique involves delivering the final cast to the same imaginary plane above the actual water, and checking the follow-through, but in the final instant the angler waggles his rod sideways to throw slack into the falling line. The result is a series of irregular slack-line loops that cushion the fly drag of conflicting surface currents.

Such complex current tongues are typical of our limestone streams and weed-rich western spring creeks riffling and eddying through their beds of trailing candelabra and nitella and watercress. Crosscurrents are also common in boulder-strewn rivers, and pools downstream from broken ledges and wild pocket water. The slack S-cast thrown across such irregular patterns of flow is often the only solution.

5. Parachute Cast

The well-known parachute cast is another method of achieving a series of slack-line loops across conflicting currents. It involves false casting enough line to reach well beyond the actual intended target point for the fly, like both the upstream check-cast and the slack S-cast. However, instead of checking the follow-through or shaking loops into the line with a side waggle of the rod, the parachute cast consists of stopping the cast short of the follow-through, and abruptly dropping the butt of the rod toward the surface of the river.

The result is a checked cast that settles to the surface in a random pattern of slack-line loops. Since a parachute cast tends to fall in a slightly different manner from the conventional delivery of either a check cast or an S-cast, it can work in some situations where the others fail.

6. Brush-Cast Technique

Few anglers seem to know the brush-cast technique familiar to the anglers who fish the spring creeks of Pennsylvania and Maryland. It is eloquently described by Charles Fox in his *Wonderful World of Trout* as the undercover cast. It is designed for fishing deep under the overhanging trees, and is extremely useful on most rivers.

Trout often hold deep in the shadows of such overhanging limbs, and only a drag-free float under the branches will take them. The cast is a long sidearm presentation designed to work a narrow loop in the line. The rod tip executes most of the action, and the false cast is worked with somewhat more line speed than would normally be required to deliver the line in the air. The final cast is executed with a driving wrist action, carrying the line low along the water, and at the final moment the left-hand slack is allowed to shoot into the guides. Perfectly executed, the shooting line and leader float back underneath the overhanging branches, settling above the rising fish.

7. Cross-Country Cast

Sometimes trout are rising beyond a deadfall or branch, or lying along an open grassy bank that makes them skittish and difficult to approach. Both situations are perfectly suited to the cross-country cast, which drops the leader and sometimes the line across the intervening barriers. The true cross-country cast is possible with wet flies and nymphs, but a cast across a downed tree or limb is best with a stiff-hackled dry fly, since its hackles permit it to come back with less danger of snagging.

The actual cast is delivered softly like an upstream or cross-stream check method, allowing the leader and line to straighten and settle to the surface gently. Since drag is inevitable and will begin quickly, the dry fly must be placed to fall almost on the rising fish. Sometimes a brief float is possible, but watching while it approaches the feeding station seems to take an eternity as you wait for the fatal drag to begin. The strike must always be quicker and firmer, to overcome the friction of the grassy banks or the intervening snag, than in a normal cast delivered over the water.

Over the years the cross-country cast has produced several big fish for me on meadow water, including a five-pound brown on the Big Hole. It was a fish I should not have tried, but once it was hooked there was little choice. The trout was rising steadily behind a half-submerged deadfall below Biltmore Springs, and its impressive rise forms sent waves down the currents trapped between the log and the far bank. It was a difficult place to cover properly.

The river is strong there, and I waded out almost chest-deep into the current, until the fly boxes in my wading vest were literally shipping water. The deadfall was still forty-five feet away, and the fish was rising beyond it, splashing water across its bleached limbs. It was a perfect place for a long-hackled spider or variant, since such a fly could be retrieved back across the log with less chance of fouling. The cast worked out past the logs, and I checked it perfectly, dropping the fly just beyond the deadfall and above the rising fish.

It reacted with a violent rise form that showered water high on the wind, and it cakewalked wildly downstream behind the log. The fish jumped several times, raking my leader back and forth over the tree, and it looked huge. The fight seemed hopeless, with a great jackstraw tangle of logs downstream, when the big trout inexplicably somersaulted out of its thicket into the open currents of the river.

The leader caught briefly, but instantly worked free of the shredding bark, and the rest of the fight went my way. However, such luck on a five-pound brown is rare—big fish seldom make mistakes.

8. Dapping, Dibbing, and Bushing

These fishing methods are centuries old. They are clearly discussed throughout British fishing literature before the first colonial settlements were established in Virginia and Massachusetts. There are a number of old names for such practices, like dibbing and shade-fishing, and dapping is a term sometimes used to describe blow-line fishing with live *Ephemera* flies on famous Irish lakes like Lough Derg and Lough Corrib. William Lawson also mentions the method in his famous edition of *The Secrets of Angling*, which first appeared in 1620:

> This flie and two linkes among wood or close by a bank, moved cleverly in the crust of the water, is deadly in the evening, if you come close. This is called bushing for trouts.

Dapping consists of lowering a fly through the streamside foliage without casting, and dancing it up and down on the surface directly above the holding lie of the trout. Dibbing is the similar technique applied to meadow banks with high grasses that sometimes make it virtually impossible to fish a likely current on the near bank without being seen. Trout in such places are often observed through a concealing screen of weeds and water grasses, and sometimes the vegetation is so dense that such fish are only heard rising. The dry fly is fished over them tantalizingly, dancing on the surface film with a nervous little rhythm beside the undercut banks. Such manipulation looks like the restless fluttering of an egg-laying caddis, and can be remarkably effective at times.

Bushing consists of the same technique executed over low streamside foliage, often to a rising fish that can only be heard splashily feeding or that has been located only from the spreading ripples generated by his rise forms. The cast is made over the screen of bushes to the unseen current beyond. Bergman describes his success in *Trout* with the bushing method along a particularly brushy reach of the Encampment in Wyoming. The rise to the dry fly fished in this manner is often relatively strong, and the strike should be delayed slightly to avoid shearing the tippet. Striking at the precise moment of the rise is likely to rake the fly from the mouth of the fish, since its direction of force is away from the jaws rather than into them. Since the leader is not lying in the surface film, its visible thickness is less critical in dapping and bushing than in more normal dry-fly techniques. Many fishermen recommend tippets as strong as .009 for average conditions, and .007 for dapping on small streams and still currents. Hooking percentages for these tactics will improve if the fisherman learns to curb his natural instinct to strike hard at the first moment of the rise; a fish still holding the fly is more likely to find itself hooked securely in the corner of its jaws if the angler waits to strike until the trout is turning toward its original holding lie.

9. Grasshopper or Bump Cast

This is a conventional cast designed to drop the fly relatively hard on the surface film in order to attract the fish when they are waiting for a big terrestrial insect like a grasshopper or fully grown inchworm to land clumsily on the water. Such a hard presentation is diametrically opposed to most dry-fly practice with its so-called thistledown settling of a perfectly cocked floater, but it is a technique directly related to the behavior of such awkward land-bred insects. When the inchworms are particularly numerous, and the meadows are alive with grasshoppers in late summer, the trout are often quick to seize them as they fall clumsily into the stream.

They're watching for a 'hopper to plop into the pool these days, explained one of my early mentors. *Give them a plop cast!*

It was excellent advice, and it has produced exceptional results over the years, particularly in late-summer grasshopper season. The cast is not particularly difficult. The backcast rises fairly high and the rod tip rides back to approximately two o'clock. The elbow drops as the backcast straightens and delivers a little more power into the forward delivery than is actually needed. The rod is driven sharply into its final follow-through, throwing an exaggerated hump into the line that rolls forward with the extending line. Checking the follow-through, the angler drives the fly forward until the fly receives the power imparted to the rolling hump in the line. It is delivered to the surface with a relatively sharp impact, like a fat inchworm dropping from the treetops, or the awkward faltering of a big grasshopper into a still trout-filled flat, and their impacts into the surface film are exactly what attracts a foraging late-summer fish.

There have been many experiences with the grasshopper cast over the years, but perhaps the most dramatic occurred on a small limestone spring creek in central Pennsylvania. It was a hot day in late August, although the steady upwelling of the limestone sink at the source of the stream kept its currents cold and rich with fly life. The grainfields along the little river were unusually alive with big grasshoppers that season, and the hot wind was getting them into the current in surprising numbers.

The lower meadows enclose two hundred yards of rich marl-bottomed flat. It lies five hundred yards downstream from the fishing house and the suspension bridge below the deep sapphire-colored sink where the stream is born. The flat is smooth and clear and sixty degrees through the heat of August. Its opposite bank is sheltered by trees and limestone outcroppings, and its shallows are bordered with a marl shelf rich with sowbugs and scuds. It is a fine reach of big trout water.

We walked down to the flat and moved cautiously along the path toward the water. The sun was high and the hot wind moved through the valley and its grasshopper meadows. We stopped short of the flat. Big wild brown trout were cruising the pool in twos and threes like bonefish on some subtropical flat.

Look at them! I thought aloud.

We crouched low and studied the rise forms to determine what they were taking. The rises were quiet and strong, suggesting both big fish and a sizable insect. Then we felt the hot wind and saw the grasshoppers. They flew up when its tepid gusts crossed the grainfields and startled them. Once they were in the air, the wind caught them and carried them clumsily over the stream. It was too wide to cross safely, and the insects parachuted helplessly when the wind gusted and died, coming down mallard-hard on the smooth currents.

It was an inexorable fate. Their shallow, faltering trajectories quickly dropped them into the water, and the big trout stalked them ruthlessly. Their relatively hard impact in the surface film triggered the cruising fish into accelerating toward each struggling grasshopper. The trout had apparently learned that these insects were incapable of flight once they fell to the surface, and their swirls were quiet and strong, completely lacking the splashiness characteristic of most grasshopper feeding. We watched the big browns attack the unfortunate grasshoppers for several minutes.

They're like crocodiles, said Charles Fox.

We took twelve fish between fifteen and twenty-three inches before a rain squall misted down the valley, cooling the wind and ending the erratic flights of grasshoppers. It was an unusual afternoon of fishing. Our fly patterns clearly played a role in our remarkable success, and I have never seen an episode of such ravenous feeding on a limestone stream since, but the grasshopper cast was a factor too. Every time we dropped our imitations hard on the surface, the big browns turned toward them like barracudas and took them greedily.

10. The Cross-Stream Mend

Although mending the line halfway through a fly drift was first developed to dampen and control fly speed in wet-fly fishing, it is also useful to postpone drag in a cross-stream or downstream dry-fly float. There are many holding places, particularly under overhanging branches in smooth currents, that cannot always be fished with a conventional dry-fly presentation from below. Such fish must be fished with a cross-stream or downstream cast, and a subtle upstream mend of the line is useful in creating additional length in its dry-fly float.

The cast is delivered across the current or slightly downstream, dropping the fly above the fish. Its duration of drag-free float can be extended by stripping left-hand slack out through the guides, but an upstream mend is useful too. It involves raising the rod tip and lifting the belly of the line, rolling it upstream in a controlled loop without disturbing the fly and its line of drift. The belly of line looped upstream acts as a cushion of slack, dampening the dragging effect of the currents on the leader and line, and improving the dry-fly presentation. Several extra inches of drag-free float can spell the difference between putting down a skittish trout and fooling it into taking the fly.

There is a productive run on a favorite stream of mine that is perfect for a cross-stream mend. The fish lie deep in the shadows of its buttonwoods, their branches almost touching the swift currents where a single stone breaks the flow. There is always a good trout lying well under the branches, between the far bank and the stone, and slightly upstream in the shallows. The overhanging branches and the stone prevent a cast from below, and the several limbs that actually touch the water prevent a quartering upstream presentation. Even a direct cross-stream cast would foul in the low branches before the fly drift could actually reach the fish.

But the downstream presentation works. It is possible to fish this holding lie with a quartering downstream cast, stripping the loose left-hand slack into the drift and mending an upstream belly into the line. Executed perfectly, the upstream mend is often the key to an extra six to ten inches of float deep under the branches, and that extra slack is often just enough.

11. The Downstream Check

Sometimes a river presents us with a holding lie that is impossible to reach from any position except directly upstream, and a conventional cast aimed downstream will result in a fly dragging almost immediately. The downstream check cast is the solution.

Every fisherman knows where a good fish can be found lying in such a place, often at the lip of a difficult pool or flat, or hanging just at the very edge of a millrace or falls. Either a presentation from downstream is totally impossible or a cross-stream cast will result in instantaneous drag. When a downstream cast is feasible, it must be delivered to a rising fish by false casting slightly beyond the fish's holding place, executing the final cast to an imaginary surface of the river about three feet above the water, and then checking the entire cast by pulling the rod back from its normal follow-through. Properly executed the cast is deftly checked, and falls back toward the angler in a series of slack loops that must extend slowly with the current, while the fly floats downstream completely free of drag. When the length of the cast is right, this drag-free drift will last until it reaches the taking lie occupied by the rising trout.

The downstream check once produced a fine five-pound rainbow for me from the millrace at Fischen-im-Allgäu in southern Germany, a free-rising trout that had frustrated me an entire season. It persisted in holding and feeding just above the millrace hatch, three hundred yards above the mill itself. The millrace above the hatch was densely grown with willows. Because of the willows and the hatch gate itself, there was no place either below or beside the mill hatch where the rainbow could be reached. The channel leading to the hatch was relatively deep, except for a small gravelly shoal sixty-odd feet upstream. There was just enough space to slip into the chest-deep current off the willows and work a downstream check; and there would be only one chance to execute a cast. The big rainbow would either take the fly or evaporate in panic when it dragged.

Several attempts that summer ended in failure, but late in the season, when we were actually stalking red stag in the evenings, my luck with the big rainbow finally changed. The cast checked and settled properly, the fly drifted right down its feeding lane, and the fish took it with a self-confident porpoising rise. It could have turned through the hatch gate and sheared my tippet like a cobweb, but the fish bolted upstream into the weedy shallows instead, and once its first wild energy was expended I captured it easily. The downstream check cast was the secret.

12. The Surface Retrieve

Ray Bergman describes this rule-breaking variation of the dry-fly method in *Trout* with an episode on the Catskill rivers. His chapter on dry-fly tactics mentions fishing out every cast until it is well free of any real holding water, both to avoid frightening the fish with a pickup of the line and to avoid taking the fly away from a trout that has followed it a considerable distance, deciding to rise only at the last possible moment.

Sometimes on a still pool or flat there is so little current that the dry fly does not drift past the fish quickly. It can sink and be retrieved like a wet fly, or remain floating and be retrieved almost imperceptibly across the surface. The fly might be given an occasional twitching movement, but it should be brought back with a retrieve so subtle that it does not make a discernible disturbance in the surface film. Sometimes a fish will take the fly at the moment it starts to move, but sometimes one will follow and take when it has travelled several feet.

13. The Skimming Retrieve

There are insect forms and behavior patterns that dictate a subtly dragging fly to fool a rising trout. Such insects skitter across the surface, in the case of certain running caddisflies and sedges, or hang dragging from their silken little threads like the inchworms and leafrollers on our eastern rivers.

When the trout are watching for such little V-shaped furrows in the surface film, dry flies fished upstream with a drag-free float are virtually useless. Such times require that our flies be fished quartering downstream, almost like wet flies, and allowed to swing in a subtle, dragging retrieve across the current. Certain current speeds will work the fly properly, but others require manipulation of fly speed with the rod and the left-hand slack. The rod tip is smoothly and steadily raised to a position above and slightly behind the head to keep the fly skimming properly. Slower currents may require a slow, steady stripping of line with the left hand and coordinating it with the gradually rising rod. It will take some practice to work both rod and left hand together, keeping the dry fly skimming in the surface film, but with a little experience it is not excessively difficult.

The skimming retrieve breaks all the rules of dry-fly fishing laid down in the books of the British writer Frederic Halford, and the American dry-fly pioneer George La Branche as well, but catches fish when conditions are right.

14. The Skater Technique

George La Branche and his colleague Edward Ringwood Hewitt are the authors of this method. It was conceived on the classic log-cribbing flats of the Hewitt camp water on the Neversink. The skater technique is based upon both fly dressing and presentation on a relatively stiff leader tippet, and since Hewitt was a remarkably cantankerous and secretive man about the critical details of his art, we owe most of our knowledge of the skater technique to men like John Atherton and Vincent Marinaro.

Fox relates the story of his experience with skaters in *This Wonderful World of Trout*. It began in the waiting room of his family doctor in Pennsylvania. There were no magazines on fishing on its tables, but in a glossy paper journal devoted primarily to golf, skiing, sailboats, and fox hunting in eastern horse country, Fox discovered an article on skater fishing written by Hewitt himself. It was beautifully illustrated, and described the Hewitt experiments with his so-called butterfly fishing in the Catskills. Fox was about halfway through the piece when the nurse called him to the examining room, and once the doctor was finished, Fox eagerly returned to the waiting room to finish it.

He subsequently wrote to Hewitt, and was answered with a letter and assortment of skater flies in the following weeks. The Hewitt dressings were simplicity itself. There were no bodies or tail fibers. Two long-fibered hackles were wound on a light-wire hook, their concave sides facing each other to create a sharp edge of stiff hackle fibers where they met. The flies were designed to skitter, skate, and jump crazily across the current, with an erratic retrieve conceived to excite a fish into chasing and taking them. Fished properly, their action suggested big fluttering sedges, drakes, and craneflies, and they were dressed in simple colors like honey and badger and brown. Fox was fascinated with the flies, but it was some time before he actually fished them.

Their baptism came on famous Spring Creek in central Pennsylvania, during lunch on a hot day in late summer. Fox and his friends had fished hard all morning, and nothing they tried had worked. Fox selected one of the Hewitt skaters, Turle-knotting it firmly to the stiff 3X tippet, and he practiced skating it with a sandwich in his left hand.

Lacking experience with skaters, Fox cast toward a deep run along a brush pile where he had often taken good trout. The first cast fluttered to the surface, and Fox ate his sandwich absently, preoccupied with making the fly skitter and twitch across the water. The second cast brought a slashing strike, and Fox took the fly away from the fish awkwardly. Another strike clumsily left the fly in its jaws. Fox was agitated now, and found a second skater after he finished his sandwich. Unfamiliar with the wind resistance of a fluffy skater, he misjudged the rhythm of his false casting and broke the hook of the second pattern when it ticked against the rod. Two of the precious Hewitt flies were already gone.

Easy does it! Fox replaced his fly again.

Two good trout were quickly hooked and released, and then he moved a trophy-size brown that splashily showered the hopscotching skater three times without taking. Fox patiently rested the big fish for fifteen minutes, hooked it soundly on the first cast after the recess, and lost the fly when the trout bored into the brush pile.

Half my skaters are gone! Fox moaned. *I'm going to fish with the rest of them in a safer place!*

Above the old mill dam he located several more good fish with his polaroid glasses. They were holding just a foot or two under the surface. The smooth impoundment currents above the dam seemed like a good place to test his skaters. Fox first tried conventional flies without moving a fish. Then he tried the stiff-hackled Hewitt patterns and consistently raised and moved the sluggish hot-weather trout throughout the afternoon. Few trout were hooked, however, and Fox left a few more of the Hewitt flies in fish that broke off, but finally he mastered the gentle, delayed strike required in fishing skaters.

Both Fox and the late John Alden Knight observed that the technique is most effective when the fish are accustomed to seeing an occasional big insect fluttering across the current, and that even the tendency of the fish to roll at the skater without taking can be turned to the advantage of the fisherman. Dog-days trout can be located with skaters, and their holding lies marked down for another time, when cooler weather and a good hatch have them rising freely.

But it was the late Paul Young who aptly described skater fishing years ago.

Fishing a skater is easy, he said. *It's just like fishing a streamer dry!*

15. The Induced-Rise Technique

Hewitt and his skaters, the slow dry-fly retrieve, and the skimming dry fly in the surface film are all techniques that break the rules of conventional dry-fly philosophy. There has long been an unspoken school of fishing dry flies with an occasional twitch, especially when fish are rising to fluttering mayflies, or egg-laying and hatching caddis.

William Lunn was the venerable riverkeeper of the Houghton Club water on the Test for forty-five years. For its blizzardlike hatches of the Caperer flies, small sedges that scuttle and leapfrog erratically on the water, Lunn devised fly dressings designed for fishing with a twitching, half-fluttering presentation. His imitations were worked out almost three-quarters of a century ago, and have been fished with both the enticing twitch as the fly approaches a rising trout, and with a fast skittering retrieve at other times. John Waller Hills tells us in his charming book *River Keeper*, the biography of Lunn and his work on the Stockbridge mileage of the Test, that the Caperer method was the most successful tactic on that river throughout the summer of 1932.

Leonard Wright has explored similar techniques for suggesting the fluttering emergence and egg-laying behavior of our American sedges. In *Fishing the Dry Fly as a Living Insect*, he describes his method of twitching a floating caddis imitation as the sudden-inch technique. The book attempts to modify the single-minded orthodoxy of American dry-fly practice, and its preoccupation with Halford's dogma of the drag-free float.

Similar techniques have existed on the British chalkstreams and rich Irish limestone rivers for more than a half century, and twitching the fly enticingly just as it reaches a rising trout is a dry-fly version of the induced-rise method that nymph experts like Frank Sawyer and Oliver Kite have long used on the Wiltshire Avon. Michael Lunn is the grandson of the great Test riverkeeper, and today holds his position on the Houghton Club water. Lunn is a primary exponent of his grandfather's Caperer technique and the induced-rise method, and Roger Foster is another skilled riverkeeper on the Maigue in southern Ireland, where the induced-rise method of fishing the dry fly is well known.

Some years ago, Roger Foster and I were fishing the water meadows of the Maigue below Dunraven Castle. It is one of the loveliest reaches of dry-fly water on earth, rich with fly hatches and trailing beds of ranunculus, its fertility born of limestone springs in the rolling, fox-hunting country that lies below Limerick. The castle beats are shrouded in history, with the ruins of a tenth-century fortress guarding the bottom mileage and the ivy-covered nave of a twelfth-century abbey only a half mile upstream. Although some of its chambers are open to the public, Dunraven Castle itself is still occupied by Lord Dunraven, and the fishing can sometimes be rented on a fly-only basis. It is a remarkable brown-trout fishery, filled with selective fish averaging about a pound or better, and there are few rivers in the world with such fly hatches.

We were hoping for good hatches of *Ephemera vulgata*, the fluttering drakes indigenous to the lakes and rivers of Ireland, but we were a few days too early. The mayfly was already emerging on Lough Derg in the Shannon watershed, traditionally its first hatching site each season, but only scattered flies were showing on the meadow flats of the Maigue. The trout were not really taking them.

They're not on the mayfly yet, explained Roger Foster, *but on rainy mornings we've got fine hatches of little Iron Blues, and the grass is alive with sedges.*

Foster was right about his sedges. There were so many caddisflies in the weeds and nettles and meadow grasses that I picked them easily, like berries in a particularly rich summer. My specimen bottles were quickly filled with dark, slate-colored little silverhorns and mottled specimens of *Sericostoma* flies and dozens of small cinnamon sedges.

Our first evening we drove down from the thatched-roofed village of Adare, past the towers and crenellated rooftops of Dunraven Castle, and wound into the man-made forest groves along the river. There were huge trees with reddish rough-barked trunks.

Those look like Douglas firs! I said incredulously. *Those big reddish-barked trees look like sequoias!*

They are sequoias! Foster laughed.

We walked down through the forest to the Maigue, where it wound out from the sycamores and willows into the winding meadow above the castle. The air above the river was alive with insects. There were thousands of tiny spinners, and an occasional chalk-colored *Ephemera* drake, and hundreds of hatching caddisflies. The fish were rising everywhere, in the swift currents below the weirs and down the silken flats.

They're probably on sedges, Foster said.

We've seen four or five kinds of caddis along the river, I grinned. *How do we know which one is hatching?*

The silverhorns hatch mostly at night, Foster answered, *and the Welshman's Buttons are almost finished.*

That leaves the cinnamon sedges? I asked.

You're right, Foster agreed.

His fly boxes were filled with elegant little sedge imitations, and I started fishing them to each rising trout in range. There were several refusal swirls and a few splashy rises, but they seemed disinterested and half-hearted. Foster was fishing below me and I watched him hook and land a fat fifteen-inch brown. The young riverkeeper released the trout and promptly caught another just above the weir. Two more trout made refusal swirls under my fly, and when a third missed it splashily, I walked downstream to watch Foster fish his sedge imitation.

Conventional tactics aren't working, I said.

Foster was drying his sedge imitation carefully. *I'm fishing what we call the induced-rise method,* he explained. *It teases the trout into taking sometimes.*

How does it work? I asked.

Foster demonstrated his method over another fish. His false-casting flicked out and settled the fly above its feeding station, and the fly dropped softly on the current about eighteen inches above the trout. The little sedge had scarcely started its drift when he gave it a subtle twitch, let it float naturally six inches, and twitched it teasingly again. It was too much for the waiting trout and it took the fly hard.

That's your induced-rise method? I smiled.

Yes, the young riverkeeper nodded and released the fish. *Sometimes it coaxes them into taking when they refuse a conventional float.*

Halford would turn over in his grave!

I'm sure you're right, Foster agreed as he dressed his fly, *but it's always the exception that proves the rule.*

It is a truth still worth remembering astream.

3. Some Strategies
in Fishing
Bucktails and Streamers

It was whippoorwill time when the old fisherman appeared at the Forks Pool Bridge. It was almost possible to know when he would come. The nights he liked were hot and dark, with the faintest sliver of a moon showing in the trees. The river had a sombre mood on such evenings, its silken currents mysterious and heavy in its cedar deadfalls, and its pull seemed much stronger on the legs after nightfall.

The old man slipped into the river like an otter. His reel stripped gratingly in the darkness as he worked out line, and I heard the swish-swish rhythm of his casting above the twilight river sounds.

Tell your father hello, his voice boomed richly.

His fishing always started when the boyhood curfew ended my fishing for another day. The old man was a streamer fisherman because he liked to catch big browns at night. He tied his own flies rather crudely on huge 1/0 forged hooks, and I still have one somewhere in my collection. The rough bodies were thickly wrapped with spun fur, and a half-dozen grizzly hackles formed the three-inch wings.

His trophy-size fish were a local legend on the Pere Marquette. Five- and six-pound browns were always lying in state in the ice-cream freezer at Baldwin, and the old man usually caught about fifty trout over twenty inches during a summer's fishing.

The river whispered in the darkness, and the old man was only a ghostly presence in its nightscape. There was no sound of his wading, and his pipe cast no glow to frighten the fish. Once he had worked out enough line to cover the river there was not even the sound of his reel unless a fish was hooked. The river sounds soon muffled the swish-swish of his big streamer as he worked the waist-deep riffles downstream.

Suddenly his reel protested with a ratchet-sharp growl as it surrendered line, and there was an immense splash below his silhouette in the darkness.

Good fish? I shouted.

It's very strong! he answered. *Very strong!*

There was another huge splash in the darkness, farther downstream where the river disappeared into an S-shaped bend. The reel shrieked gratingly as the fish took more line, and the old man was forced to follow. His shape was gone into the night.

Good luck! I shouted.

But there was no answer, and I waded out of the pool. The path up through the willows was barely visible, and I turned my rod butt-first to protect it from the branches. My father was already in camp, and the glow of his cookfire was ahead among the trees. We had just finished our supper when the old Scotsman came up into the firelight with the tail of a great trout dragging in the sand.

My God! I thought. *That fish is huge!*

Its spots glittered in the flickering light, its thickly muscled bulk still glistening with water that dripped on the path. It was the biggest trout I had ever seen in those years.

Gentlemen! said the old man, like a fanfare.

That's some brown trout! my father said.

Yes, the old man cackled happily. *It is the biggest I've ever caught in all my years on this river—and 'tis a wee bit bigger than anything I caught years ago on the Whitadder and the Tweed!*

How big is it? I stammered.

Perhaps the use of your scale will tell us the weight of this sea monster, he laughed heartily. *May I borrow it?*

I slipped inside the tent and came back with a fifteen-pound scale. The old man seated it firmly in the gill cover, and its spring creaked as it took the weight of the fish.

Almost nine pounds! my voice was filled with awe.

Nine pounds, said the old Scotsman softly. *It's a time for sharing a dram from the pewter flask in the truck!*

Congratulations, my father extended his hand.

The old man laid the big trout in the grass and walked back in the darkness for the whisky. It was an impressive fish, but in those days on the Michigan rivers there were a lot of men who caught big browns at night with bucktails and streamers. They knew every hole and deadfall and boulder in the river, covering it as easily at midnight as the summer people fished it at noon.

Several years ago my good friend Lee Wulff was talking about the old days on rivers like the Battenkill and Ausable in New York. His memories drifted back to the years when both were renowned big-fish rivers, the years when he developed the White and Gray Wulffs.

You know, he leaned forward and frowned, *years ago every river had its bucktail artists, men who fished nothing else and were locally famous for the big fish they caught. Now they're all gone, and we're left with the hardware throwers!*

Although we cannot be certain who invented streamers and bucktails, or even if they originated in the United States or Canada, they are unquestionably a fly type and method that originated on this side of the Atlantic. Some angling historians credit the Algoma Indians of the Canadian subarctic with deer bucktails, while others argue that polar bear flies evolved on the rivers of Alaska. Emerson Hough is generally believed to be the fisherman whose expeditions into the north country discovered bucktail and polar bear flies in use among the native fisherfolk.

However, there is better evidence that bucktails originated at the feather-littered workbench of William Scripture in New York, and other authorities argue that streamers probably had their genesis in the Piseco Lake patterns of the nineteenth century.

Guy Jenkins is a skilled angler who fished the Catskills in their golden age, and who knew men like Theodore Gordon, Edward Ringwood Hewitt, and George La Branche. Jenkins points out that Theodore Gordon originated a bucktaillike pattern he called the Bumblepuppy, and that Hewitt and La Branche were not always dry-fly purists.

They were not always the saints their disciples imagined, Jenkins observed puckishly over lunch at the Anglers' Club of New York. *They fished wet flies and nymphs fairly often—and even a big Scripture bucktail or two when they discovered a good fish minnowing.*

The recorded history of such flies is relatively recent. Roy Steenrod was a close friend and fishing companion of Gordon's on the Catskill rivers, and Steenrod recalled that the Bumblepuppy bucktails were dressed as early as 1880. Gordon demonstrated in his correspondence that he knew these primitive bucktails were baitfish imitations.

Others were experimenting with bucktails and streamers too. Smallmouth-bass flies were fashioned of bucktail on the headwaters of the Tippecanoe and Maumee about 1886, and at the turn of the century Carter Harrison and Alfred Trude were fishing hair-wings on the Henry's Fork of the Snake. Herbert Welch constructed smelt imitations with feathers as early as 1902, and although these flies were tied with wings of married feather sections, they were undoubtedly the prelude to the full family tree of New England streamers.

During this same period, William Scripture was tying surprisingly modern bucktails on the rivers west of Albany. One of his prototypes is unquestionably similar to the Blacknosed Dace developed years later by Arthur Flick on the Schoharie farther south. Harvey Donaldson was also fishing bucktails on the headwaters of the Mohawk in these years, and on the brook-trout waters of the West Canada and the Cedar. The best-known Scripture pattern had a red crewel tag, tinsel body, and a wing of natural brown bucktail. Although our history of the Scripture school of fly tying is limited, it is apparent that the smallmouth bass and brown trout of New York were the catalysts that produced the bucktail.

Popular legend tells us that the slender trolling streamer had its origins in Maine at the Grand Lake Stream. Alonzo Stickney Bacon was a guide on those waters not long after the turn of the century, and his spur-of-the-moment use of saddle hackles protruding from a canoe cushion led to a feathered lure that took an impressive catch of landlocked salmon. Since the fish had been dour and uncooperative for days, word of his feat spread like wildfire in Maine. Bacon may well be the father of the hackle-feather streamer, and from those beginnings in Maine our fly-pattern dictionary has been greatly enriched with a galaxy of baitfish patterns.

New England was the region that produced the classical patterns in the history of bucktails and streamers. Fly tiers like Herb Welch, Carrie Stevens, Bert Quimby, and William Edson were archetypical of this school of thought. Lew Oatman, Bob McCafferty, John Alden Knight, Don Gapen, Herb Howard, and Ray Bergman followed in a succeeding generation of bucktail and streamer theory, and in our western mountains men like Don Martinez and Dan Bailey carried the philosophy with them when they abandoned earlier lives in the eastern cities. Bucktails and streamers worked extremely well on the Pacific Coast watersheds, and the original fly patterns developed by Polly Rosborough, Roy Patrick, Don Harger, Jim Pray, Peter Schwab, Gary Howells, and Roy Donnelly have quickly become modern classics.

However, streamers and bucktails have been common coin among American anglers for only forty-odd years. Before that time, fishermen used conventional wet flies, and the first period of dry-fly purism had begun. Sometimes big fish were taken on such insect imitations, but minnow feeders were another matter.

Meat-and-potatoes, the old Scottish streamer fisherman explained that evening in the firelight years ago. *These old sea monsters like to eat meat-and-potatoes—not those wee river flies!*

It is often true of big trout. Their diet includes a lot of smelt, candlefish, dace, chubs, shiners, sticklebacks, sculpins, and other bait fish. Big fish always take a lot of small fish, including a cannibal diet of baby trout. Over the years many stomach autopsies have revealed a lot of baitfish specimens. I once stripped more than two hundred tiny dace from a big brown taken at night on the Beaverkill; and there was a six-pound fish on the Battenkill that disgorged an eight-inch brookie like a cake of soap when I dispatched it with my priest knife. Such minnow-eating is not too unusual.

It has been argued in many books that trout take our flies through motives of hunger, curiosity, playfulness, and sometimes through territoriality. The fish that trails our retrieve does seem almost curious, and the fish that virtually attacks a bucktail is usually defending a primary holding lie or spawning site. Such examples of territoriality are common. Life in the depths of the river, however, is a precarious equilibrium between ingesting food and expending energy, and I have never accepted the common theory of playful behavior. Most of the tail-chasing behavior I have observed looks playful to fishermen, but it has always been the result of competition for prime holding lies, shelter, ripe henfish, or prime spawning gravel—and most strikes on bucktails and streamers are from feeding behavior.

Such behavior permits us to separate bucktails and streamers into two primary categories. There are the brightly feathered fancy patterns that date themselves to the days of unsophisticated brook trout and landlocks in Maine, richly colored flies whose ornate dressings continue to fascinate modern fishermen—much as we admire an oriental carpet or a stained-glass window or the scrollwork on a Victorian house. These intricate flies have gradually lost favor as fishing pressure has increased. Replacing them on our hard-fished lakes and streams are the imitative patterns, which attempt to fool a fish that is feeding on the smaller bait species.

There are many such imitative flies. The ubiquitous Muddler is perhaps the best-known baitfish imitation, owing its success to the tiny madtoms and sculpins that inhabit our rivers. Some of the classic fancy patterns like the Supervisor and Gray Ghost and Nine-Three unquestionably owe their success to the smelt populations in our northeastern waters. Lew Oatman was perhaps the first streamer expert to embrace the theory of baitfish imitation systematically, and he worked out a series of conscientiously tied streamers that suggested the forage species of New England and New York. Oatman fished the Battenkill from his summer house at Shushan in upstate New York, and I met him there some years before his death. We had stopped to fish a swift stretch between the Dutchman's Hole and the ledgerock pool at Buffum's Bridge. It was a night when I had moved a big brown along an underwater ledge, but the fish had only followed without taking.

Oatman listened quietly while I described the problem. *What fly were you using?* he asked finally.

Black Ghost, I said.

Oatman rummaged in his fishing coat for a worn fly book. *Here's a little perch pattern,* he offered me an exquisite streamer tied with olive-yellow grizzly hackles. *It's big enough to coax an old buster—and he sees a lot of perch in a warm summer like this!*

Thanks! I waded back into the smooth current.

The warm sunlight and late afternoon shadows were a rich chiaroscuro on the pool upstream. The big fish had appeared above me in the shallows, scattering frightened minnows like a barracuda. Three times it had charged my streamers, its bulk forming a bow wave behind my retrieve, but each time it turned away. Its immense refusal swirls were positively unsettling each time they boiled to the surface.

It seemed most likely that the fish usually held in the deepest run along the sunken ledge, where the current scoured shoulder-deep and strong. The line delivered the streamer about thirty feet above its suspected holding lie, and I let it settle back toward me, sinking deep in the current. When it had bellied deep, riding into the dark water along the ledge, I began stripping it back downstream. It was about twenty-five feet away when there was a boil, followed by a slashing strike on the surface.

The weight of the fish telegraphed back into the rod and I struck it sharply.

He's got it! I shouted. *He's on!*

It was a hook-jawed male of almost six pounds, and I owed it entirely to the gentle generosity of Lew Oatman. He was as happy and excited over the fish as I was, and after I released it we sat talking in the gathering darkness. Oatman gave me samples of his baitfish series, and talked about methods of fishing them. He dressed streamers so beautifully that they were as exquisite as the most elegant dry flies of the Catskill school, and his imitative theories made him the father of the scientific approach to baitfish patterns—just as Alfred Ronalds originally introduced a disciplined entomology to the dressing of his wet-fly patterns in his British *Fly-Fisher's Entomology* of 1834.

Oatman's example has been expanded in the imitative patterns of contemporary fly dressers like Keith Fulsher, Dave Whitlock, Roy Patrick, Polly Rosborough, Don Harger, and Gary Howells. Their variations on Muddler and madtom patterns, along with the Pacific baitfish imitations dressed with multicolored polar bear hair, are superb flies. Woven mylar tubing and sheet mylar have been used extensively by fly dressers like Arthur Fusco, Robert Boyle, Tony Skilton, Kani Evans, and Dave Whitlock. Its flash makes minnow imitations possible that truly suggest the dazzling silver or golden flash of shiners, candlefish, and smelt.

Except for the wilderness brook-trout fisheries tributary to Hudson Bay, and draining the interior of the Labrador, this trend toward disciplined imitation in bucktails and streamers will continue. Although I still carry the bright Mickey Finn in my fly books, including small versions for working hard-fished rivers in bright weather, my approach to bucktails and streamers is primarily imitative—and, in my experience, the baitfish patterns are so deadly on back-country trout that there is no need for the bright-feathered traditionals.

Our baitfish species are the key to such fly patterns, and their distribution and importance as trout forage are the basis for my preferences in streamers and bucktail flies. The various Muddler bucktails, and the baby trout series of imitations developed by Sam Slaymaker in Pennsylvania, are recent examples of imitative patterns that have enjoyed considerable success. On the Pacific Coast, Roy Patrick and Polly Rosborough are the authors of a number of smelt and candlefish imitations dressed with polar-bear hair. My own experiments with baitfish patterns have worked in similar directions, attempting to imitate the major forage species found on our American trout waters.

Bucktails and streamers should be dressed both to imitate the minnow species indigenous to a reach of water and sized to its scale as well. Hook sizes are related to the average growth of the species in question; the size of the water is a factor too, with bigger dressings most useful on brawling rivers like the Madison and Yellowstone and Delaware. Smaller patterns are optimal for average rivers, and tiny bucktails and streamers about an inch in length are superb on tributary streams and under low-water conditions. Current speed and character are also factors in fly size. Heavy water demands big flies, and broken chutes in a relatively small river pose similar problems. Smooth currents and tail shallows are often the place for smaller dressings, even in surprisingly big rivers.

Bucktails and streamers should be big enough to attract and hook large trout, although even big fish are insect feeders, since insects offer more calories per gram ingested. The myth that big fish eat only baitfish is based on a precarious foundation in fact, and there will be times when a man who fishes only bucktails and streamers will catch little or nothing.

But there are also times when the cycle of the season or some inexplicable mood of the fish make them the solution. Most anglers have experienced days when the trout have not settled into a uniform pattern of behavior, with one fish chasing minnows and another sampling random insects. There was such an afternoon a few years ago in the pastoral meadows of the lower Musconetcong in New Jersey. It is a rich valley of limestone springs and generous stonework barns. Cattle were fording the river when Arthur Morgan wound his station wagon down toward the sycamores where the meadows meet the river. August sunlight glittered on the riffles downstream, and there were locusts in the trees.

There was nothing hatching. The current flowed over the pale stones in the riffles, gathering against a limestone outcropping downstream, where it tumbled in the shade of the trees. There were no rises.

What should we fish? Morgan asked.

We studied the riffling pockets and the run below the ledge. *It's pretty hot,* I said. *You see anything working?*

Sunfish over there, he pointed across the river.

The stream thermometer read seventy-one degrees, almost too warm for the trout and ideal for panfish.

You say there are springs along the outcropping? I asked. *Might be some trout working there.*

The current is definitely colder there, Morgan said.

Let's fish nymphs along the ledge, I suggested. *There could be fish lying deep in the colder water.*

You fish the ledge, he insisted.

It was a reasonable solution, but it did not work. Weighted nymphs in several patterns were fished deep in the current without moving a trout. There were still no rises anywhere. Finally I stood in the swift thigh-deep currents below the ledge, studying my fly books. There was a single Mickey Finn tucked into the lamb's wool, and suddenly I decided to try it in the deadfall runs downstream.

Can't work any worse, I thought wryly.

Alders brushed against my left shoulder, and I roll cast the little bucktail across the main current tongue. It had just started a teasing swing in the sunlight, when a foot-long rainbow darted from a boulder pocket and nailed it hard.

Arthur Morgan saw it hopscotch across the shallows and waved.

What'd he take? he yelled upstream.

Would you believe a Mickey Finn? I waved back happily.

No, he laughed, *I wouldn't.*

Sometimes a hot-weather fish does strange things, I said. *The sun in this red and yellow hair works wonders!*

It continued to take fish steadily that day.

The fish that had refused everything turned easy, and we both took them from every inviting pocket and run. There were a half-dozen browns from twelve to fifteen inches in the next one hundred yards, and then I hooked a strong three-pound fish under a deadfall. It was a good stopping place, and I reeled in the line with satisfaction.

Arthur came wading upstream with a fine brace of brown trout.

They wanted the Mickey, he said. *Can you explain that?*

No, I grinned. *But it worked!*

Such behavior is difficult to explain, but sometimes the fish hunt the baitfish shallows in bright weather. More often they hunt minnows in high water or just after daylight or late in the evening shadows; and sometimes they stalk their prey on warm, moonless nights like that long-ago summer on the Pere Marquette in Michigan. These are trout foraging in average populations of minnows, unlike the fish that feed ravenously on seasonal baitfish cycles. Such periods of baitfish feeding are remarkable. Familiar examples are caused by the downstream migrations of sockeye salmon fry at places like Babine Lake in British Columbia and the travelling schools of candlefish and herring that draw feeding coho salmon in the tidal currents of the Juan de Fuca Straits. There is also the periodic abundance of smelt and alewives in the Great Lakes, and the legendary runs of lake smelt in the watersheds of New England—in fishing places with ancient tribal names like Mephremagog and Mooselookmeguntic and Kennebago.

Basic streamer and bucktail fishing is simple. It can be executed with a rudimentary cross-stream cast, allowing the fly to swing on a fixed length of line. Fast currents bring the fly alive by themselves, and no rod work is necessary to tease its swing. Rhythmic teasing with the rod tip is important to give the fly life in slower reaches of water, but no left-hand strip is needed in basic techniques.

Such basic tactics should impart a regular half-darting rhythm to the fly swing, simulating a minnow working across the current. Bucktails and streamers are just like wet flies, except that a dead drift is only useful in suggesting a half-dead minnow trapped in the currents. The fly should be kept in the water as much as possible, and the entire river should be covered, from chutes and deep pools to surprisingly shallow riffles and flats. Since minnows are primarily found in such shallow water, big fish often stalk their prey in water scarcely deep enough to cover their dorsal fins. The late Joe Brooks was a fervent believer in fishing baitfish imitations in all types of water.

The last time we fished together, Brooks showed me some favorite mileage at Emigrant Flats on the Yellowstone. It was a bright September morning with fresh snow in the high country, and he squinted upriver into the glittering sun, pointing as he described the character of the Emigrant Flats and its gargantuan pool.

There're some real busters in that chute. Brooks' soft voice echoed his Chesapeake tidewater heritage. *The good fish lie along the willows, and down the deep flat for about two hundred yards—but sometimes the big fish drift back into the tail shallows and you should cover everything.*

Brooks really understood the swift Yellowstone, and we took several fish from the chute and its spreading flats that morning, but the best fish we hooked was lying in shallow water. We had already covered the most promising water, and I had fished well down into the tail shallows when my fly swing came around below me, and I briefly glanced back upstream toward Brooks. We had taken and released more than a dozen fish between us, brown trout between twelve inches and four pounds.

Shall we walk back and fish through again, I yelled, *or should we saddle up and try something else?*

Suddenly the smooth shallows below me erupted, and I snapped my eyes back downstream. The fly swing had passed a smooth boulder, and as it worked across the ankle-deep water, a big fish awakened with a threshing turn and chased it across the gravel flat. It pushed a spreading wake and bow wave, and it took the big Muddler in a bold, head-wrenching strike. It threshed angrily when it felt the hook, and bolted swiftly back up into the deepening spine of the pool.

It shook itself and stopped in the smooth chest-deep flat. The rest of its fight was a sullen stalemate, with the fish bulldogging angrily on the bottom, too strong and heavy to control with the four-ounce parabolic I had chosen that windless October morning.

Big fish? Brooks yelled.

It feels pretty strong, I answered. *Can't seem to budge him with this gear. You think it's a brown?*

Probably! He was wading downstream.

The wrenching, head-shaking spasms continued, telegraphing back along the line into the harshly straining rod. It was a brief one-sided struggle. The fish moved out a little farther into the current and stopped again. It felt as strong as a salmon, and it never surrendered a millimeter of line until the fly suddenly pulled out.

Too bad! Brooks said gently.

You're right, I reeled line unhappily. *But we never would have hooked that fish without covering the shallows too—just like you suggested!*

It was a valuable lesson in bucktail tactics. Our coverage of that pool on the Yellowstone was also an exercise in the basic techniques of fishing bucktails and streamers. Tactics at typical levels of water require working across the current and slightly downstream. Like a basic wet-fly cast, its angle of presentation should vary with current speed. Slow currents are best fished with a cross-stream cast about ninety degrees to the current flow, increasing the life and fly speed of the swing. However, such a cross-stream cast in fast water will generate too much fly speed, dragging the bucktail harshly in the surface currents. It should be cast quartering downstream in swift chutes and runs, dampening fly speed enough to fish the fly enticingly. It should be worked in rhythmic, pulsing movements imparted by the rod tip. These swimming patterns made on a fixed length of line suggest a hapless baitfish in the current. However, in very broken currents the tumbling flow itself is often enough to impart life to the fly.

Fish each cast out as completely as possible. Most anglers are too impatient, and lift their flies much too soon for another cast. Sometimes a curious trout has followed a swinging bucktail, waiting until it stops its arc and hangs directly downstream before it decides to take. Sometimes a bucktail riding deep, and undulating lazily in the bottom currents, can tease a fish into taking. Picking up the fly too soon can lose both opportunities, and a lazy retrieve is often wise when a cast has been fully fished—the odd fish that has followed your swing and not taken the fly may decide to take it when it has stopped and finally started back in its final upstream retrieve.

Skilled bucktail and streamer fishermen keep feeding slack and mending line and retrieving, to keep their flies in the river as long as possible. Many types of animation are possible with upstream and downstream mends, retrieves of varying speeds, and manipulation of the fly with tip action. Some of the bucktail artists I watched on my boyhood rivers in Michigan seemed to cast very seldom, and worked a fly tantalizingly along undercut willows and logjams and deadfalls almost as patiently as a bait fisherman.

There are times when a bucktail or streamer will have periods of missed and refusal rises. Such behavior is often true with bright confections like a Mickey Finn or the marabou patterns that were designed to excite fish with their pulsing filaments rather than imitate specific baitfish. Missed rises should be covered with a quick repeat cast while the fish is still visible, and such fish can often be excited into a second try. Refusal rises are another problem. Sometimes a trout will follow the fly swing or retrieve, mimicking its speed like a carbon copy, before refusing it when it comes close to the angler or the pickup point. Such fish can sometimes be induced to take with a gradual acceleration of the retrieve, and then an abrupt drop in fly speed—the fish has been coaxed into overrunning the fly, and like a pickerel following a spoon, it suddenly has been forced into the choice of veering off or taking.

Varied tactics and retrieves should be tried. Sometimes a deliberate retrieve of subtle rhythm will draw the most rises. Other times the fish seem to like erratic movements, and still other times the trout are excited by skittering or fast-strip methods. Cold weather and high water usually mean working a bucktail or streamer slow along the bottom. Hot weather in midsummer can mean the fish are more active, their digestive processes accelerated by the temperature of the river, and hungry enough that they will pursue a swinging bucktail eagerly. Such behavior can merely be a question of mood, but it can also result from baitfish behavior.

Sculpins and madtoms stay near the bottom, and move sluggishly in comparison with the nervous behavior of dace or darters. Silversides and freshwater smelt move in relatively swift, graceful patterns quite unlike these other species. Fishermen can learn valuable lessons in observing the behavior of the forage species most common in their local waters. Their patterns of movement are the key to manipulating bucktail and streamer imitations.

Study the minnows! the old bucktail fishermen used to tell me on the Pere Marquette. *You watch the minnows in the river—and they'll tell you how to dress your flies and fish them!*

Mixed colors of both feathers and hair have long been a basic principle of dressing bucktails and streamers. Slender feathers and delicate filaments of marabou move and work enticingly in the water, and like the red-and-yellow color mix of the Mickey Finn, this fluttering seems to excite the fish. Their behavior in following the pulsing retrieve of a feather streamer or marabou certainly seems to arouse a mixture of curiosity and excitement.

This ability to excite fish does not always result in a strike, but its powers of attraction often tempt fish to show themselves. Sometimes they only shift position deep in the current, revealing themselves with the brief flash of light catching their sides beside a boulder or in the shadow of a deadfall. Sometimes a fish shows itself as a shadow that starts from its hiding place under the bank, ghosting briefly behind the fly before it turns back. Fish that follow a retrieve or actually false rise behind the fly are easily detected—and the ability to tease fish from their hiding places can be used to prospect a river and mark the prime holding lies of its big trout for future reference.

Mixing hair, hackle feathers, or marabou in a modern baitfish imitation is a little like the light-spectrum color theories developed by the late Preston Jennings. Tiers like Polly Rosborough and Roy Patrick are expert at achieving such chromatic effects in polar bear fibers, and mixed color is blended with the breathing action of marabou or a splay-winged feather streamer. Woven mylar tubing can be used for bodies of minnows having silvery coloring, and sheet mylar overlays can be seated outside the mylar or feather wings to simulate a species with silvery or gold flanks. Fins can be imitated with throat hackles and tails. Species like the redfin shiner, which has bright orange fins and tail coloring, can be suggested by dying the tips of a streamer wing with a waterproof felt-tip pen—in addition to the hackle and tail fibers.

Dave Whitlock is a skilled fly maker and theoretician of fly dressing who is rethinking bucktails and streamers. Whitlock likes to leave a touch of scarlet rayon showing between the body material and the head. It imitates the brightly colored gills. Since a crippled baitfish does show its gill coloring in its terminal spasms, and few fish can resist a crippled prey, it is not implausible to include this blood-colored rayon and incite the trout's killing instincts. Red hackles and tail fibers are included in the dressings of many traditional bucktails and streamers for this same purpose.

Big trout can't resist a bleeding minnow, Whitlock argues.

Perhaps some general observations about bucktail and streamer patterns are in order before we explore specific techniques for fishing them. Marabou flies can be dressed both weighted and unweighted. Weighted versions are useful in both marabous and bucktails for fishing deep in heavy cold-water currents. Dark roily currents suggest a white marabou dressing, while milky spates are often best fished with extremely dark flies. Bob McCafferty and Charles Fox were some of the first fly tiers to experiment with marabou stork-feather wings on their streamer patterns. They liked yellow or white for silt-gray or coffee-colored water, and McCafferty preferred black marabou for the chalky currents of limestoners like Penns Creek and Spring Creek.

The easiest way to work a bucktail or streamer deep is to weight it carefully under the body and fish a sinking line. Too much weight will distort the action of the fly and make it difficult to cast. It is also possible to weight a fly in the field by tying the leader knot with an unclipped strand of nylon trailing under the hook. The trailing nylon can then be clamped with a lead shot. Weighted in such fashion, a bucktail or streamer will fish deep with an erratic pattern quite similar to the action of a saltwater jig.

Marabou stork feathers entrain so much air in their fluffiness that they are difficult to sink unless false casting is kept to a minimum. This property is useful for suggesting a dying baitfish that is half floating in the surface of a river or lake. Sometimes big trout cruise a calm lake, picking such crippled minnows from the surface like a fly hatch. Experienced still-water fishermen will place such a half-sinking marabou ahead of a cruising fish, allowing it to hang slack until the trout approaches. It should then be retrieved suddenly, suggesting the desperate adrenalin-triggered panic of an injured fish that has seen a predator begin its deadly stalk.

The partially floating characteristics of marabou stork are also useful in shallow water. Dressed with light-wire hooks, such flies will remain near the surface until a retrieve is started. They will expand and contract, with their breathing stork fibers echoing the rhythmic retrieve, and will seldom sink enough to foul in the bottom.

Baby streamers should not be ignored. They are especially killing flies in low-water conditions, and are dressed on tiny long-shank hooks as small as sizes twelve and fourteen. Such flies are about one inch or slightly longer in length, and are intended to imitate fingerlings and fry. Sparse dressings are most effective.

Leaders of ten to twelve feet tapered to 4X or 5X at the tippet are superb for fishing small streamers in low water. Bigger flies will require heavier tippets to cast and fish properly, and large bucktails and streamers are best combined with tippets of 1X or 0X. Even heavier tippets are sometimes needed with a 1/0 bucktail or marabou in strong winds.

Experience will quickly demonstrate proper tippet size, when nylon that is too thin refuses to turn over a big bucktail or snarls in frequent casting knots. Sinking lines and big water demand a shorter leader, perhaps only eight or nine feet in length, because too long a leader of nylon will ride back toward the surface, cancelling the effect of the deep-riding line.

There are about fifteen variations on basic bucktail and streamer tactics that should be part of an angler's repertory of skills. The fisherman should choose a technique that is attuned to his local baitfish.

1. The Basic Bucktail Swing

The basic swing method of fishing a bucktail or streamer is relatively easy to learn, and since these minnowlike patterns are easier to follow in the current than a conventional wet fly, it is sometimes a good method for starting a beginner. It involves a rudimentary cross-stream cast, allowing the fly swing to work back across the current. The swing is followed with the rod by pointing its tip at the apparent position of the bucktail.

Follow it around! the old-timers used to tell me in Michigan. *Follow it around and stay in touch with your fly!*

The basic swing operates with a constant length of line. Since it does not add left-hand manipulation of the line to its technique, and merely lays out repetitive casts a step or two downstream, its methodology is ideal for a beginning flyfisher. Fast currents usually impart enough life to the swimming bucktail or streamer that no tip action is needed to improve the retrieve and just following the fly swing with the rod is enough. It is not difficult to judge when the fly is fishing right, since too fast a swing will force it to skitter crudely in the surface.

Don't let it swing around raw! the old-timers added.

Slower currents mean the fly must be worked to suggest the swimming movements of a forage fish species. Its pulsing fly swing is achieved with a raising and lowering rhythm of the rod tip, and the length and timing of this rhythm is determined by the behavior of the fly in the current. The rate of current flow can also be used to control fly speed. Relatively slow currents should be fished with a cast directly across the current, which exaggerates the bellying line and increases the speed of the fly swing. Fast currents mean the fly should be cast quartering downstream, decreasing both line belly and the velocity of the fly.

When a cast and its subsequent fly swing are being fished out, the rod should be kept low and the line held between the index finger and its cork grip. No complicated left-hand twist or stripping of line is used during the fly swing itself, and since a fish will occasionally follow the swinging fly into the slack currents immediately below the angler, it should not be picked up too quickly. Many skilled bucktail men will allow the fly to trail at the bottom of the swing, and then retrieve with two or three line strips straight upstream. It is a familiar technique on salmon rivers, but it also has its usefulness on a trout stream, since a fish that has followed the swing will sometimes take when the fly starts moving again.

Covering a spreading flat with this method is particularly effective, since it patterns a series of concentric fly swings over the bottom. Fished correctly, this method will work a fly swing over every fish in the pool as the angler moves patiently downstream a step at a time.

2. The Hand-Twist Retrieve

Sometimes a bucktail fished with a deliberate hand-twist retrieve is a deadly method. It can be used to work the fly directly downstream, probing under the bank willows and logjams and deadfalls. The angler permits his fly swing to parallel the overhung bank, and may even strip out more line to allow it to drift deeper into the fishable currents before retrieving it slowly back upstream with the hand-twist method.

Ray Bergman liked the subtlety of the hand-twist retrieve, and first described using bucktails with this method in his book *Just Fishing*. Sometimes the fish take a streamer or a bucktail pattern fished this way because they are feeding on bottom minnows that swim slowly. However, they seem to strike at other times because they cannot resist such a tantalizingly slow retrieve. It has often been extremely effective for me on still-water sections of rivers, where there is insufficient current to swing the fly. It is often deadly when fished from an anchored boat, or wading in the shallows of a lake or impoundment. Such tactics involve casting clockwise around an imaginary clockface on the surface of the lake, and fishing the bucktail back with a hand-twist retrieve. Such casting patterns can start at nine o'clock, and be placed about a yard apart until the final cast is fished back from the three o'clock position. The first series of casts should be fished in a semicircle about forty feet out, and each succeeding series of casts adds approximately five feet, until the angler has reached his maximum distance. Such pattern casting should cover any cruising fish within range.

Bucktails fished with a hand-twist retrieve have produced some big fish for me in many parts of the world. There were the big rainbows we took one opening day in the San Cristobal Reservoir in Colorado, as we fished our bucktails on the ledges in the upper shallows of the lake with a deep hand-twist retrieve. It is a productive meadow in the weedy inlet channels of Henry's Lake in Idaho, and the marl lagoons of Wade Lake in Montana. This past season, fishing a weighted bucktail with a hand-twist clock-face method took three five-pound brookies in forty-five minutes at the black-sand mouth of the exotic Pichi Traful in Argentina.

3. The Left-Hand Strip

Although similar to the hand-strip method recommended for wet-fly fishing, the left-hand strip for bucktails and streamers is most useful when used to execute an erratic, rapid retrieve. It is achieved with the line held under the index finger, against the cork grip of the rod, and stripping back lengths of line with the other hand.

Such stripping pulls can vary from six inches, similar to the maximum hand-twist length of line but more rapid, to a quick arm pull at full length.

can swiftly retrieve from two to three feet. The
n simulating the erratic behavior of crippled
t when it senses a predator. It is also the only
ing an upstream bucktail back fast enough in

seful in any fisherman's bag of tricks, for it will
t cannot be achieved any other way. It is perfect
agile baitfish, and for exciting fish in wilderness
chery.

d length of line with the rod itself. Although it
l or streamer with changing lengths of line as do
ieving a fly, it will manipulate them differently.
fly moving without the pause required in a
ction is a series of rapidly connected swimming

seful in keeping a following trout interested, since
ere the fish can get too good a look at the fly.
s its drawbacks. Its swimming rhythms are started
ne locked under the index finger, or drawn back
cert with the rod. The position of the rod is pointed
rallel to the water, at the start of the retrieve. It
activates the fly with a fluid sequence of rod movements, ending with the
rod held beside and slightly behind the angler. It is an awkward final
position, and if a trout has followed the retrieve all the way and decides to
take at the last moment, the fisherman often finds he has worked the rod so
far back that a hook-setting strike is almost impossible.

Sometimes a fish can be hooked with the rod in that position if the
fisherman has the line in his left hand, and can either execute his strike
with a hand pull or a draw across his body.

5. The Rod-and-Line Strip

Working a bucktail or streamer in this fashion is not unlike a simple
left-hand strip, except that it adds a teasing rod-tip rhythm between the
line pulls. The result is a fly that swims with a contrapuntal rhythm of
draw-and-twitch-and-draw movements. The line should be held under the
index finger for optimum control. Since the rod-and-line strip involves a
complex pattern of hand and rod control, it is a bit more difficult than
other methods of manipulating a streamer pattern.

6. The Cast-and-Strip Method

This is a useful tactic for getting more depth with a sinking line in strong
rivers, lakes, and impoundments. It involves executing a long cast, to get
the fly and the line belly riding deep, and then stripping still more line off
the reel. The extra line is then paid out with a brisk side-to-side shaking of

the rod tip. When the line begins to straighten, and the fly is swimming against its tension in the water, the cast can be fished out with any of the basic retrieves. Sometimes a trout will take one of the imitative baitfish patterns while it is still sinking.

It happened to me several years ago on the Caleufu in Argentina, and the surprise of its strike was almost comic. The river churns through an earthquake fault in the lava that blocks its course below Meliquina, spreading into a slow-flowing pool at the foot of the Paso de Cordoba. It was a pool I had never fished, since it lay close beside the road, and I had always passed it on my way south to the Traful, or enroute to the famous Boca Chimehuin farther north.

This morning it looks good! I thought.

The sun sparkled on the surface of the pool. Its light penetrated deep into its emerald green currents, revealing a jumble of great boulders on the bottom. The four-inch marabou worked out with its lazy double haul, the sunlight glittering on its mylar wings, and it dropped well across the pool. It quickly started to sink, and I stripped off a few yards of line and shook them out through the guides. The marabou drifted deep, catching the sunlight as it fluttered toward the bottom, when I glanced down and discovered that I had forgotten to finish lacing my wading brogues.

Careless! I thought aloud.

The rod lay among the boulders, and I had just started to tighten the laces when the reel suddenly came to life. The rod jumped and started sliding toward the water, clattering noisily against the stones. The fish had taken the sinking bucktail like a dying minnow, hooked itself soundly, and started downriver in mere seconds.

Scrambling over the rocks with one brogue still unlaced, I soon recovered the rod, and the fish cartwheeled when it felt the pressure. It was a bright rainbow of almost six pounds. It fought well, jumping again and again down the pool, and I finally released the fish with admiration for its acrobatics and courage, along with some doubts about its wariness. Except for the depth achieved by using the cast-and-strip technique, it was a rainbow that had virtually caught itself.

7. The Upstream Dead Drift

This method is surprisingly effective at times, especially with imitative patterns like the Muddler. It involves casting upstream, or upstream and across the current, allowing the fly to drift back without extra manipulation by either the rod or left-hand line. Such tactics will get the fly deep in swift water, letting it drift tantalizingly along the bottom, where a fish may pick it up for a dead minnow.

Sculpins and other bottom-feeding forage species are a major part of the trout diet, and fishing a bucktail upstream dead drift is a superb method of suggesting their behavior. It is an especially effective tactic for large western rivers, although I have also used it in swift pocket-water reaches of small eastern streams where the tumbling current was enough to bring the fly alive—and the character of the water made a normal downstream coverage of the fish impossible without frightening them.

8. The Upstream Strip

This is another technique that has proved itself on relatively small rivers over the years. It permits a careful stalk of a pool or run from below, with a cast like an upstream dry-fly presentation to likely looking places in the current. Unlike a dead-drift approach, the upstream strip fishes the fly back downstream rapidly enough to work it quickly, in spite of the countering current speed.

It is a demanding method. Like most left-hand strips, the line is held under the index finger against the cork grip. The stripping itself is executed with the other hand, and in fast water, the rhythm is a series of brisk pulls made as quickly as possible.

The upstream strip produced my best fish this past season on our Brodheads water in Pennsylvania. It came on the Buttonwood Run, where a smooth riffle breaks into seventy-five feet of deep water under a stand of sycamores. The branches shelter the holding channel, their leaves almost trailing in the current. Fish hold everywhere in their leaf-flickering shadows. The deepest place is just below the throat of the pool, where the current swells and slides past the roots of a medium-size tree. It always holds a good fish.

It was a dull morning at midweek, with a light rain misting down the valley. The current was a little milky and there were no hatches. Conventional wet-fly and nymph tactics moved nothing, and finally I decided on a small mylar streamer. It moved a good brown on the first cast, and I decided to stay with it into the Buttonwood.

It soon started to rain harder. *It's pretty gloomy!* I thought. *The fish are pretty moody—but it's the kind of day for moving a big fish!*

The marabou dropped tight against the roots and teased swiftly back across the main current. It had just escaped the shelving hole, working into the gravel shallows just below me, when a big fish slashed out of the deep water and boiled around the fly without touching it. The trout finally bolted back into its hiding place.

He saw me that time! The fish had charged the fly aggressively, changing its mind at the last moment when its greed carried it close to my waders. *Maybe he'll come again if I rest him!*

I waded slowly out of the pool and sat down under the big oak that shades the gravel shallows across the current. The rain slowed and stopped after twenty minutes. It was time to try the fish again, but I studied its lie before wading back into the pool. The current flowed still and smooth.

Maybe from below him, I thought suddenly.

It made sense to fish the place with an upstream cast, since my position would be behind its holding lie. The little marabou sliced out low, hooking close to the undercut bank about fifteen feet above the trout. It settled back deep on the current, and when it seemed that the fly must have reached the

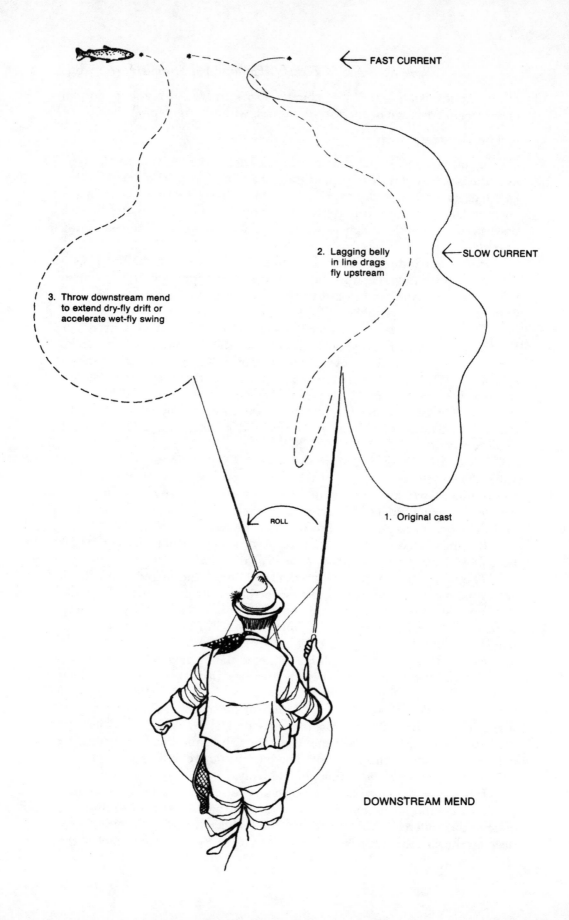

FAST CURRENT

SLOW CURRENT

2. Lagging belly
in line drags
fly upstream

3. Throw downstream mend
to extend dry-fly drift or
accelerate wet-fly swing

ROLL

1. Original cast

DOWNSTREAM MEND

deepest place under the roots, I started a fast left-hand strip. The fly had travelled about six feet when there was a wrenching strike, and the fish was solidly hooked. It fought hard, splashing and probing deep under the sycamore trees—and it measured slightly better than twenty-two inches when it came to the net.

9. The Crippled Strip

This is a deadly rhythm of fishing a strip retrieve rather than a fully separate method of bucktail fishing. Few big trout can resist a dying or injured minnow. Fishing a bucktail or streamer to suggest that it might be hurt consists of breaking the pattern of the retrieve. It was a lesson taught me years ago by the skilled minnow fishermen in Michigan.

They were artists at swinging a minnow into a promising run, letting it tumble clumsily in the current, and then giving it an occasional darting pull that caused it to flash as it caught the sunlight. It always seemed to work. Any fish lying in the run seemed unable to resist that erratic light-catching shiner working past them, and a streamer or bucktail fished that way is deadly too.

It takes a little skill to simulate a crippled fish as it sinks helplessly and tumbles slackly in the current, giving an occasional darting roll as it struggles with the last of its energy against the flow. Its pathetic behavior is suggested by a combination of using the pull of the current, stripping with the left hand, and working the rod irregularly.

10. The Panic Strip

Sometimes a fish lying visibly in a pool or run seems disinterested in everything, but it can be triggered into taking a fly worked with a skilled panic strip. The technique is simple enough.

It involves casting the fly slightly above the fish, judging the distance to insure that the fly will ride fairly close to its position along the bottom. The fisherman manipulates his fly in a manner to suggest a minnow that is drifting casually with the current, unaware that the big fish is there. The fly should be allowed to blunder like an empty-headed shiner into mortal danger—and then wildly stripped away like a minnow that has suddenly sensed its peril.

The method works best when the target fish is visible, but it can also be used to prospect through a holding lie that is likely to shelter a good trout. The bucktail or streamer is cast to fish a promising pocket in exactly the same way: it is allowed to swim deep into a suspected holding place, and then it is stripped back like a terrified dace or darter. The panic strip sometimes results in an explosive strike, because few predatory trout can resist faltering and helpless prey.

11. The Skittering Retrieve

Sometimes a bucktail or streamer fished back wildly across the surface, after its delivery with a relatively harsh cast, will move fish when nothing else works. Such a skittering retrieve is a little like the way a minnow flees a marauding trout, and it is a useful change-of-pace presentation.

12. The Sink-and-Draw Method

This is a technique borrowed from salmon fishing, like the panic strip and the greased-line method. It is a favorite tactic on the Vatnsdalsá in Iceland, where John Ashley Cooper has perfected it over the years, using his favorite salmon tube flies.

The sink-and-draw is a fine big-water method for trout too. It is a downstream method which involves pulling back on a cast to settle it with enough slack to get some depth. When it reaches its full length of line, it is allowed to swim against the current and is then teased back with an upstream draw of the rod. The result is a bucktail or streamer trailing in the current, sometimes at the swift tail of a major pool, and a lazy rhythm of sink-and-draw handling with the rod. The fish that strike such a fly seem angry, almost as if they had been irritated into attacking or defending their feeding lies or territory.

The method can also be used in a relatively small stream by allowing the fly to work in a swift chute or swirling pool, or under a logjam or willow-hung channel—since the strikes are relatively hard, fishermen should not fish too fine a tippet.

13. The Boat-Swing Technique

The boat swing simply uses the tension of the water and the speed of a boat or canoe to create a line belly that works the fly well. It is simple enough to master. The bucktail or streamer is cast slightly ahead of the boat and allowed to sink a few counts, while the boat continues along the shoreline or weedbed being fished. The result is a line bellying slightly behind the angler, who fishes out his cast until it comes back toward the boat. Both the angle of the initial cast and the point of pickup depend upon the depth of the water being fished and the speed of the boat. Deep water requires more sinking time, and the cast should be placed farther ahead. Faster rowing or paddling speed means a cast should be placed ninety degrees to the course of the boat or canoe, dampening line belly and fly speed.

Similar manipulation of the bellying line and its fly speed is possible from a river boat or canoe. The fly should be placed in a quartering cast downstream in relatively swift water, slowing its swing in the currents. It can be placed higher in the current on more quiet reaches of the river, accelerating its teasing swing. Skilled boatmen know just how to maneuver their craft, pausing to make sure a fine piece of cover is fished carefully, and lowering the boat systematically downstream, so each successive cast falls a foot or two below the last. Such tactics cover a pool with a series of concentric swings and are used by boatmen around the world—on European salmon rivers like the Alta in Norway, on American rivers from the Allagash in Maine to the Au Sable in Michigan and the swift MacKenzie in Oregon, and on the Tolten and Calcurrupe in Chile.

14. Diving and Bobbing

Sometimes crippled fish lie in the surface film of a lake, hanging exhausted or struggling to swim deeper, and cruising fish pick them up like hatching flies. Such injured minnows are tempting to the bigger fish, and bucktails and streamers are often effective imitations when fished with the diving and bobbing technique.

It is executed by lightly dressing the flies with silicone and casting them out to lie on the surface. They should be allowed to rest like a bass bug for several seconds, and then pulled under the surface sharply with the rod. The silicone will buoy them up again, where a pause of several more seconds is allowed to pass before the fly is pulled under again. Such diving-and-bobbing behavior will often induce a fish to strike eagerly when more conventional techniques have failed.

15. The Greased-Line Method and the Crosfield Pull

Our earlier discussions of wet-fly tactics pointed out the origins of these techniques in the salmon-fishing methods of Arthur Wood and Ernest Crosfield in the United Kingdom. Both methods were conceived to control and modify fly speed. Wood used a dressed-silk line—which gives his method its name—to extend the duration of optimal fly speed for each cast.

It involves casting almost directly across stream, or even slightly upstream, increasing line belly and accelerating the speed of the fly. Each time the fly begins to swing too fast, its speed is dampened slightly with an upstream line mend, bringing it back to its most enticing swing. It tends to give the fish a side or quartering view of a bucktail or streamer, and a skilled hand can increase the duration of proper fly speed as much as fifty percent. Joe Brooks liked to call this technique a broadside drift.

The Wood greased-line method also has its opposite coin: the downstream mend designed to increase fly speed. It will pick up the swinging fly speed of a bucktail or streamer that is beginning to fish too slack through a quiet reach of water.

Ernest Crosfield developed his pull technique for an undressed fly line, which is difficult to mend when it works under the surface. The line is held firmly under the index finger, and is retrieved in a steady pull designed to pick up fly speed with a smooth acceleration. The method is usually employed to fish a fly swing properly in relatively slow currents. Crosfield also perfected a corollary technique designed to diminish fly speed by paying small lengths of line to dampen its bellying swing.

You have to tease the fish! the bucktail fishermen on the Pere Marquette liked to tell me years ago. *It's exactly like getting a lazy cat to play with a string—pull it too fast along the floor and they won't bother to try, but work it too slow and they ain't excited!*

Since I was then primarily interested in fly hatches and relatively small daytime trout that fed on them, my boyhood experience with bucktails and streamers was limited. My parents refused permission for night fishing with bucktails, and when the old-timers who fished the river after whippoorwill time were first starting out it was always curfew time for me to stop fishing and start for home.

My education in big-water tactics with bucktails and streamers has really come since *Matching the Hatch*, and the subsequent opportunity to fish sprawling mountain rivers from the Labrador to Tierra del Fuego.

However, I had some success with these flies in my early years in Colorado. There was one good morning on the Roaring Fork in the heavy water below Basalt and Emma, but perhaps the most amusing experience occurred on the Frying Pan in a neighboring valley. It was the first summer I fished the river. We were staying at the guest ranch on the Frying Pan at Ruedi, with its famous half-mile still water and the footbridge pool right across the road. The valley was relatively open there, spreading into wide meadows between gentle mountains. The slopes were dotted with lodgepole pine and ponderosa, with small groves of aspen above the valley. The mountains were almost maroon-colored basalt, with the dramatically sculptured formations at Seven Castles on the lower river; but there was a strangely chalk-colored mountain of gypsum at Ruedi. It was a favorite boyhood place, but it now lies under almost three hundred feet of water, entombed at the bottom of Ruedi Reservoir.

We were fishing the Frying Pan itself, and its morning and evening fly hatches were awesome. Colorado regulations in those days stipulated that the limit was twenty fish or ten pounds, and night fishing on public water was not permitted. Curfew came at eight-thirty, but the Frying Pan supported an incredible population of fish in the days just after the war. It was difficult to catch a twenty-fish limit, not because trout were scarce, but because it was virtually impossible to avoid the ten-pound limit after landing five or six fish. We were dressing our own flies in the cabin, matching the hatches we collected on the river each day. We were catching a lot of big trout—far more than the other cabins were taking on their fancy patterns, and the rancher came by just before breakfast.

You fellows are catching a lot of fish! he said.

We poured him a mug of steaming coffee. *Hatches are good and we're tying our own imitations of the flies.*

Got a proposition for you! He stirred his coffee.

What's that? I asked.

He stood up and walked to the back porch and pointed toward the cattail sloughs below the outbuildings.

You fellows seen my ponds? he asked. *Them ponds are the old stream channels, before the Colorado & Midland built its roadbed down the valley and diverted the Frying Pan into the still-water channel along the county road.*

You mean the county road was the railroad?

Exactly! the rancher continued. *The railroad used the old channel to raise trout for the tourists and the hotels—like the Hotel Colorado down the valley to Glenwood Springs and the Jerome up to Aspen.*

You still keep them stocked? I asked.

He nodded and sipped his coffee. *And that's where you fellows come in!*
How so? I asked.

Well, he smiled, *most times my tourists ain't seen trout before, and they fish my stocked ponds at a dollar a fish—but your catches on the river's got everybody fishing there the last few days.*

You want me to fish your ponds? I laughed.

Not exactly, he said slyly. *There's only twelve or fifteen inchers in them stocked ponds—but there's some really big browns in the bottom sloughs I want you to catch.*

But why? I asked.

We'll lay them brutes in the ice chest, the rancher explained slyly and winked. *And I'll tell the tourists you caught them in my dollar-a-fish ponds.*

It doesn't seem right, I began nervously.

Hell, boy! the rancher laughed. *There's six and seven pounders down in them sloughs—and you don't get charged nothing to fish them!*

Six and seven pounders? I wavered slightly.

Now we're talking turkey! he grinned broadly. *How do you think we can fool them big browns?*

Bucktails at night, I suggested, *but the Colorado fish laws have an eight-thirty curfew that forbids night fishing.*

Not on a private fishpond! the rancher grinned.

Okay, I succumbed.

That night I dressed several big marabous with the Coleman lantern burning white-hot on the oilcloth table. It was getting dark when I finally came in from fishing the river. We had released our trout that evening, since a heavy morning hatch of big *Ephemerella* flies had filled our ten-pound limits easily, and one of the fish I released went eighteen inches. It was unusually warm in the valley that evening, and no wind stirred the surface of the ponds.

The rancher was waiting. *Let's fish the sloughs.*

I rigged a heavier leader with a fluffy two-inch marabou, and we walked down through the water meadows below the cabins. The surface of the slough was mirror-still, reflecting the dark silhouette of the mountains and the stars. There was a rotting canoe pier, and the rancher suggested that I fish the old Frying Pan channel from there.

The line worked out into the gathering darkness, and I dropped it at nine o'clock to start the clock-face pattern of hand-twist retrieves. The pattern had almost reached a twelve o'clock cast straight into the old channel when there was an immense splash in the stillness. The fish had missed, and I picked up the rhythm of the retrieve. Suddenly there was such a wrenching strike that I snapped the rod down sharply, and when I tightened, the fish jumped wildly in the darkness. It fought stubbornly and well, and when I finally netted it and walked back into the grass, it threshed powerfully in the meshes. It was huge, well over two feet and deep-bellied. The rancher dispatched the big fish with a stone, and held it up against the night sky.

You bring a scale? he asked.

Yes, I whispered, *but a flashlight will frighten any other fish that are cruising and feeding in that slough.*

Weighing this one can wait—get another one!

I'll try, I said.

We took three big browns that night, and I lost another that fouled the leader in the weeds. The first fish went better than seven pounds, the second trout weighed four, and the third scaled exactly six pounds. We dressed them back at the house and placed them in crushed-ice splendor in the cooler. The next morning the dollar-per-fish ponds were lined with tourists from the other cabins, derricking stocked twelve-inch rainbows up the bank with salmon eggs. The rancher was smiling broadly when he stopped at our cabin that evening.

It was beautiful! He laughed. *They saw your three trophies in the ice chest—and there was a stampede!*

Did they catch many? I asked.

The rancher waved his arms happily. *Two hundred and thirty-one!* he cackled. *Two hundred and thirty-one!*

My God! I swiftly calculated the profits.

Guilt haunted me all night, and finally sleep came when the morning sun glowed pink on the pale gypsum hills behind the ranch. The fishermen in the other cabins were generous in their praise that week, and they never guessed our night-fishing secret. It was a week of pure torture, and I still remember it guiltily almost thirty years later. It was the end of my career as a fishing shill.

4. The Secrets of
Fishing the Nymph

It is a country of round-topped church towers and walled villages filled with charming half-timbered houses. Mill wheels turn lazily in the smooth cress-filled currents on the trout streams. There are limestone plateaus where we hunted stag and roebuck and partridges above the rivers, and precipices and outcroppings with ruined castles. Timber frames are found in the hops fields, and the old women gather sticks in the forests, carrying their rough bundles back along the cobblestone roads into the towns. German rivers were the classrooms for my postgraduate years in fishing the nymph, and the quality of the trout fishing was a revelation in those years after the war.

The stone-paved road winds south toward Regensburg, into the pastoral Vils country below Amberg. It passes through narrow streets of intricate brickwork houses, where the April rains glitter on the roof tiles. The church towers have the graceful onion-topped domes sometimes found in Bavaria, after the Ottoman campaigns that reached deep into central Europe. Ducks and geese forage in the millraces, waddling through the marketplaces in the rain. Storks construct their tangled, roughly textured nests in the chimney pots, and every feeder brook and river and millrace holds a fine population of free-rising brown trout. It is a lovely and pastoral part of the world.

April winds from the south stir the alders along the rivers, smelling of snowmelt in the Bavarian Alps and freshly plowed earth in the fields outside the villages. The winds are perfumed with orchards and wildflowers too. The farmers are building new hops frames on the hillsides, and dairy cattle are grazing in the river bottoms. Later the fly hatches are heavy at Schmidsmühlen.

71

The Lauterach is a classic German stream. Its winding meadows and alder-lined pools were the laboratory where I first really learned to fish nymphs well. More than twenty-five seasons have passed since those postwar April mornings, although it all seems as fresh as yesterday.

Before that first summer in Europe that gave me the opportunity to polish eager boyhood skills on the difficult fish of German rivers, nymphs seemed only a half-understood version of conventional wet-fly themes. The nymphs in my fly books were strange creations in those early years. Some had been dressed in England, echoing the experiments of Skues and Sawyer, but I had developed little faith in them. The fault lay principally with my ignorance of nymph fishing and not with these British patterns, but the American nymphs that I fished half-heartedly were fanciful creations that had no obvious insect counterparts in aquatic entomology on either continent.

Except for the odd trout that took some roughly dubbed British pattern or accepted a small nymph I had copied from the flat-bodied Hewitt style of dressing, my first attempts at nymph fishing were unproductive. Bergman was my first real instructor in nymph fishing theory and technique, since Hewitt and his writings were little known beyond our eastern trout streams. Bergman's *Trout* introduced an entire American generation to nymph fishing, although our writers had not yet studied the subaquatic naturals and their behavior, like the discipline of the British fly-fishing experts on the chalkstreams.

Still the lessons found in Bergman were sound, and I devoured both *Just Fishing* and the later *Trout*, even if his observations on nymph fishing were incomplete. There was no inkling in my mind that these books fell woefully short of a comprehensive treatment of nymph fishing in those years. Sometimes the slow hand-twist retrieves recommended by Bergman produced impressive baskets of fish, like one summer morning on the Pere Marquette in Michigan, but the so-called nymphs that appeared in the color plates of *Trout* were more lures than workable imitations.

However, there were many experiences when certain dressings of conventional wet flies seemed to work on nymphing fish. Sometimes I caught trout easily on a worn hackle pattern when they were working in the film. Weathered wet flies like a March Brown or Hare's Ear or Greenwell's Glory often took fish well when they were porpoising softly to a hatch. It never occurred to me in those early years that such patterns worked as well as they did because, when they became shredded, they imitated the emerging nymphs and pupae.

Bergman outlined simple nymph-fishing tactics.

His methods were primarily extensions of conventional wet-fly methods. They included the dead-drift presentations, downstream wet-fly swings, fly swings with an additional teasing rhythm of the rod tip, and a patient hand-twist retrieve. These basic approaches often produced fish, and I can clearly remember my first trout with a nymph in the high-country headwaters of the swift **Taylor** in Colorado.

During those early summers in Michigan and the Rocky Mountains, the painstaking collection of aquatic insects that formed the basis of both *Matching the Hatch* and *Nymphs* had already begun. The unexplained successes of the nonimitative Bergman patterns were puzzling. The catches of those days always seemed a complete accident; the rational patterns of cause-and-effect were tenuous, having little real relationship between insects and imitative fly dressing, unlike my early experiences with the dry-fly method in Michigan.

Fishing the Lauterach in Germany changed everything.

The riverkeeper at Schmidsmühlen was a skilled tutor who soon ended my confusion about nymph fishing. His patient example in the water meadows of the Lauterach began a whole new cycle in my fly-fishing education. My father and I first met him in a half-timbered *Gasthaus* near the river on a late spring afternoon. There was a late lunch of fresh sausage and thick potato soup and red cabbage, and we finished over coffee with considerable talk about his river and his flies.

His fly boxes were filled with delicate little slate-colored uprights and mottled sedges and long-tailed mayflies. The old riverkeeper was particularly proud of his nymphs. His favorite pattern had a pale dubbing body ribbed with brown crewel, with wing cases and legs of partridge. It looked much like the March Brown nymph popular on our Catskill rivers.

This dark little nymph is best, the old man picked a fat partridge-legged nymph from the box. *It is my favorite pattern.*

Are they hatching now? I interjected.

The old riverkeeper nodded and explained that the hatching nymphs migrate into the shallows and fly off quickly when they emerge.

So the trout must pursue them? I asked.

The old man nodded and filled his intricately carved pipe.

The hatching flies are pretty difficult to catch, the keeper continued once the pipe was smoking properly, *and the fish concentrate on the swimming nymphs instead.*

Let's try them, said my father.

We rigged our tackle and walked upstream through the cherry orchards above the village. There was a long reach of river where the mayflies were already coming off the riffles. Two fish were working where the swift shallows shelved off into the currents along an undercut bank.

They're rising over there, I pointed.

Nein! the old man shook his head forcefully. *The trout are taking the nymphs just under the surface!*

How do we fish them? my father asked.

The old man pointed to the riffles upstream. *The hatching nymphs are there,* he explained. *The nymphs drift down from there, wriggling and working just under the surface.*

Shall I move the fly?

Ja! the old man answered. *These hatching nymphs can swim and you should work your flies with the rod.*

Petri dank! I said.

The first cast along the grass went fishless. The second cast dropped the nymph tight against the bank, where the swift riffle deepened in a bend, and I teased the fly swing with the rod. Its drift worked deep where the fish had been rising. Suddenly there was a strong pull and the trout hooked itself and jumped twice.

The fish like your nymphs, I laughed.

We took many fish easily that afternoon, killing a brace of fat two-pounders for supper at the *Gasthaus*. Later stomach autopsies confirmed their diet of big hatching *Siphlonurus* nymphs; and the naturals were almost perfectly matched by the little partridge-legged nymphs dressed by the riverkeeper and his sons. It was a fine lesson in basic nymph-fishing techniques, and the Lauterach was my proper baptism in the method.

During the weeks that followed, the old riverkeeper carefully taught me the lessons of his Bavarian river, pointing out what kinds of nymphs lived in the different types of water. Although his own flies were unprofessional and roughly tied, he painstakingly tried to match the color and configuration and size of the naturals, and he insisted that his nymphs be fished to duplicate their movements and behavior in the river. Tactics keyed to the behavior of both the naturals and the fish were a revelation after the diet of fancy patterns and mere fly manipulation recommended in Hewitt and Bergman.

Their somewhat casual approach to the imitation of natural nymphs and their emphasis on the dead-drift and hand-twist presentations had not always worked. Many times obviously-nymphing trout had ignored such tactics completely. Yet we had taken fish in the Lauterach meadows that afternoon, moving each feeding trout with the clockwork regularity that comes only when you have really solved the problems. Such a degree of effectiveness is the true measure of success on trout water; and it had eluded me in those first, fumbling experiments with the Hewitt and Bergman fly patterns.

It is certainly no accident that many American anglers are relatively baffled and uninformed about nymphs. Our books have not examined the naturals and their behavior systematically and have limited their discussions of fishing nymphs to dead-drift and hand-twist techniques of presentation. Some writers have also discussed fishing them with the timeless chuck-and-chance-it tactics, but our American literature on the subject remains fragmentary and relatively incomplete. Most pieces of the puzzle are still missing, and many fishermen already skilled in the dry-fly method readily acknowledge their singular lack of success with the nymph, particularly with trout that are porpoising in the film.

They're nymphing all over the place! they shake their heads unhappily. *Tried nymphs and they didn't work!*

It is a surprisingly familiar chorus on trout water. Fishermen seem to believe that trout are not selective when taking nymphs, and that any nymph pattern will work. Nothing could be farther from the truth. It is like the old story about the Broadway showgirl who read her first book, found it difficult and boring, and subsequently declined to start another.

Using any nymphal pattern when the fish are nymphing, just because it happens to fall into the category of nymphs, is doomed to failure in most cases. It is surprising to find men who thoroughly understand selectivity in the context of dry-fly fishing and its relationship to aquatic entomology, yet are often totally unaware that trout are equally selective to wet flies and nymphs. Trout have more time to examine their subsurface foods readily and at relative leisure, without the visual distortions of the film and its broken-surface turbulence; and they see nymphs rather better than diet forms floating on the meniscus itself. Therefore, selective fish are perhaps more critical of nymphs in terms of color, configuration, and size than they are of both naturals and dry flies floating on the surface.

Our preoccupation with the more fashionable dry-fly method is the reason for our relative ignorance about nymphs. The awesome influence of Frederic Halford on subsequent American writers like Theodore Gordon and George La Branche has led us into a pair of surprisingly common mistakes. Our first error is the commonly-held attitude that the dry-fly method is the most difficult, and that its difficulty and complexity make it the moral superior of other fly tactics. Knowledgeable anglers all enjoy the surface rise to the dry fly immensely, but no one can build an airtight case that the dry-fly method is more difficult or subtle than the full spectrum of tactics for wet flies and nymphs. Since approximately ninety percent of the trout diet is based on subaquatic nymphal and pupal forms, floating adult insects obviously play a relatively minor role in their feeding; but Halford ultimately convinced himself that the dry fly was not only the moral superior of the other fly methods, but also the most effective technique on his chalkstreams. The second error familiar to contemporary anglers, in their dry-fly myopia, is the rather simple-minded assumption that a visible surface rise automatically means a surface-feeding trout.

Fish commonly porpoise and swirl to hatching nymphs and thread-worms and pupae in the surface film. These insect forms are nymphs about to emerge as adult flies, pupae struggling to escape their pupal skins, and other ecotypes that breathe in the oxygen-rich meniscus of the water. Each of these forms is still lying under the surface, yet when a fish takes one, his movements are betrayed by a showy surface rise or bulge. Such rises are to nymphs and pupae, and must be fished with nymphal and pupal imitations that settle just under or ride in the film. Other visible rises, particularly dimpling swirls in lakes and slow-flowing streams, are indicative of feeding on the larvae and pupal forms of the minute Diptera, which often hang motionless under the surface film, their minute gills pulsing in the meniscus layer.

Although many anglers are still confused about nymphs and nymph fishing, our methods of fishing them are quite ancient. Such methods include each of the primary wet-fly techniques, depending on how the specific nymphs and pupae move in the water, and have their origins deep in angling prehistory. Most of our primitive fly patterns and many that originated in the past three centuries were fished under the surface—they were often taken for emerging mayfly nymphs and hatching pupae.

The rods and other tackle required for optimal nymph fishing are quite similar to those found in our earlier discussions on wet-fly tactics. Floating, sink-tip, and full-sinking lines are all valuable depending on the feeding level of the fish. Leaders of relatively fine limp nylon are important for nymph fishing in order to provide a relatively free character of drift. Generally speaking, nymph-fishing rods should be delicate enough to handle relatively fine tippet diameters, and have sufficient length to facilitate line mends and other manipulations of fly speed. Such rods might vary from seven to eight and a half feet, with matching lines from five- to eight-weight tapers. Their actions should provide the relatively slow rhythms of a semiparabolic taper, proportionately delicate tip calibrations, and oversize guides. Such tackle is capable of false casting nymphs without costing them moisture, can lay the imitations softly on the current, and can fish a fine nylon point without breaking it off in a good fish.

Our first conscious knowledge of the relationships between nymphs and aquatic fly hatches is found in *Certaine Experiments Concerning Fish and Fruite*, which the British writer John Taverner published in 1600. Walton did not mention such topologies in his *Compleat Angler* in 1653, and his collaborator Charles Cotton also omits mention of nymphs in his *Being Instructions How to Angle for a Trout or Grayling in a Clear Stream*. However, Cotton was later aware of nymphs, and his narrative poem titled *Wonders of the Peake* includes an unmistakable reference to such subaquatic flies.

The first conscious speculation on the importance of nymphs and larval forms in the trout diet appeared when John Younger published his *River Angling for Salmon and Trout* in 1840. Twenty-three years later, H. C. Cutcliffe wrote his book *Trout Fishing in Rapid Streams*, a classic based on a lifetime of experience on the rivers of Devonshire. Cutcliffe offers a concise account of west-country flies and the techniques of fishing them in swift water. His stratagems include stalking the fish carefully, and fishing the upstream dead drift to keep out of sight. His book unmistakably defines the differences between the reaches of water where exact imitation is necessary, and the swift pockets where a fish must take quickly or go hungry. Cutcliffe thoroughly understood the behavior of the small-stream trout as well as the life cycle of the aquatic insects, and in his book we find the following speculation:

> I find so much spoken about the natural fly and its imitation, but little about the insect before it is arrived at maturity. How seldom does one imitate the larva or pupa of the several insects.

However, it was not until the close of the nineteenth century that the genius emerged who would fit together these disparate pieces on the classic Itchen in England. George Edward MacKenzie Skues conceived and painstakingly hammered out the full theory and practice of modern nymph fishing himself, and quickly refined it to a surprising level of maturity. Skues was a solitary bachelor who fished and loved the Itchen for more than fifty years, and he was certainly the conscious progenitor of modern nymph-fishing techniques.

Skues first published his evolving philosophy in *Minor Tactics of the Chalk Stream*, which first appeared in 1910. It was based on a penetrating logic, healthy distrust of past dogma, thorough knowledge of fly-fishing history and theory, and considerable original thought. *Minor Tactics* made a point for retaining wet-fly tactics on the chalkstreams, and although it aroused a chorus of vocal opposition from the dry-fly acolytes around Halford, its brief for nymph fishing was so subtly and convincingly argued that it has never been successfully refuted. However, Skues faced strong opposition, and the quarrels still continue, more than fifty years later, at the Flyfisher's Club in London.

Skues was so successful with the chalkstream fish that he became a full-blown legend in his lifetime. His willingness to adapt himself and his tactics to the moods and rhythms of the river was his secret, and made him consistently more effective than his skilled dry-fly rivals on both the Itchen and the Test.

The studies outlined in *Minor Tactics* were enlarged in 1921, when Skues published his major book *The Way of a Trout with a Fly*, which polished and refined a consistent philosophy of nymph tactics. *Nymph Fishing for Chalk Stream Trout* codified a lifetime of experience along his beloved river above Winchester. It should be understood that Skues fully grasped the limitations of his work, and his books are filled with intimations of that awareness. Skues recognized that the spectrum of fly hatches on the chalk-rich rivers of Hampshire was limited, just as the insect populations of our eastern limestone streams and western spring creeks are often limited to relatively few individual species as well.

Most still-water insects are swimming ecotypes, ranging about freely in the current both during their everyday underwater lives and during actual emergence. There are infinitely more insect species and ecotypes found in other biosystems, such as the swifter rivers throughout the United States and Canada. However, such exceptions to the Skues philosophy of nymph fishing in no way weaken its importance. The conditions endemic to the British chalkstreams are also found on our slow-flowing rivers, alkaline spring-fed streams, and lakes and impoundments everywhere. Skues is still the sole father of modern nymph fishing, and his conceptual innovations stand as the principal bench mark of all subsequent work on nymphs, even if his pioneer thought falls short of the full scope of modern nymph-fishing problems in the United States.

Since manipulation of the artificial nymph depends upon the physiology and behavior of the natural, stream entomology is unquestionably the key to frequent success. American stream entomology poses a considerable problem in observing and imitating the plethora of diet forms indigenous to an entire continent, rather than the relatively limited palette of fly hatches found in the British Isles.

The considerations of American entomology are extensive. When the collections I made for books like *Nymphs* and *Matching the Hatch* grew larger and larger, it became obvious that our fishing poses galaxies of fly-hatch problems not found in Europe—writers like Skues, Sawyer, Harris, and Kite have written exhaustively about their chalkstream nymphs, while our American writers have primarily concerned themselves with tactics rather than making a serious study of the nymphs themselves.

Both Oliver Kite and Frank Sawyer are superb nymph tacticians whose studies have been focused on the Wylye and Avon a few miles above Salisbury. Kite compiled his experience in *Nymph Fishing in Practice*, and Sawyer published his knowledge in the better-known *Nymphs and the Trout*, which includes the following perceptive observations on a nymphing fish:

> While after fish which are plainly visible one learns just how a nymph is taken, and it becomes increasingly obvious that sometimes the indication shown on the surface is so slight, that without very close attention, a trout can have your nymph in his mouth and spit it out before you realize a chance was missed.
>
> One develops an awareness which is not even a sixth sense. It is something which just cannot be explained. You see nothing, feel nothing, yet something prompts you to lift your rod tip, some little whisper in your brain to tell you a fish is at the other end of your line. But this feeling only comes if you are intent on your work, for though it may not be possible to see through the surface, it is possible to visualize the position of the fish and anticipate his reactions to your nymph.

My recent book *Nymphs* has sought to provide a foundation for nymph-fishing techniques on American waters, carefully based upon an extensive catalog of the actual nymphs themselves. The experience gathered since the publication of *Matching the Hatch* in 1955 has made me fully aware that trout are as selective in their nymphing as in their feeding on floating insects.

However, fishing nymphs properly is not only a problem of dressing imitations to match the naturals, but also of understanding how these subaquatic insects behave and move at various depths of water. Knowledge concerning their preferences in water types, their behavior in the subaquatic growth cycle, and the character of the nymphs during a hatch is critical. The skilled nymph fisherman must have an understanding of their typical bottom-dwelling habits, their movements at the intermediate depths of water, wriggling a few inches beneath the surface, and their final hatching moments in the film itself. Such knowledge will make precise imitation and presentation possible, keying our handling of the flies to the behavior of the naturals. There are fifteen basic fly-manipulation techniques in nymph fishing.

1. The Dead-Drift Swing

The dead-drift swing is perhaps the oldest basic fly technique adapted to simulate certain types of slow-swimming nymphs working toward the surface to hatch. It is executed by casting across or quartering downstream, depending upon the current speed, and then simply allowing the fly to work back across the current tongue with a fixed length of line. Such a presentation is effective on a nymphing fish, or can be used to cover the water in a series of concentric quarter-circles.

Experienced nymph fishermen will use this technique to fish imitations of clambering stonefly and mayfly nymphs that swim clumsily toward the shallows before hatching. It is also useful in imitating the slow-swimming little *Paraleptophlebia* nymphs, and other tiny mayflies in their hatching periods. Tiny swimming mayfly nymphs of the *Baetis* flies are particularly numerous on American trout streams, and the dead-drift swing is especially good when they are emerging. There are also times when a dead-drift swing is effective on fly hatches that are partially winged before they reach the 'surface and emerge from their nymphal shucks. Such hatches include the two-tailed *Epeorus* flies, which split their wing cases before they leave the bottom, and the ubiquitous *Ephemerella* mayflies found throughout American waters, which begin to escape their nymphal skins a few inches below the surface film. The large swift-water *Stenonemas* are a group of mayflies that hatch clumsily, working toward the shallows and struggling with half-dried wings in the film; their emergence behavior is ideally suited to the dead-drift swing.

My fishing diaries are filled with experiences focused on each of these nymphal forms, but perhaps the most pervasive memories are those of the heavy *Baetis* hatches on the famous Frying Pan in Colorado. These tiny mayflies are many-brooded, with several hatches during each season. The first cycle usually comes in early season, but the subsequent hatches of August and October seem more important to the fish. The *Baetis* hatches at the Ruedi still-water on the Frying Pan were like tiny slate-colored snowflakes in those years before college, but they are lost now, drowned forever under the waters of a reservoir.

It was an accident that I discovered the dead-drift swing on the still-water at Ruedi. There was a heavy hatch of *Baetis* on the sprawling half-mile flat, and I was busily working a tiny dry fly over the rising fish, when friends stopped to talk from the road. There were rises everywhere on the still water but few fish had taken a floating imitation of the naturals.

What are they taking? my friends called.

They're not taking the dry fly very well, I shouted back. *They seem to be nymphing or taking something else tonight!*

Work it out! they laughed.

My tiny dry fly had drowned and drifted past me while we talked, and it began a dead-drift swing across the current downstream when a good fish took it and was hooked.

You fish better when you're not fishing! one friend called, from across the pool. *Why'd he take it sunk and downstream?*

Let's try it again and find out, I suggested.

The tiny dry fly was bedraggled and soaked with fish slime, and without cleaning it or drying its hackles, it was cast again and worked past another rising fish. The fly came across its feeding lane, swinging against the tension of the leader, and there was a soft little swirl. The leader twitched suddenly and I tightened.

He took it! my friend said excitedly.

They're taking the nymphs of these little flies! I said. *Two fish in a row is no accident—it's the solution!*

It was a happy discovery that produced a cornucopia of selective trout that afternoon; and the fish we killed for the frying pan were filled with tiny *Baetis* nymphs. It is a technique that has proved itself over the years.

2. The Swimming-Nymph Swing

This approach is a subtle variation on the simple dead-drift swing, which introduces a teasing rhythm of the rod tip into the fixed-length manipulation of the line. It consists of casting directly cross-stream in slow-moving currents, and quartering downstream in most cases. The fly swing is allowed to work back across the current on a fixed length of line, with a contrapuntal teasing of the rod tip. The rod rhythms can be varied in frequency and character to suggest various nymphal and pupal behavior.

Such fly swings have a wide range of usefulness.

They work to suggest small swimming nymphs found in currents of good flow speed, like the big *Leptophlebia* nymphs that hatch on our eastern rivers in early spring. Such nymphs often migrate along the river in schools, and the swimming nymph swing is particularly effective then.

The approach is also effective fished on a sinking line with big stonefly nymph imitations, particularly on our large rocky mountain rivers where such diet forms are numerous. It is a little like salmon fishing, casting a long quartering angle downstream, and allowing the big nymph to ride deep in its swing. It should be teased through the swing with a subtle rising and falling rhythm of the rod tip. Each cast should be fished out until it hangs directly below the angler, and then it should be repeated a half step downstream.

Emerging caddis pupae are another diet form perfectly imitated with a swimming-nymph swing. Such pupal flies leave their sacs, struggling free from the shucks while they work in a slow rhythm toward the surface. The subtle, teasing rhythm of the rod tip is ideally suited to imitating Trichoptera, and it is a valuable method during caddis hatches.

Such caddis behavior is often the solution during impressive rises of fish both in Europe and the United States. Many flies are coming off at such times, and a large number of fish are working at the surface, but dry flies are surprisingly ineffective. The key to the puzzle is often a simple **soft-hackled** imitation, fished downstream to specific rising trout with a rhythmic fly-swing method. Fished properly, such trout often become unusually gullible.

Thoughts of such hatches inevitably turn to a summer evening years ago on the venerable water of the Brooklyn Flyfishers, which lies on the Beaverkill headwaters above Rockland. It is some of the loveliest water in the Catskills. It has been protected, stocked, and painstakingly restored over the past seventy-five years by releasing many trout and fishing only with flies. Several times the members have been forced to rebuild their banks and log cribbings, binding up the wounds of hurricane flooding. The quality of the fishing on their brief mileage of the Beaverkill is eloquent testimony to the stewardship of the Brooklyn Flyfishers—just as the superb no-kill water on the lower river below Roscoe clearly demonstrates the only viable method of providing good sport over decent-size trout on our hard-fished public waters.

The last evening I fished the Brooklyn water, I drew the upper riffles and the deep run along the county road. It was a soft evening with a warm wind moving up the valley. Normally, I would have expected a hatch of pale *Stenonemas*, and I began fishing under the willows with a pale little nymph. Two fish took it lightly and came off after a momentary struggle. One brown trout porpoised to the teasing nymph as if it were lazily taking a dry fly, and I hooked it firmly.

The next fifty yards were unproductive. There were no trout rising anywhere in the wide riffling reach of shallows, and then suddenly the Beaverkill came alive. It was the miracle of a heavy *Psilotreta* swarm, coming just after five o'clock. There were more and more of the little slate-colored sedges rising from the current now, and the birds were dipping to them. Swallows were wheeling high above the river, while the restless little phoebes and flycatchers darted down into the hatching swarms.

There were hundreds of sedges now. The fish were working heavily, too, and the birds became highly agitated. Thousands of caddis flew along the river on the gentle wind. Some were as much as sixty feet above the current, judging from the darting chimney swifts and swallows, while other hopscotched enticingly along the surface.

The fish went crazy. Trout were rolling and porpoising in the current everywhere. The run along the county road was alive with rises. Fish rolled and dimpled and splashed along the rocks, fed eagerly in the cribbing backwaters, and rose greedily in the smoother currents. Many of the rise forms were slashing and eager, and I guessed that the expenditure of such energy indicated the difficulty of capturing a fluttering caddis.

The little sedges were difficult to catch. When the fish clearly rejected a dozen dry-fly imitations, I spent several minutes trying to catch one of the naturals. It was some time before I was successful. It had a dark brownish body, darkly mottled legs, pale antennae, light grayish rear wings, and dark speckled forewings.

That's strange, I puzzled. *These darkly tied little dry flies are good imitations—they should have worked!*

Carefully observing the trout, it soon became evident that their rise forms were becoming vigorous and greedy, but that they seldom were focused on a fluttering adult. Occasional canddisflies did disappear unhappily in a surface rise, and then I saw the solution. There was a strong swirl across the current, and an adult sedge emerged from the rise form, and scuttled clumsily into the air. Another hatched from a second splashy rise, but was instantly taken as an adult fly, before it could escape the surface. It happened again upstream.

Caddis pupae! I thought happily. *They're taking the little pupae just before they hatch and fly off!*

The fish were still rolling and splashing eagerly, expending the kind of energy usually involved in surface rises to a fluttering adult, but these fish were taking the swimming pupae. Such rises could only be triggered by a fluttering or swimming subaquatic ecotype. The ability of a caddis pupa to swim toward the surface explained the relatively energetic rise forms, and I searched my fly books for a soft-hackled little wet with a darkly dubbed body. For several past seasons I had been experimenting with partridge and woodcock hackle flies in the tradition of British writers like Stewart and Pritt, and had found them effective during caddis hatches.

There was a good fish porpoising above a flat rock in the gathering currents toward the tail of the pool. I selected a small, dark brown partridge pattern with a body of hare's mask, and cast to its position. As the fly began its swing, I teased it gently with a rod-tip rhythm. It came swimming through the holding lie, and there was a quick rise above the rock.

The fish was securely hooked. *That's it!* I thought. *That's what they're doing and I've matched it!*

The fishing was suddenly easy. Trout that had consistently refused my dry flies took the little soft-hackled wet readily. It was a clear lesson in reading rise forms for all kinds of fly hatches that emerge from swimming nymphs and pupal forms, and it is especially true of hatching sedges. There was no question about having matched the hatch. Thirty-six trout were caught and released while the sedge hatch lasted, and when the sedges stopped emerging and disappeared from the river, it flowed smooth and silent in the gathering darkness.

3. The Hand-Twist Retrieve

American fly-fishermen are perhaps most familiar with the hand-twist retrieve, because Ray Bergman devoted considerable attention to its importance in *Trout*, and taught its rudiments to a whole generation of anglers. Bergman described his faith in the hand-twist retrieve in an episode that took place on Cranberry Lake, the logging impoundment on the Oswegatchie in the Adirondacks. The method was to cast out across the drowned channel of the river, let the wet flies or nymphs sink toward the stumps and deadfalls at the bottom, and then retrieve line rhythmically around the fingers of the left hand.

The technique requires holding the line between thumb and forefinger and reaching for additional line with the last three fingers; then the hand is oscillated counterclockwise to the palm-up position, again lacing line around the fingers. The last fingers reach again for another few inches of line, rolling the hand palm-down, and oscillating again. The hand works like a rolling shuttle, lacing the line through the fingers in a figure-eight wrapping. Bergman placed great importance on the rhythm of his hand-twist retrieves; he liked them as slow as twenty-five to thirty turns per minute, although one turn per second is about average.

The hand-twist retrieve is particularly valuable for imitating slow-swimming insects. These behavior groups include backswimmers and aquatic beetle larvae and dragonfly nymphs, as well as the freshwater crustaceans like sowbugs and scuds. It has been particularly successful in fishing the thick-gilled *Leptophlebia* nymphs, the smaller fringe-gilled nymphs of the *Paraleptophlebia* flies, and pond-dwelling mayfly nymphs like the *Callibaetis* and *Caenis*.

Perhaps the most dramatic example of such success with the hand-twist retrieve came some years ago on the weedy, slow-flowing Nissequogue in April. It has its source in a series of spring-fed ponds and marshes on eastern Long Island, and is a quiet little river with an old and distinguished past in the history of American sport.

Daniel Webster once fished its Wyandanche Club, the century-old membership that controls its headwaters. Its roster over the past one hundred years has included some equally famous captains of industry and shipping and finance, and its present members are no less distinguished. Webster still dominates the club's history, just as he once dominated the Washington political landscape, and local legends remember his huge baskets of brook trout taken on the Nissequogue.

Its beats are carefully marked in the woods along the river, with duckboard walks in the marshy places. The beats are drawn among the members from a leather dice cup at breakfast, although the guests are often given preferential treatment. My good friend and host Lester Brion rolled Beat Five for me. Beat Five is a long reach of still water that winds upstream from the boat landing for Beat Six, which is essentially the millpond above the dam. The smooth currents of Beat Five shelter some big brown trout, and it is challenging water. There are a number of fine holding lies. Fish cruise the open waist-deep reach above the boat landing, often lying in the pickerelweed backwaters. The smooth currents work along the alders, sweeping the silt from a brief expanse of pale gravel. Upstream there are dense beds of eelgrass, where pale stones cause some eddying currents. It is a place where I once took a deep-bellied three-pound rainbow in early spring.

There is a deep hole under the alders above the upper boat dock, and good trout are lying there. Thirty yards of smooth, relatively shallow flat are next, sometimes good for cruising fish, and then come three hundred feet of undercut holding water that is some of the best on the entire river. It has deep pockets along the willows and alders, with brushy deadfalls that break the currents. It is a deep dark-water stretch that has often surrendered brown trout between sixteen and eighteen inches.

It is a perfect slow-flowing run for an upstream hand-twist retrieve, and it is rich with *Leptophlebia* nymphs. These subaquatic insects are unique still-water species, somewhat sluggish in their swimming motions, and they congregate in the backwater shallows. They scuttle and clamber there in the bottom detritus, swimming laboriously from place to place. These nymphs cruise together in schools like minute baitfish, foraging rather boldly along the bottom. *Leptophlebia* nymphs also display the habit of mass migration just before their emergence. Such schools can number several hundred nymphs in an optimal habitat like the Nissequogue, a river ideally suited to the genus; and these nymphs can travel as much as a mile. The slow rhythms of their swimming before emergence make them easy prey for the trout and perfectly suited to the slow hand-twist retrieve.

It was an April morning years ago when I drew Beat Five and a large migration of these mayfly nymphs was moving along the undercut banks below the swamp maples. The big fish there were making the most of the opportunity, and I watched them taking the nymphs along the bottom, the weak sunlight flashing on their sides when they captured a swimming *Leptophlebia* below the tangled deadfalls. There had been an occasional hatching fly that morning, and I had collected several *Leptophlebia* duns downstream.

It was a good guess that the concentration of working fish in the sixty-five yards of water above me was the result of a migratory school of nymphs, and I tried an imitation in the run where I had seen a deep-feeding trout turn several times. The first cast dropped a few feet above its holding lie, and as it settled deep on the sinking line, I started a deliberate hand-twist retrieve. My left hand had completed less than a half dozen turns when there was a strong pull, and the light caught a turning fish along the roots. It was a fine eighteen-inch brown trout, and its throat and gill structures were crammed with dark *Leptophlebia* nymphs. The sixty-five yards of water under the willows and alders produced almost thirty good fish that morning—to a patient hand-twist retrieve along the sheltering willows.

4. The Hand-Strip Retrieve

There are a number of nymphal species that swim too erratically and move with considerable darting movements for effective imitation by the hand-twist retrieve. Such nymphs include swimming nymphs of the *Siphlonurus* and *Siphloplecton* genera, and many of the larger subaquatic forms that inhabit still currents, lakes, and impoundments. The hand-strip retrieve is used to create a pulsing rhythm of the nymph in swimming movements from five inches to twenty-odd inches in length. Fish taking such nymphs typically display a relatively bold rise form, since the agility of the nymphs makes them difficult to capture.

The technique involves holding the line under the index finger at the rod grip, with the left hand then manipulating the rhythm and length of the stripping retrieve. The frequency of the retrieve should employ a slow series of five-inch strips, executed at a rhythm of thirty per minute, suggesting a nymph that swims with such pulsing behavior patterns. Much faster rhythms are also possible, although the minnowlike movements of some nymphs are perhaps better imitated with the rod-and-line strip.

Several years ago in Wyoming I experienced some exceptional fishing in a sheltered bay of Yellowstone Lake. It is an immense ecological world in itself, its incredibly blue and unpolluted water lying in an amphitheater of smoke-colored mountains. Boiling springs bubble and steam in the September mornings along its timbered shoreline. The dense forests of spruce and lodgepole pine and fir are beautiful. Pewter-colored deadfalls lie bleached and slowly rotting in the shallows, along with dense phalanx of tules and reeds. Gulls and pelicans crowd the food-rich bays of the most remarkable cutthroat fishery in the world. There is exceptional fly-fishing where the remote headwaters of the Yellowstone enter the lake, in the bays where feeder streams join its waters, and in the outlet flowages where the river gathers itself and slides into the huge cutthroat flats below the famous Fishing Bridge.

It was below the headwater inlets that I once encountered a heavy hatch of big *Siphlonurus* drakes, in numbers that only the rich alkalinity of such waters can sustain, and the fat cutthroats began rising vigorously. There was one fish that began working along the reeds, and its rises were big enough to suggest size. Several times it rose boldly in the shallows, but its rises were so scattered that it was sometimes difficult to predict its movements. Random casting with a dry fly to its single rise forms proved fruitless, since it seldom remained in one area and had a 360-degree range of options for leaving its last position. Any cast could be wrong and there were considerable percentages against its being right. Fishing an imitative nymph in such a situation is a little more effective, since its retrieve can cross the feeding routes travelled by any number of foraging trout. The hatch increased steadily until the still surface of the bay was covered with sailboat-shaped mayflies, and the fish's rises became steadily more frequent. It was possible to watch for two or three rise forms in relatively quick succession and, from their sequence of quiet swirls, plot the direction the fish was working. Its rises were coming faster.

They're like beads on a string, I thought suddenly. *You can tell where they're going from two or three swirls.*

The big cutthroat rose again along the reeds. Its second rise came three seconds later and was about six feet toward the right. The third rise came at about the same rhythm and spacing, and I cast my nymph about six feet ahead of its last swirl, dropping it slightly beyond its probable line of direction. The retrieve was a steady left-hand strip, working the fly back slowly in a series of six-inch swimming motions. It had just about passed the spot where I had anticipated its next rise form, when a bulging wake appeared behind my nymph and it disappeared in a heavy swirl.

He's taken it! I shouted to myself.

It was a fat cutthroat that weighed almost five pounds, rich golden yellow and delicately spotted, and it fought hard through the weedy shallows. Its capture was typical of the tactics in both lake fishing and the hand-strip retrieve.

5. The Rod-and-Line Strip

Some nymphal forms are so agile in the water that their movements can rival those of the fish themselves. Such nymphs cannot be imitated with a simple hand-strip technique and some action of the rod tip is required. One solution is a rod-and-line strip not unlike the manipulation of a bucktail or streamer. It is a technique that requires some experimenting, like the hand-twist retrieve or a similar method, to discover a rhythm of fishing that fools the trout.

Damselflies, burrowing mayflies, and fast-water swimming nymphs like the agile *Isonychias* are all nymphal types that move with erratic, darting motions in the water. Sometimes their swimming rhythms are deliberate and slow, and can be suggested with more conventional techniques. Sometimes their movements are so rapier-quick that an exaggerated rod-tip action interjected into a hand-strip retrieve is needed. The fish are often as attracted to the erratic retrieve suggestive of the nymphs, provided the size and configuration and color of the nymphs is right, as the imitative character of the fly pattern itself.

There was an evening on the Esopus twenty years ago that demonstrated this fact. It was the middle of June, and my father and I were fishing a broken reach of water above Phoenicia. The river suddenly came alive in late afternoon when a number of good trout began working along the shorelines and below a large boulder at midstream, but the symptoms were a mystery in those years.

What are they doing? my father yelled.

Several big leadwinged drakes hopscotched along the rocks and finally got airborne.

See those big mayflies starting to hatch? I shouted back. *It could be their swimming nymphs!*

It was a lucky guess, but I understood so little about the habits of the *Isonychia* nymphs in those years that the reason the fish were working along the rocks puzzled me. The secret lay in the migratory behavior of the nymphs before a hatch.

The agile, little fast-water nymphs swim and dart swiftly among the rocks through most of their life cycle, and about an hour before emergence, they migrate toward the rocky shallows. The nymphs migrate and gather in hatching schools, moving restlessly from stone to stone near the rocks they will climb when actually emerging. It is strange that the nymphs congregate around specific rocks for hatching, since the differences between one stone and another are not apparent to the human senses. Such rocks are surrounded with darting, restless *Isonychia* nymphs waiting to hatch, and when emergence actually comes they crawl up their hatching stones to the waterline, waiting for their nymphal skins to split.

Preston Jennings recommended a big leadwing Coachman fished wet during these hatches, working it in the rocky shallows where the nymphs congregate. His *Book of Trout Flies* is the genesis of our American studies in disciplined trout-stream entomology, and I selected a big Coachman from my fly books.

This should work if they're taking the nymphs of those big slate-colored drakes, I yelled downstream.

The big wet dropped along the rocks where several good fish were working, and I watched the leader for a telltale movement that would signal a taking trout. The leadwing drifted back downstream and nothing happened. Several more casts produced similar results, and I retrieved the wet fly to shorten its wings in the hope it might look more nymphlike.

It's not working. I shook my head while the line drifted past me. *It's supposed to match these nymphs, but it's not working.*

The bellying line began working across the current downstream and a good trout took the swinging fly hard. It had been chasing the relatively fast fly swing from the shallows, and its rise was a splashy swirl that showered water across the current. It seemed like a lucky accident.

You've solved it! my father shouted.

It was only an accident, I laughed. *I wasn't even fishing when it took the fly!* The fish went fifteen inches and I released it.

You sure it was accidental?

My father had a point and it started me thinking. Perhaps these nymphs moved swiftly in the shallows, darting minnowlike among the rocks, and my bellying line had accelerated its speed to suggest the naturals. It seemed worth trying, and I placed the bedraggled fly above a rising fish, stripping it back with both the rod tip and my hand. The fly had come only a foot past the fish when it took with a savage swirl and promptly cartwheeled in a series of staccato jumps downstream.

Rainbow! I yelled. *Fished it fast!*

My father cast across the stream to another rising fish, stripped back line, and hooked it immediately. *Got one!* he laughed. *I think we've solved the problem—with a little help from the fish!*

6. The Cast-and-Strip Method

This is primarily a method of fishing a nymph deep in a swift current, using both line manipulation and a sinking line to achieve the desired depth. It involves casting across a deep current tongue and then shaking additional slack out through the guides as the line settles into its swing. This tactic will get deeper on a downstream drift, and it is useful when the fish are foraging along the bottom.

Another version of the cast-and-strip technique will work a nymph even deeper, and is useful in fishing strong currents and extremely deep pools. It involves casting upstream and shaking the additional slack into the fly drift before it bellies past your position and swings downstream. This technique will buy considerably more depth if the stripping-out is properly timed to take advantage of the sinking slack-line drift. The bellying line swings past, working below your station in the current, and the tension of the line against the rod tip indicates when the nymph is swimming deep. It can either swing on the line tension without additional action from the rod or fish with a teasing rhythm across the current.

The downstream cast-and-strip method once produced a heavy hook-jawed brown on the Big Hole above Twin Bridges. Gene Anderegg and I were fishing together when we reached a temporary irrigation weir on the river, and I cast well down its deep-flowing pond, stripping out a dozen feet of sinking line into the settling cast. We allowed it to belly deep into the impoundment, and then I fished a big beetle larva back along the bottom with a patient hand-twist retrieve. The four-pound brown took the nymph as it was literally ticking along the stones.

Fish like that are worth the trip! Anderegg said.

There was another morning years ago on the Roaring Fork in Colorado when I had gone fishless for almost two hours. There were few hatches and fewer rising fish, although conditions seemed perfect for both. The swift run along the railroad slide looked good, and two bait fishermen were patiently fishing its throat with salmon eggs. They were using several split shot and working their bait along the bottom, and I stopped to admire their catch.

Got some good rainbows. The older man raised his metal clip stringer from the river. *Pretty nice?*

They look strange! I said.

Each fish had rubbed its nose raw on the bottom. The bait fishermen agreed to let me dress a fish and examine its stomach contents, and I discovered its digestive tract was filled sausage-tight with fat little caddis larvae. The trout had been rooting them out of their hiding places among the stones along the bottom and a larval imitation fished deep with the cast-and-strip quickly produced two dozen rainbows.

7. The Upstream Dead-Drift Technique

The upstream dead-drift presentation is another nymph-fishing method described in considerable detail in Bergman's *Trout*; and along with the conventional hand-twist retrieve, it is perhaps the most basic tactic in the strategy of a practiced nymph fisherman.

Since a large number of subaquatic insects clamber and crawl along the bottom, totally unable to swim throughout their larval existence or during emergence, the upstream dead drift is the best method for suggesting their behavior. Such tactics closely imitate the clinging or clambering mayfly nymphs. The two-tailed *Epeorus* and three-tailed *Ephemerella* nymphs are the immature forms of our most important fly hatches, and their nymphs reach the surface buoyed with the gases generated inside their splitting nymphal skins. Some wrap their half-emerged wings around themselves, trapping a galaxy of tiny bubbles, and others split their immature shucks with the gentle pressures of similar gases. These hatching nymphs are fished with half-winged emerging fly types, by casting the imitations upstream on a floating line. It is a difficult technique to master, perhaps the most subtle problem in all of fly-fishing, since a nymph drifting back on a completely slack drift is difficult to follow in broken currents. The fish often come to the dead-drift presentation so softly that a taking trout goes completely undetected.

Anything can mean a fish! the old riverkeeper on the Lauterach repeatedly lectured me that golden summer years ago. *The line can twitch or pause in its rate of drift or stop its swing imperceptibly—any of these things can tell you a trout has intercepted your nymph!*

You really mean anything? I laughed.

The old riverkeeper was quite right; and in the years that I gained more experience with nymphs, it became apparent that really skillful nymph fishermen have an almost extrasensory ability to feel the moment a fish has taken. Sometimes a taking fish reveals itself with a subtle flash of light as it turns along the bottom, or its swirl along the bottom transmits itself back to the surface currents in a minuscule change-of-flow. These clues are almost imperceptible, like the half-seen tumbling of a drowned leaf along the bottom or the brief shadow of a passing kingfisher, and such false clues can frequently trigger an experienced nymph man into striking. It is a hair-trigger quality of judgment that only hours and hours of nymph fishing can develop, disciplining and honing the senses to an exquisite degree of skills.

Our earlier discussions of wet-fly tactics have outlined how Bergman recommended the fly-bobber method in *Trout*. His technique involved a dry-fly dropper attached at the butt of the leader. It becomes a crude but effective bobber, while it floats on the surface, and the indicator fly pauses or twitches when a taking fish interrupts the drift. It was a method I often attempted in boyhood years, even filing off the hook bends to keep them from tangling in my casts, and using a pale bivisible dressed as a highly visible indicator. It was a method I promptly dropped after I raised an immense fish to the hookless bobber on the swift-flowing Pine in Michigan. Modern nymph fishermen use a similar indicator technique in fishing the upstream dead drift, with either a tiny Whitlock fluorescent tube or a touch of bright lacquer at the leader knot—although I once had a hatchery brook trout take that too on the waters of an exclusive fishing club in Pennsylvania.

The upstream dead-drift method is also used with weighted nymphs and larval imitations almost literally bounced along the bottom. Such fishing is always done with a relatively short floating line, stripping back the slack like a dry-fly presentation, staying closely in touch with the fly. Staying in touch aids in both sensing a strike and in tightening in time to hook the fish. Such tactics are particularly valuable in heavily broken currents, or in the cold water of early season, when the fish are sluggish.

Heavily weighted nymphs are preferred, and leaders loaded with split shot or twisted fuse wire are common on many rivers. Such tackle handles awkwardly, and I seldom choose such methods, but no one can deny their effectiveness when the trout are bottom feeding.

Some anglers who are expert in fishing a weighted leader recommend a split shot on the tippet, with one or more nymphs on dropper strands farther up the leader. Another variation involves two dropper strands, with flies attached to the first dropper and point tippet, and the weighting fastened to the second dropper strand. Placing the weight in these positions on the leader means that the flies will come free when the lead fouls on the bottom, since only the split shot or fuse wire is snagged, and will slip off the nylon with a steady pressure.

Perhaps the most skilled practitioner of the weighted-leader nymph technique is Charles Fothergill, the famous fly maker and guide at Aspen on the Roaring Fork. Fothergill is remarkably proficient with the upstream dead drift on its Colorado rainbows, and has tutored a whole circle of Aspen fishermen in his methods. Gardner Grant is another fly-fishing friend particularly adept at fishing such weighted leaders, and his catches are impressive when our eastern rivers are still cold with April rains and snowmelt, although he takes a merciless ribbing from companions who refuse to fish such weighted terminal tackle.

It really works on the Beaverkill when the river's high and cold, Grant was explaining over lunch in Manhattan. *It's a little clumsy, casting the split shot on the leader, but it really takes trout when they're bottom feeding!*

Ed Zern looked up from his salad, fixing Grant in midsermon with a puckish frown. *What happens when a hatchery fish takes the lead?*

You've got trouble! Grant admitted.

8. The Still-Water Dead-Drift

The dead-drift method on lakes, impoundments, and beaver ponds is often the best technique for imitating the minute larval and pupal forms of the *Chironomus* midges, one of the most important insects in the still-water diet of the trout. Although these midge larvae and pupae are minuscule, they are available literally in the millions, and even large trout cruise lazily to take them in the meniscus film with tiny little dimples. Such rises of fish are extremely frustrating to most fishermen, since there are dimpling swirls everywhere across the still surface, yet no insects are visible. British fishermen call these midge forms duck flies and buzzers and reed-smuts, and their so-called smutting rises make for difficult times when conventional fly patterns and tactics are doomed.

Ain't nothing hatching! the old-timers used to complain when the fish were smutting on the Colorado lakes. *Them fish're only playing out there tonight!*

Trout are never playing. Their existence is a perilous equilibrium between calories ingested and energy expended, as our earlier chapters clearly demonstrate, and predators lurk everywhere. Smutting fish are usually taking tiny larvae and pupae imprisoned in the surface film in such incredible numbers that even a large fish can collect more calories from sipping these minutiae than it expends in its feeding efforts.

Such midge forms pass through several cycles each season. During periods when the midge pupae are readily available, trout can ingest as many as forty to fifty pupae per minute. Smutting often involves such frequent feeding that its rhythms dimple a still lake with countless little rise forms, even though no insects are apparent anywhere.

Fishing an imitation of these minute subaquatic insects is both subtle and simple. The larval and pupal patterns are small flies, with hooks ranging from about sixteen through size twenty-eight, dressed on delicate light-wire hooks that hang in the surface film. Fishing a wet fly pattern is usually a problem in saturating the leader and the fly dressing so that it will sink readily, but this is not the case in fishing these tiny midge imitations with the still-water dead-drift technique.

The still-water dead drift is most effective when the imitation neither really floats nor sinks, but rides clumsily awash in the surface film, and the leader is often partially dressed to float like a bobber. The tippet should sink readily, unless it is finer than about .005 in diameter, but the fly must ride suspended just at the surface. Smutting trout often rise so frequently that it is difficult to cast to them, although it is possible to read their direction of feeding from the sequential pattern of their rise forms. It is typical of still-water fishing.

Since the naturals are virtually incapable of motion, the fish are not attracted through either manipulation of an imitation or its impact on the surface. Such trout must simply encounter the larval or pupal imitations on their foraging rounds, hanging motionless just under the film, or the presentation will not appear natural. Such tactics obviously demand patience. The angler must wait for a cruising fish, observe its rhythm and direction of feeding, and then make a soft cast well ahead of its route. The fly should perhaps be placed one or two rise positions ahead of the cruising fish and allowed to hang dead-drift from the floating leader. The trout often swim just under the surface, pushing a little bulge or bow wake ahead of their passage, and their rise to the artificial in the film is accompanied with a darting twitch of the nylon. It is a subtle and challenging method of fishing the smutting rise.

9. Cast-and-Countdown Method

The cast-and-countdown method is another primary technique of fishing lakes and impoundments. It is the optimal system of working a nymph deep in the channels of a still-water habitat. Perhaps the best places to find trout in such biosystems, particularly the larger trout inhabiting our lakes and reservoirs and ponds, are the shelving dropoffs and outlet and inlet channels. Such places are the primary source of forage baitfish and other lacustrine diet forms for the trout population. Such foods are principally concentrated in relatively shallow waters, because photosynthesis is dependent upon relative turbidity and the penetration of sunlight into the water and because the myriad diet forms find both food and shelter in the shallows.

Most lakes, impoundments, and ponds are inhabited primarily by still-water ecotypes, except in their wind-swept zones where virtually continuous wave action on the reefs or rocky shorelines produces oxygen saturations that rival the parts-per-million counts found in a tumbling stream. However, the swift inlet shallows and gathering outlet currents also shelter organisms requiring relatively high oxygen counts, and such zones sustain a richer spectrum of life than adjacent waters. It is no accident that the fish gather in these places, since trout simply forage where food is most plentiful.

The countdown method of fishing a beetle larva, dragonfly nymph, or freshwater shrimp imitation in such places is designed to present such fly-patterns in a natural manner. It is a matter of discipline and patience. The countdown is effective in widespread waters, from the reedy outlet of Lago Maihue in Chile to remote Indian House Lake in the Labrador. It is particularly well known in the rich weed-bordered channels at Henry's Lake in Idaho, where the big cutthroat hybrids and brook trout forage along the bottom for the fat *Gammarus* shrimps.

Weighted imitations should be fished deep on a sinking line. The cast should be made well across the weedy channels, and allowed to sink while the fisherman counts off the seconds. His count may range from ten to twenty seconds, depending on the estimated depth of the channels. The purpose of this calibrated reconnaissance is defining the length of time required for an imitation to reach the weeds or bottom. Should the first several casts work back without actually touching the moss or ticking gently into the bottom gravel, the angler must cast again and add enough seconds to his countdown until the retrieve touches the bottom growth; its depth is the critical bench mark. With that depth accurately established, the fisherman shortens his countdown slightly so the weighted fly hand-twists back slowly, just above the weeds or gravel.

The rest is more discipline and patience. Each cast is allowed to sink to the proper depth, and the skilled angler covers the channel carefully, with a clockwise fan-shaped pattern of casts. Each should fall about two feet farther around the imaginary clock face. Such a properly executed pattern should intercept any cruising trout, and the cast-and-countdown technique will settle the fly to the correct fishing depth.

Hooking a fish against the drag of a sinking line fished at such depths is not difficult if a few brief points are mastered. The fly should be worked with either a firm hand twist or a slow line strip, with the running line held under the index finger of the rod hand. The rod tip should always be pointed directly at the retrieving fly, and held relatively low over the water to gain maximum depth. The strike on feeling the tugging pull of a deep-feeding trout must be firm enough to tighten the deep-riding belly of the line, compensating for hydraulic drag and slack to hook a fish that takes half-heartedly.

10. The Multiple-Nymph Method

Although my own experience had always pointed toward the use of a single fly pattern, recent experience with midge forms and heavy sedge hatches have made me aware of the multiple-nymph technique. Such three- and four-fly leaders are still common on the Irish and Scottish lakes, and on the subarctic lakes of Scandinavia, where the dropper loop and snelled fly remain in fashion. Such tackle was common on the Gunnison and Frying Pan and Roaring Fork during my early summers in Colorado.

Some big western rivers like the Deschutes and Yellowstone and Snake are still fished with snelled flies in their tumbling white-water stretches, but such tackle is much too crude for the trout in most of our hard-fished waters. The dropper loops and snells are far too visible for the brown trout in most of our rivers now, although cutthroats and brook trout and rainbows are still somewhat easier to catch, particularly in broken water and the back-country lakes of our western mountains.

However, modern two- and three-fly rigs should be fabricated with a little more subtlety than the old loop snells could offer. It is possible to make up a leader for a three-fly cast by tying its final two tippets in eighteen-inch lengths, leaving the heavier strand in each barrel or blood knot about four or five inches too long. The lighter strand should be trimmed neatly. The dropper strand, fashioned of the heavier nylon, will tend to project out from the leader, both because of its larger diameter and its relative position in the tippet knot. Its attitude will keep the dropped flies from tangling in the leader itself, which is a problem with multiple-fly casts, particularly if the droppers are too delicate or too long. Dropper strand diameters of .006 are perhaps the smallest calibrations possible, even in the so-called hard nylons, and in the modern limp materials the droppers should be .007 nylon or larger. Experience with fly sizes, and their relationships to dropper length and diameter, will help you rig effective multiple-fly leaders that fish without constantly tangling.

Scottish and Irish lakes are still commonly fished with six- and eight-fly leaders, particularly in the Hebrides and Killarney, but such tackle is not recommended on American waters. However, there are times during heavy fly hatches of sedges and stoneflies when enough nymphs are emerging that a two- or three-fly leader may be more effective than fishing a single imitative pattern. Perhaps the multiple flies catch the attention of a trout feeding on the swarming natural nymphs and pupae, and surprisingly enough, the three-fly rig is sometimes effective when the fish are gorging on tiny midge forms—although multiple-dropper strands seem ill-suited to fishing such minute imitations.

11. The Skimming-Nymph Method

The skimming-nymph method is similar to fishing the riffling hitch on Atlantic salmon, and it is important at times when emerging nymphal and pupal forms are moving visibly in the surface film, making a tiny bulge or subsurface wake as they hatch. Such insects are usually large sedge pupae, or damselfly and mayfly nymphs, since smaller species barely disturb the film during emergence. It is certainly the disturbance of the surface film that attracts the fish, both in river flats and smooth-topped lakes, and I have seen them turn and come considerable distances.

Such conditions are best fished with a floating line, and with a partially greased leader, to work the nymphs just under the film. These imitations should not really sink too readily, and should almost fish awash. Dressing them on relatively light wire hooks will help work them at the surface. It is a combination of fly dressing, line and leader preparation, and manipulation of the cast and the fly.

Sometimes it is useful to employ a nymph in similar fashion on tumbling trout water, fishing a relatively short line to maintain control over its subsurface skimming. The skimming-nymph method has also worked well for me in lake fishing in Ireland, when the soot-colored mayflies are hatching on Lough Corrib and Lough Sheelin.

12. The Greased-Line Method

Greased-line tactics are extremely important in fishing nymphs, perhaps more important than in manipulating wet flies and bucktails. There are many situations in nymph fishing when a selective fish is taking the natural nymphs and pupae in quiet currents, with a stronger current tongue flowing between the angler and his prey. It calls for a presentation not unlike the drag-free float required in fishing the dry-fly method, except that the nymph is obviously fished wet and across or downstream. The dry-fly technique resorts to the hook cast, throwing upstream slack to fall across the intervening current tongues in order to extend the length of drag-free presentation.

The greased-line method is similar. It does not create a completely drag-free nymph swing, but it was originally conceived to mute the speed of the swinging fly when the floating line bellies and is caught in the swifter current tongues. It is a relatively difficult technique to master, since it involves an upstream mend so subtle that the path of the swinging nymph is scarcely interrupted. The cast is delivered across or slightly quartering downstream, and just as the primary currents start to catch the bellying line, the fisherman lifts it from the water and loops it upstream with a lateral oscillation of his rod tip. Such an upstream mend is difficult to perfect, but it is extremely valuable in both nymph and wet-fly fishing. It has a corollary in the downstream mend, which loops the bellying line downstream to increase fly speed in slack currents.

13. The Crosfield Pull

Our earlier chapters on wet flies and streamers have pointed out that Ernest Crosfield was a notable salmon fisherman on the British rivers at the turn of the century, and his Crosfield pull was designed to increase sinking-line fly speed in slack currents too slow to fish properly. His techniques are also extremely useful in fishing a nymph, particularly in big water on our western rivers, and a skillful nymph fisherman should master them—since precise fly manipulation is the key to success.

Like the greased-line method, the Crosfield tactics are geared to dampening or accelerating fly swing, but are perhaps easier to master than the upstream and downstream mends. Crosfield achieved a slower fly speed by stripping out a little line into its bellying swing, or increased his fly speed by stripping in line with the left hand. Both methods are controlled with the line under the forefinger of the rod hand, and since the length of line strip required to dampen or increase the nymph swing in any particular situation varies, considerable experience is required to judge its precise timing and length. Really skilled fishermen can almost sense proper fly speed through the slight tension of current pull transmitted into the rod tip, but such sensory skills are not developed and polished overnight.

14. The Leisenring-Lift Technique

James Leisenring was a legend on the Brodheads in Pennsylvania; and his theories are laid down in *The Art of Tying the Wet Fly*, in which he adapted British wet-fly theories to American conditions.

His method is equally effective in fishing nymphs. Leisenring fully understood that a nymph-feeding trout often takes a swinging fly at its three-quarter point, that the fly was most enticing at that moment, and that it was deadly because it suggested a hatching insect as it left the bottom. Leisenring had often observed nymphing fish in his favorite river, watching them hover just over the bottom gravel. Such trout would suddenly turn and rise in the current, taking some struggling nymphal form before it reached the surface, and Leisenring reasoned that such nymph behavior was common before and during a hatch.

When a quartering downstream cast is made, and the line settles deep into its swing, it reaches a point of maximum depth before the bellying line is forced back toward the surface by the pressure of the current. It is this moment that suggests a hatching nymph enroute toward the surface, and in *Trout* Bergman calls this moment the critical point in the entire fly swing. Bergman did not equate his hot-spot theories with the behavior of hatching nymphs and pupae, but Leisenring fully understood this causal relationship. Leisenring also developed a method of lifting his rod subtly as the fly reached its critical point in the swing, exaggerating the illusion of a hatching insect.

It is remarkably effective on selective fish, and twenty-odd years ago it solved a hot-weather problem on the Ausable in the Adirondacks. Mac Talley and I were fishing the East Branch near the pastoral village of Keene Valley, and the river was unusually low and clear. The trout had moved into the springholes and congregated in the cold seepages of the tributary creeks. The main river was much too warm for fishing, and there were absolutely no trout in the usual holding pools. Finally, we understood the temperature problem, concentrated our fishing in the springholes and the flowages of colder tributaries before breakfast, and went swimming in the famous pools of the river itself in the afternoons.

We caught enough trout in these spring-fed places, but the unseasonably hot weather continued until we were fishing at just daylight and hibernating at midday. Finally the evenings themselves became too hot and muggy to cool the river to fishable temperatures, and all activity ceased. It seemed likely that our fishing was finished when we discovered the springhole trout at Upper Jay.

Twenty years ago, the bridge in the village of Upper Jay was a steel Warren-truss structure spanning the entire river. Above the Upper Jay bridge, a small brook tumbled through the village and added its cold currents to the Bridge Pool. It was a justly famous reach of river in earlier years. Upper Jay was the village where the late Byron Blanchard operated his memorable little Adirondack Mountain House. The river there had a prominent role in the books of writers like Bergman, and in *Trout* we encounter the following observations on the Ausable at Upper Jay:

> Trout of a pound and a bit more were then really quite common, and almost any sort of day produced enough fish to make a catch that under present-day conditions would be raved about. It was a bad day indeed when at least two or three fish of two pounds and more did not come into camp, and repose in cold grandeur in Byron Blanchard's icebox. And we fished with dry flies too. We disdained such things as streamers, spinners or bait. It wasn't necessary to do so.
>
> As I delve into the recesses of my memory and read some of the many notes I made in those days, I find the following flies were outstanding in their performance: Brown Spider, Fanwing Royal Coachman, Light Cahill, Whirling Dun, Badger Bivisible, Brown Bivisible, and Gray Bivisible.
>
> I believe that I introduced the first spiders to the Ausable, at least I have notes to the effect that I was badgered unmercifully at By Blanchard's Adirondack Mountain House when I exhibited them, and it was demonstrated that Ausable trout not only would take them, but that they liked them better than many of the other patterns we had come to think perfect.

Modern anglers familiar with fishing the East Branch in our time can only smile at such observations, since its trout are infinitely more difficult today. Except for the pale-hackled Cahill during the summer *Stenonema* hatches or the Whirling Dun in the *Epeorus* and *Ephemerella* hatches earlier, these fly patterns would move only hatchery fish in the smooth-flowing pools and flats of the Ausable.

Mac Talley and I were facing the problems of selectivity and warm river temperatures, and even when we located trout in a springhole or the mouth of a tributary creek, the fish were shy and difficult to take. It was a week of doldrums until we stopped for a late lunch in Upper Jay.

It was late afternoon when we finished coffee, and walked idly across the trusswork bridge. It was still hot and the bridge pool flowed tepid and smooth. We leaned on the railing, watching the current riffle down the shallows upstream and lose itself in the pondlike still water of the pool. It was already evening, and the shadows reached out across the smooth current tongues above the bridge. Suddenly a good rise disturbed the current sixty-odd feet downstream from the mouth of the tributary above the bridge.

That was a trout! Talley pointed.

You're right, I said, *but look at the bottom below the feeder creek—it's almost black with fish there!*

My God! he said. *Look at them!*

The pale bottom was literally layered with trout, holding in the cold seepage of the tributary to escape the marginal temperatures of the river. There were several hundred fish crowded into some one hundred feet of bottom, holding in a weaving phalanx of trout that ended twenty yards above our position on the trusswork bridge.

This ought to be easy, Talley grinned.

Maybe so, I laughed, *but I doubt it in spite of that tin of sardines down there!*

Let's give them a try, he said.

We walked back to the diner and rigged our tackle at the car, selecting light rods and lines that would sink deep to the springhole fish where they lay on the bottom. The night before there had been a fair hatch of pale little mayflies in the valley, and I suggested we try nymphs, working them deep over the trout and fishing them back like a hatching dun. There was only an occasional dimple below the springhole flowage when we finally slipped into the twilight currents above the bridge.

You'd never know there were more than a hundred trout out there. Mac gestured toward the still currents.

The darkening river whispered past and a car rattled across the old trusswork bridge, scattering gravel from its planking, with its lights glittering on the current. There was no wind but the night seemed imperceptibly cooler now, and the western sky was bright with afterglow beyond the trees.

What do you think? Mac asked.

They're a little sluggish when they're schooled like that, I answered. *We have to get the nymph down deep and tease them.*

Lead on! Mac suggested.

The pool flowed smooth and still, and from the bridge I had noted two stones that marked the position of the tightly-clustered trout. Dim lights from the few houses across the river were reflected in the river, and bats were starting to chase the insects that hovered over the pool. We waded very slowly into position, carefully moving to mute our disturbance and prevent it from alerting the trout.

I'll try a regular fly swing first, I explained.

The cast worked out into the twilight and dropped my nymph slightly above the fish. It teased back on a conventional fly swing, and nothing happened until it had worked well past the springhole trout, when a fat shiner took it hard. Several identical casts failed to interest a fish where dozens were lying.

Why isn't it working? Mac asked.

Not sure, I said, *but it's probably because they won't leave that cold current tongue along the bottom.*

Can't we get the nymph deeper? he suggested.

Modern sinking lines had not been developed that evening more than twenty-five years ago at Upper Jay, but I had an old line of undressed silk on a reel in my rucksack. Sometimes I fished it in the spring to sink my wet flies in the cold currents, and I walked back to our car to get it. Mac waited waist-deep in the smooth current, its flow scarcely visible past his waders.

No rises, he reported. *Nothing!*

The silk line was fully rigged, and I waded out deliberately toward his shadowy form.

The undressed line should get the fly a little deeper, I said.

The cast was postponed until the line and leader were thoroughly soaked at our feet, and then I dropped it beyond and well above the holding lie of the springhole. It started to sink and drift deeper, and I hoped it would reach its deepest point of drift just above the fish. It bellied deep into its swing, and I lifted the rod tip and teased it pulsingly. The little nymph fished through the entire run without moving a trout.

Well, maestro, Mac laughed, *what now?*

The second cast reached twenty feet farther upstream and settled deeper into the springhole currents. The line bellied in the slow currents and started swinging the nymph over the fish, and when the rod tip worked the nymph back toward the surface with a tantalizingly slow rhythm, there was a strong pull.

Fish! I grinned in the darkness.

It was no trophy, but a fat twelve-inch brown at the conclusion of a long and almost fishless day is more than welcome. It finally surrendered and we rested the pool for fifteen minutes before making another cast. The silk-line presentation was repeated, and when it bellied deep and worked the nymph back like a hatching fly, the line darted suddenly and another trout was hooked.

You're doing better, Mac said happily.

The fish bolted downstream, stripping line from the reel, and wallowed in the shallows at the bridge. It was a richly spotted brown of fifteen inches, and it fought stubbornly against the fragile tippet. Finally I netted the fish in the shadows of the rattling trusswork span.

You try them, I suggested.

Talley took my rod and dropped a cast well above the fish, where the little tributary creek trickled out into the pool. Once more the silk line settled deep along the bottom, its belly catching in the sluggish currents as the fly swing started. The nymph had reached the perigee of its bottom swing when Talley raised the rod tip and started the teasing retrieve toward the surface. The fly had almost reached the surface when there was a heavy swirl and the reel ran shrilly in the darkness.

The fish stripped off twenty yards and stopped, and Talley began backing toward the gravel shallows above the bridge. The trout fought stubbornly, jumping once in the shadowy light across the pool, and finally we worked it close to the beach. It was still fighting hard when I netted it in the darkness, and it came grudgingly ashore, writhing and threshing in the meshes.

Big fish? Talley asked in the darkness.

Pretty good one, I laughed. *From its weight I'd guess it's probably seventeen or eighteen inches.*

You're joking! he gasped. *I've never caught a fish that big—let alone fished a nymph before!*

Congratulations! We shook hands.

It was a strong eighteen-inch brown, and we took several fish between ten inches and two pounds that night. It had been a virtually fishless day before we tried the hatching-nymph retrieve on the Bridge Pool at Upper Jay; the same method became extremely productive the remainder of that week at several springholes along the river. It was a fine lesson in basic nymph tactics.

15. The Sawyer Induced-Rise Method

Frank Sawyer is widely considered the best nymph fisherman in the world, and books like his *Keeper of the Stream* and *Nymphs and the Trout* firmly establish him as the midcentury heir of George Edward MacKenzie Skues. Sawyer is the famous riverkeeper on the Officer's Association water of the Wiltshire Avon above Salisbury. Like his antecedent Skues, Sawyer fishes his nymphs only to rising trout or to fish visibly lying beneath the surface watching for subaquatic naturals; it is the British philosophy of refusing to fish the water blind, perhaps a reaction to the dry-fly purism common on the chalkstreams.

Skues liked to fish his nymphs to rising trout, much like a conventional dry-fly presentation, and Sawyer likes to fish his imitations to trout visibly nymphing below the surface. His induced-rise technique involves casting a nymph well above a working fish, letting it sink back into its field of vision, and then teasing the fly subtly to make the waiting fish take. Sawyer himself eloquently describes his technique in *Nymphs and the Trout:*

> Remember you are after a wild creature and creep stealthily to a position where the light gives you the best chance to see the head of the fish and an area of about two feet in front of him. Judge the depth of water and the pace of the current. Remember that the slower the current the faster a nymph will sink. Forget all your dry-fly tactics. The correct presentation of a nymph is a separate technique. With a dry fly the aim is to place the artificial

accurately and delicately on the surface and not more than one foot in front of the rising fish. If cast properly it settles gently on the water without disturbance and you wait for the head of the fish to appear as a signal that he has been deceived. This signal is quite plain to see. You get a signal when a fish takes a nymph beneath the surface, but this can only be appreciated fully when the eyes have been trained to understand and interpret the underwater movements of a fish.

With a nymph the most important thing is to concentrate on the fish, to watch its head and especially its mouth. Try to pitch the nymph into the water well to the front, placed so that any ripples caused by the entry will not distort your view. Already you will have judged the level at which the fish is lying and also the speed of the current. As the artificial sinks and drifts so you prepare for the take and the hooking. Presentation is quite simple and it is not difficult to deceive trout and grayling with nymphs. But, unless you can see the fish take, or some indication that he has taken an artificial, it is only by luck that you will catch more than one in a hundred, and then only because the fish has usually hooked himself.

Few American nymph fishermen would fully agree with that last observation, since we seldom have the opportunity to fish the Sawyer method on our open pocket-water streams. His induced-rise technique is extremely effective on our eastern limestone streams, like the Big Spring and Falling Spring Run and the famous Letort, and on the spring creeks found throughout our western mountains. Their fish lie in the pale gravel channels between the watercress and weeds, and a skilled Sawyer method will take them, for Skues and Sawyer developed such tactics on the equally smooth Itchen above Winchester and the Wiltshire Avon above Salisbury.

However, most American rivers are quite unlike these British chalk-streams—yet our skilled nymph fishermen regularly take fish without seeing them actually come to their flies. It requires an even more highly developed sensory skill than the induced-rise method, although like the dry-fly technique, watching a fish clearly take our nymphs is perhaps the most satisfying form of fly-fishing.

There have been many experiences with the nymph and the induced-rise over the years, from the headwaters of the Connecticut in New England to the poetic little Cumilahue in Chile, but perhaps my most memorable exposure to the Sawyer method occurred in the Allgäu mountains in southern Germany.

Fischen-im-Allgäu is a charming village of red-tiled rooftops and a steepled bell tower, and it lies in a narrow alpine valley with the high snow-capped Austrian mountains beyond. Oberstdorf is a famous ski town just below the border, and the swift glacier-silt currents of the Iller have their source in the snow fields of the Nebelhorn and its sister mountains in the Tyrol. There are both brown and rainbow trout in the river, but its chalk-colored currents make it a relatively poor river for fly-fishing.

The sport is better at Fischen-im-Allgäu. Its silken little Grundbach is formed in a millpond below its cobblestone marketplace, where a flotilla of white ducks is always rooting for sowbugs in the watercress. The millpond is formed by gathering the tumbling flow of several tributary streams. Its mirror-smooth currents flow calmly for almost a mile between the village of Fischen-im-Allgäu and its hatch weir at the millrace. It is a classic mile of water, with channels of fine gravel between beds of trailing weeds, and it has good fly hatches from March through October.

The Grundbach and its trout taught me about fishing the Sawyer induced-rise technique the first morning I fished it. We found the little river completely by accident, since we had originally intended to try the Iller for its spring-running rainbows, but had found it bank-full with chalky snowmelt. There was an old man riding a bicycle on the Sonthofen road, and we stopped him to ask about fishing.

Where is there good fishing? my father asked.

Bachforellen? the old man frowned thoughtfully. *Perhaps below the millpond at Fischen-im-Allgäu.*

Dankeschön! we waved and drove off.

The village lies between the road and the river, and we drove down through its tidy houses to the millpond. It flowed across watercress shallows below the marketplace, gathered in a swifter channel above its waving beds of rannunculus, and finally spread into a rather broad millpond below the footbridge. Ducks and geese were foraging in the shallows. We parked the car and walked out on the bridge to observe the little river.

From the railings we could see a number of trout lying in the channels between the weeds and over several open beds of gravel. The fish were all between twelve and sixteen inches, except for one lying in a deep watercress channel above the footbridge that appeared larger.

We've really found something! I whispered excitedly.

Sie haben recht! my father agreed.

While we watched from the bridge, two of the twelve-inch trout began feeding deep along the bottom gravel. These fish would move forward, or slightly to one side or the other, to intercept something drifting in the bottom currents. Sometimes they would drift back without taking anything, but other times they would quickly open their jaws, revealing a momentary flash of white. Once the mouth closed on the unseen prey, their forward or sidewise swimming momentum ceased, and they seemed to settle back toward the bottom. We watched these two trout feeding below the footbridge for some time.

What are they doing? my father asked.

I think they're nymphing, I said guardedly. *Maybe there's going to be a fly hatch later this morning.*

Perhaps you're right, he nodded.

When we stopped watching our two fish below the bridge, it was apparent that several others were nymphing now, and the first dark little mayflies were already hatching. We walked hurriedly back to the Mercedes to rig our equipment. Before we reached the water again there was a heavy hatch of small *Baetis* flies coming down the currents. Many fish were visibly porpoising at the surface, while others held at various depths, still busily feeding on the nymphs.

My father chose to cast a dry-fly imitation over the visibly rising fish, since he had always felt a little uncomfortable fishing the nymph technique, and I passed him a half dozen darkly hackled Iron Blues. Since there were many fish working steadily above the footbridge, he left with considerable optimism, but after a half hour he came back downstream.

You sure this fly matches this hatch? he asked.

It's the right dry fly for these Iron Blues, I laughed, *but they may not actually be working on the surface.*

But they're rising all over the place! he insisted.

They could still be nymphing, I suggested, *taking them at the surface just before they hatch from their shucks.*

They look like they're rising! he insisted.

During the first half hour, I had tried several nymphs over free-rising fish without results. There was still one small English nymph in my fly books, dressed entirely from pheasant-tail fibers and slightly weighted, and I clinch-knotted it to my tippet.

Let's try it on that fish, I suggested.

There was a good trout lying tight against a dense bed of rannunculus just downstream from the bridge, and it was visibly taking a nymph every few minutes. My first cast dropped about two feet above its station, but I had misjudged its depth and the fly swing came past its position too near the surface. The fish rose slightly in the current when the nymph drifted through its taking lie, but it settled back as if rising high enough to intercept my fly were too much effort. My second cast settled about six feet above the trout, and I briefly lost sight of the nymph before the drift actually reached its station.

The trout shifted its position slightly and rose almost imperceptibly in the current, and when its mouth opened and closed about the time my fly would have reached its position, my reflex involuntarily raised the rod tip. The fish had taken and was securely hooked.

You've got him! my father exclaimed.

We spent the next two hours searching for such clearly visible trout in the crystalline little Grundbach, and I took more than twenty with virtually the same tactics. Sometimes I watched the nymph through its entire drift, teased its swing slightly with the rod tip as it approached, and watched fascinated while the fish either inspected it or took it readily. Sometimes I lost its fly swing in the current reflections. It was difficult to calculate and time my strike, but several times I saw the trout take something at about the moment my nymph should have reached its position, and I hooked a good fish. The day was most instructive, and I learned much about fishing the nymph with the Sawyer induced-rise technique.

Fishing the beautiful Grundbach was a postgraduate laboratory in nymph-fishing methods, and I travelled there almost every weekend for two entire seasons. It offered rather large trout with good fly hatches in quiet currents. The Allgäu is a beautiful countryside, with steeply forested hills and snowfields on the higher mountains beyond. The mountain herdsmen took the cattle to their summer pastures in late April, when our seasons of fishing had just started, and in the autumn the herds came back down from the high country. The cattle carried ornamental bell frames and garlands of flowers in October, and the herds were led through the narrow streets of Oberstdorf with their delicate bells tinkling in the morning sunlight. It was a good time, with breakfasts on the scrollwork balcony of the Hotel Luitpold, and I still fish there often in the time-mellowed weather of the mind.

5. Terrestrials and
the Trout

It is a gentle landscape of manicured fields and brick-patterned Pennsylvania barns and grazing dairy cattle. Ringnecked pheasants cackle and forage in the rich cornfields. The pastures are broken with outcroppings of limestone, and the whitewashed fences are as immaculate as the clapboard farmhouses themselves. It is a countryside of carefully tailored fields, its valleys sheltered between the folded hills and tree-covered ridgelines of the Appalachians.

It is a world of well-filled granaries and silos. Herds of fine cattle graze lazily in the meadows and stare curiously at the fishermen from the sheltering elms and buttonwoods. The barns are painted white and bright red, their cantilevered hay-wagon floors sheltering cattle stalls that open toward the south. Their design permits the cattle to be gravity-fed from the haymows above; and the stored grain and ensilage and hay above these livestock pens insulate the winter cattle, and hold their body heat inside the barn while the low sun angles of midwinter slant deep into their stalls. The hay-wagon floors shelter these same cattle stalls from the hot summer sun.

The barn builders always sited their structures on a slope exposed to the south, sheltered by higher ground to the northwest and the worst winter storms. On the best-planned farms, the fields were on the higher ground, so a loaded wagon could travel downhill toward the barn.

The builders mixed their primitive functionalism and knowledge of climatology with witchcraft, covering their bets both ways with hex signs on their barns to protect the farms and their livestock and families from evil spirits and demons.

The trout streams are also unusual.

The most famous stream rises in a series of rich limestone springs in the pastoral countryside below Carlisle. Its waters emerge full-blown from fissures that surrender the hydrology of vast underground caverns. These limestone springs are remarkable for their clarity and volume, bubbling thousands of gallons per minute to create these gentle meadow rivers. The result is a habitat uniquely rich in fly life, currents that remain ice-free in winter, and water temperatures so constant that the fish feed and grow steadily through the entire year. Its currents are so rich with lime salts that its fertility rivals that of the chalk streams of Europe, rivers like the Risle and Andelle in France, and the better-known Itchen and Test in the chalk downs of Hampshire.

It is the classic Letort Spring Run.

The river is almost tiny in its watercress beginnings, and it flows smoothly over bright-gravel shallows where the two principal feeders join above Carlisle. Beyond this pastoral junction, among the barns and stonework farmhouses, there is a fine half-mile of water below the lime quarries. The railroad trestle follows, and farther downstream there is a simple farmhouse and the reach of water called Otto's Meadow.

It is a marvellous half-mile of stream, flowing through the leaf-flickering shadows of the swamp willows, deeply undercut banks, beds of watercress so dense they will support the weight of an angler on his knees, and brushpile bends long known for their big trout.

The famous Barnyard stretch is next, with its lovely mason-work farmhouse and barn above a willow-bordered bend. The channels in its watercress and elodea have witnessed many angling experiments and epic struggles with its selective brown trout. Highway construction has destroyed the Thorntree Meadow below the Barnyard water, and a four-lane bridge spans its grassy bottoms with massive abutments and post-tensioned beams and piers, forever eradicating its serpentine banks with a straight channel. The sitting bench where Charles Fox and his circle of skilled limestone fishermen gathered to talk and watch the river is still under the buttonwoods downstream; and nearby is the blind where Vincent Marinaro took his famous photographs of rising trout. The river carries a tradition unique in our fly-fishing history.

Fishing the Letort Spring Run in central Pennsylvania has become as much a matter of pilgrimage as sport. Its hatches are composed of small flies and its fish are unusually selective. The smooth currents are silken among the watercress and elodea, and the trout dimple almost imperceptibly. It was my principal laboratory for learning about the growing importance of terrestrial insects in the trout diet, and its regulars taught me much about ants and leafhoppers and beetles on fine tippets.

Although our preoccupation with terrestrial insects on American waters is relatively recent, and the innovations in imitating ants and leafhoppers and beetles worked out on Letort Spring Run are already legendary in our own time, many anglers are unaware that land-bred insects have played a role in fishing and fly dressing virtually since the fifteenth century. Some historians have argued that the flies described in

Macedonia during the second century by Claudius Aelianus were tied to imitate terrestrials, although there is some evidence they might have been sedge imitations instead.

The classic twelve fly patterns found in the *Treatyse of Fysshynge wyth an Angle*, which Dame Juliana Berners assembled in the fifteenth century, include several terrestrial imitations like the Shelle Flye and the Waspe Flye. These patterns were recommended for the midsummer months:

> Thyse ben the flyes wyth whyche ye shall angle to trought and grayllyng, and dubbe lyke as ye shall now here me tell.
>
> The Donne Flye. The body of the donne wull and the wynges of the pertryches. Another Doone Flye. The body of blacke wull: the wynges of blackyst drake: and the jaye under the wynge and under the tayle.
>
> The Stone Flye. The body of blacke wull and yelowe under the wynge. And under the tayle and the wynges of the drake. In the begynnynge of May and a good flye. The body of roddyd wull and lappyd abowte wyth blacke sylke: the wynges of the drake and of the redde capons hakyll.
>
> The Yelowe Flye. The body of yelowe wull: the wynges of the redde cocke hakyll and of the drake lyttyd yelowe. The Blacke Louper. The body of blacke wull lappyd abowte wyth the herle of the pecok tayle: and the wynges of the redde capon wyth a blewe heade.
>
> The Donne Cutte: the body of blacke wull and a yelowe lyste after eyther syde: the wynges of the bosarde bounde on wyth barkyd hempe. The Maure Flye. The body of darke wull the wynges of the blackest mayle of the wylde drake. The tandy flye at Saynt Wyllyams Daye. The body of tandy wull and the wynges contrary eyther ayenst other of the whytest mayle of the wylde drake.
>
> The Waspe Flye. The body of blacke wull and lappyd abowte wyth yelowe threde: the wynges of the bosarde. The Shelle Flye at Saynt Thomas Daye. The body of grene wull and lappyd abowte wyth the herle of the pecoks tayle: wynges of the bosarde. The Drake Flye. The body of blacke wull and lappyd abowte with blacke sylke: wynges of the mayle of the black drake wyth a blacke heade.

Excepting the fly pattern described by Aelianus in second-century Macedonia, the Waspe Flye and the Shelle Flye are probably our first historical examples of terrestrial fly patterns. The history of fly-fishing is filled with similar patterns, from the list of flies that Charles Cotton added to *The Compleat Angler* in 1676 to almost all of the subsequent authors who discussed fly dressing for the next two centuries.

Alfred Ronalds carried our knowledge of the trout and the land-bred insects in its diet still farther, with *The Fly-Fisher's Entomology* and its copper plates of both British hatches and his own imitative fly patterns. His collection of aquatic fly hatches was the first made with both scientific discipline and first-rate watercolors of the natural; and his use of proper scientific nomenclature in identifying these insects has been the yardstick of quality measuring all subsequent work. Most of Ronalds's *Entomology* devoted itself to the mayflies, sedges, and stoneflies found on British rivers, but his catalog of trout-stream insects also includes beetles, gauzewings, ants, *Pachymerus* flies, two-winged flies, and caterpillars. Surprisingly it also includes two leafhoppers more than a century before Vincent Marinaro and his *Modern Dry-Fly Code* solved the problems of their imitations with the silhouette theory of his jassid.

Grasshoppers and flying-ant swarms have long been imitated in the history of fly-fishing, and many writers have speculated about their importance. However, the importance of ants through the spectrum of the entire angling season, rather than peak seasons of mating flights, was never emphasized in earlier books on fly-fishing. Ants are continuously on the water in great numbers as the season progresses, even during warm weather in early spring and late fall, and their considerable role in the trout diet has been virtually ignored. Except for the brief mention and an unworkable imitation in the Ronalds *Entomology*, the place of the minuscule leaf hopper, one of the principal diet forms on forest and meadow water, was virtually unknown to anglers.

These concepts are the source of the Letort legend.

The evolution of workable leafhopper imitations, and the discovery of the importance of minute Hymenoptera, is an angling breakthrough that makes the studies of Charles Fox and Vincent Marinaro on the Letort the modern equivalent of the Halford-Marryat collaboration that codified dry-fly theory on the British chalk streams.

Modern terrestrial imitations of ants and leafhoppers and beetles are an angling event. The frustration of casting conventional flies over terrestrial-feeding trout is ended. Classic patterns for such smutting fish were merely tiny conventional dry flies, and most anglers called them midges. Yet true midges are minute aquatic insects, and imitations of these *Chironomus* flies are consistently refused by selective trout taking terrestrials. Such behavior unquestionably results from the fact that conventional midge-type flies do not provide an imitative silhouette, the unique light patterns and opaque outlines that identify a floating ant or leafhopper or beetle to a terrestrial-feeding trout.

The discovery of such fly-dressing concepts is described at length in my book *Remembrances of Rivers Past*, and the following passages recount their beginnings on Letort Spring Run:

> The day of discovery is eloquently recorded in Marinaro's *Modern Dry-Fly Code*, which describes fishing the meadows with Charles Fox near the little fishing hut. There were no visible insects on the water, but the fish were busily working. Conventional methods

had failed miserably in the past, and were no better that afternoon. The rise forms were the familiar bulges so frustrating in the Letort meadows. Fox and Marinaro tried fish after fish, resting one and casting to another, exchanging helpless shrugs as they passed.

Marinaro writes that his frustration finally proved too much. He stopped fishing to study the current. Prone in the warm grass, Marinaro watched the slow current pattern slide hypnotically past. Some time elapsed in pleasant reverie before he was suddenly aware of minute insects on the water. He rubbed his eyes but they were really there: minuscule mayflies struggling in their diaphanous nymphal skins, tiny beetles like minute bubbles, ants awash in the surface film, and countless other minutiae pinioned in the smooth current.

His mind stirred with excitement as he hurried toward the fishing hut. There he quickly fashioned a fine-mesh seine with sticks and mosquito netting. Its meshes were not long in the water before his suspicions were confirmed by the thin residue of tiny insects that collected at the waterline. There were mayflies with wings less than an eighth-inch in length, beetles less than three thirty-seconds of an inch in diameter, tiny reddish-gold and black ants an eighth-inch in length, and leafhoppers of minute dimensions in astonishing numbers.

It was the moment of discovery. Charlie Fox came downstream and examined the tiny insects. Both men searched their boxes for flies of proper color and size. Several good fish were quickly caught, and autopsies of stomach contents confirmed a diet of minute forms. The puzzling frustration of the bulge rises was over on the Letort.

But modified conventional flies were often rejected in the days that followed. New concepts were needed. Many experiments were tried before a workable fly-dressing formula was perfected. The basic concepts were slow in coming, and the early attempts were less than fruitful.

Beetle imitations are typical.

Small coffee beans were tried first, filed and mounted on hooks with cement like tiny bass bugs. They floated too low and landed too hard and the trout wanted none of them. Cork and balsa wood were no better. Clipped and folded deerhair beetles were too water absorbent. Black sponge rubber actually worked sometimes, but tended to twist on the hooks and made it difficult to hook the fish. All worked fairly well on other streams, while the selective Letort fish remained suspicious and skeptical.

The full shape and thickness of beetles was ultimately forgotten and a fresh theory of fly dressing evolved. Silhouette and light pattern in the surface film were its essence. Marinaro used large jungle-cock eyes first. Their opacity was good and the fish came well to imitations with the jungle-cock wings tied flat, but the feathers were fragile and tended to split after a few trout were taken. They are now prohibited from entry into the United States and stocks are dwindling.

Ross Trimmer and I were sitting in the Turnaround Meadow one August afternoon. I was tying flies and noticed some pheasant-skin pieces in a hackle cannister. There were a few dark greenish throat feathers on one fragment. We tried them instead of jungle-cock, soaking several feathers together with lacquer to get toughness and opacity. The lacquered feathers were trimmed to proper ovoid shape and tied flat over trimmed hackles. Success was remarkable and immediate. We tried them in the meadows above the trestle and took twenty-one fish. Such a score on the beetle-feeders was unbelievable.

Although the jungle-cock beetles proved too fragile, the jungle-cock wing proved marvelously successful in another context. It is the key to imitating the ubiquitous leafhoppers with a remarkable series of patterns called Jassids. These diminutive flies are one of the great all-season solutions for difficult, dimpling trout. Much of the surface feeding in the hot, low-water months of summer is concentrated on leafhoppers. Alfred Ronalds mentions leafhoppers in his *Fly-Fisher's Entomology*, but his imitations are poor for selective fish. Jassids have proved excellent, and their development will make Marinaro an angling legend wherever big midsummer browns feed quietly in flat, mirror-calm water.

Both the ringneck feathered beetle and the minute jassid are proof of the same theory: that fish cannot sense the thickness of small insects floating above them, and that proper opacity and silhouette and light pattern in the surface film are the critical elements in successful terrestrial imitations.

There have been countless experiences with both beetles and tiny leafhopper imitations. The fat little *Popillia* beetles on the Letort Spring Run were my first profound experience in fishing trout that were selective to tiny Coleoptera forms. Such Japanese beetles have largely been decimated now, since their inadvertent arrival in the United States in 1916, as stowaways in the root soils of some oriental azaleas. Their expanding migration from that hapless nursery in New Jersey had already reached approximately 2,500 square miles in only six or seven years. The Japanese beetles had spread westward more than two hundred miles when they reached the limestone spring creeks at Harrisburg, and expert fly-fishermen like Marinaro and Fox began attempting to imitate them as a staple of the trout diet. Their experiments with silhouette imitations have taught everyone some priceless lessons, and my own experience along the Letort is typical.

Japanese beetles were clustered on the grapevines and wild rose bushes like crawling little bronze berries. Beetles droned in the sycamores like bees. The males were active first, and the females followed. They were numerous at midday, flying across the stream and getting into the water, and the trout were taking them regularly in the weedy channels.

Below the limestone quarries, the current was divided into two deep channels in the watercress. The primary channel was on my side of the stream, where the smooth current eddied over a bottom of gravel and marl. The smaller current tongue was across the stream, little more than twelve inches wide, and channeled through the watercress and elodea. There were wild grapevines immediately upstream, feeding beetles into this secondary channel in the weeds.

The heat was oppressive and I stopped to rest. Wetting my face and neck felt good, and sitting with my legs in the current was pleasant. My lassitude was broken by a subtle rise upstream. The rise form was audible, but not visible, and I searched the narrow channel for its post-rise disturbance. The sucking sound came again. There was no visible rise form, but my eyes were ready this time as it came up along the watercress. The rise was gentle. It bulged out imperceptibly against the current and its disturbance was quickly absorbed against the weeds. The rises were small, but the sound spelled a heavy fish, and it was working steadily. Beetles were thick in the grapevines above its station.

There were plenty of imitations in my fly box, since Ross Trimmer and I had spent an earlier afternoon dressing flies in the Turnaround Meadow, and I waded stealthily into position. The dense beds of elodea cushioned the waves of my wading. The fish was still working.

Checking the delicate 5X leader for casting knots, I tied a tiny beetle to the tippet. Then I waited and watched for the big trout to come up again, marking his exact position. The leader was all right and my little beetle was dressed with silicone paste. Finally I was ready and poised.

The trout came up again. *He's there,* I thought.

My cast dropped nicely above its feeding station against the watercress. The beetle fell flat and dark on the current, riding flush on its trimmed hackles. It flirted with the weeds. There was a shadowlike bulk that appeared and evaporated under its float. The fish had rejected my beetle. I reduced the tippet to .004 diameter, and the fly dropped softly and drifted right against the weeds. It disappeared in a quiet rise.

The trout bolted upstream along the watercress channel and wallowed on the surface. It jumped twice then, suddenly stitching my leader precisely through the weeds on both sides of the narrow channel, and it was gone.

Four pounds! I sighed unhappily.

It was a typical Letort seriocomic episode, since heavy terrestrial-feeding trout on gossamer leaders are difficult to handle in weeds. But the real challenge and accomplishment lay in getting such a fish to rise in the first place, and since that hot afternoon no one has seen that beetle-eating trout again. The little river has changed.

Although the Japanese beetles have been finally checked and are no longer a major factor in the trout diet, there are still many land-bred Coleoptera that are important. The slender little click beetles provided some superb fishing in the grainfields along Spring Creek in central Pennsylvania several years ago, and the tiny *Platysonia* beetles are often numerous in our eastern deciduous forests. These black beetles measure one-eighth to one-quarter of an inch in length, and I have experienced exceptional hot-weather fishing with their imitations on smooth pools from the Musconetcong in central New Jersey to the Battenkill in Vermont. The fishermen along the Letort Spring Run are convinced that their trout occasionally eat fireflies, which are the uniquely phosphorescent *Photinus* beetles. The slender grain beetles are less than one-eighth of an inch in length, and are important on farm-country waters, just as the quarter-inch post beetles are common on forest rivers. Flea beetles are found along trout streams from Minnesota and Maine, to the rivers of the Smoky Mountains in the southeastern states. These handsome little black insects are many-brooded, measuring three thirty-seconds of an inch, with two generations each season. Flea beetles are often quite numerous, and just this past weekend, I experienced some excellent sport with good browns taking these *Altica* flies on a shallow flat of the Brodheads. The fish were dimpling softly over the amber-colored gravel, partially concealed in the dappled light of the sycamores; and after rejecting everything else in my fly boxes, they eagerly took a black beetle imitation tied on a tiny size twenty-two hook. Small beetles are important not only on eastern and middle-western rivers. I have often found the trout taking little bark beetles on still flats of surprisingly large rivers from Colorado to Montana.

There was a hot September morning many years ago on the lower Big Hole when I was fishing with Gene Anderegg, and the soft rises of the fish frustrated us for two hours before we tried a tiny beetle imitation—and the difficult trout suddenly became easy.

Where are the beetles coming from? Anderegg asked.

Watch the trees and the wind. I pointed to the cottonwoods above the flat. *When the gusts move in the branches, the rises are more numerous. It's blowing them onto the river!*

Maybe you're right, he said.

Such conditions always produce the best terrestrial feeding, when hot weather makes the land-bred insects highly adventurous and active, and the wind gets them into the water. It is typically good weather for ants and leafhoppers and beetles, and it has produced some remarkable midsummer fishing to terrestrials.

Since boyhood summers on the rivers of Michigan, we have had good fly-fishing with imitations of the apple green inchworms. Paul Young used to dress green deer-hair imitations for the fishing on the South Branch of the Au Sable. When the trout first began taking them each summer, the worms were pale yellowish green and hung from the trees on their delicate, silken threads. It was always exciting to watch a good fish waiting under a dangling inchworm to take it when it fell haplessly into the river.

Sometimes the fish jumped to catch them before they actually fell to the current, and sometimes they hung trailing in the surface, making tiny V-shaped wakes in its film. The fish were often attracted by the gentle disturbance of the trailing worms, and came considerable distances to take them when they touched the water. It triggered some dramatic fishing each season.

Later the inchworms reached full growth, and when they became too heavy for their silken threads, they fell into the water clumsily. The trout were now watching for their impact; the spreading surface rings could attract them from many feet away, and provide relatively easy fishing.

When the little half-grown worms are trailing in the current, a dragging imitation on a fine nylon tippet is deadly. Since a drag-free float becomes less important, these early inchworm-feeding trout are often less difficult to catch. Unlike other dry-fly presentations, dragging the flies can even prove an advantage, their visible wakes triggering a rise when a conventional float would be ignored. It is good novice fishing, and I once brought a beginner to the Beaverkill in inchworm season. His clumsy casts and dragging flies only served to attract the fish from under the trees, and they were anything but shy.

Thought you said trout were hard to catch! he laughed euphorically. *They're easy as sunfish!*

They are today, I had to agree.

Like the Japanese beetle, the gypsy moth caterpillar is a recent immigrant, this time inadvertently transported from Europe. It has spread quickly from its tragic introduction into Massachusetts, until it threatens forests from New England to southern Pennsylvania. The trout did not take the gypsy moth caterpillars on our eastern streams the first two seasons they hatched there, but this season has been different. The gypsy moth caterpillars are slate-colored with sparse filaments of pale grayish brown and measure less than an inch in their early weeks. The fully-grown worms are apparently unpalatable to the fish, since the trout usually ignore them. It is gypsy moth time as I am writing this chapter, and I have been observing the trout feeding ravenously on them.

The current has been covered with their little caterpillars, and the first days that our fish took them were strange. Aquatic hatches were sparse, with virtually nothing emerging or riding the currents, yet there was an occasional showy rise. Under the sheltering branches, the fish would take something in a strong swirl. Finally I saw the baby caterpillars in the surface film, black and wriggling and less than half an inch in length, and I realized the fish must be taking them. There was no other explanation for such feeding activity.

Just a half inch of black polypropylene dubbing on a light-wire hook, I thought. *Maybe a dun hackle palmered and trimmed short.*

It worked beautifully for two weeks.

But finally the caterpillars grew too large, with long and dense filaments and multicolored markings, and our fish soon stopped taking them. The fish consistently refused the full-grown worms. Yet there was an occasional rise form showy enough that only something relatively large was taken, and in a young sycamore I discovered there were still a lot of the half-grown larvae.

That explains it, I thought.

The small black imitations worked on such rising fish, and whenever I found a strong rise form downstream from some oaks or buttonwoods, I changed to a caterpillar pattern. It took seven or eight trout that were not taking the occasional hatching sedge, yet were working.

There are seasonal variations in the populations of all insects, especially the terrestrial species, and their role in the trout diet varies accordingly. Some years the bright green inchworms have been extremely important, providing as much as two weeks of superb dry-fly fishing. This season they have been scarce, and the fish consistently refuse imitations, although the gypsy moth larvae have replaced them these past few weeks. The tradition-minded angler is sometimes offended by trout that are selective to caterpillars, since fly-dressing theory is based on elegant insects like mayflies, and there is nothing elegant about an inchworm.

It's not right! Stinson Scott laughed in mock horror one afternoon along the Brodheads. *Turns us into worm-fishermen!*

Dry-fly worms, I agreed.

Similar fluctuations in seasonal populations occur in all terrestrial species, although ants are always found in good numbers. March flies are a perfect example. These little two-winged terrestrials are often found hatching in incredible numbers from their pupal burrows in the banks. They look a little like slender house flies, with rust-tinged legs and pale dun-colored wings folded flat over their backs. Hatches are usually too sparse to trigger a selective rise of trout, but a half-dozen years ago there were so many *Bibio* flies coming off on the eastern rivers that the fish gorged on them. It was the only time I ever watched trout take so many flies that they finally stopped rising altogether, although the current was still covered with the wriggling little insects.

We tied imitations of these *Bibio* flies with black fur bodies and a bluish gray wing tied flat over the body. The furnace hackles were trimmed flat on the back, the wing seated in a drop of cement, and then the hackles were trimmed out under the thorax to float flush in the surface film. The thorax of black dubbing completed our imitations, and they were extremely productive, taking one brown of almost twenty-three inches on a still Brodheads flat.

Other Diptera are distantly related to these little March flies, and include both terrestrial and aquatic species. Craneflies are imitated successfully with both a skittering spider or variant, like the British Red Variant so popular on the meadow rivers of Colorado and Wyoming in my youth. Sometimes a big parachute-style dressing with spent wings is effective when trout are taking these craneflies; and such imitations have long been dressed for fishing the Irish loughs—the so-called Daddy

Longlegs, with its legs imitated by knotted strands of condor quill or pheasant tail.

Similar roles in the trout diet are played by other two-winged genera, like the houseflies, deer flies, snipe and robber flies, soldier flies, grass flies, picture-winged flies, blowflies, tachinas, humpbacked flies, and cowdung flies. It was this last genus that caused an apocryphal incident along the Beaverkill many years ago.

It happened on the famous pool at Cook's Falls, where two hundred yards of tumbling boulder-filled river flow the length of the town. Its iron trusswork bridge is high above the current, and there was a skilled city fisherman taking fish regularly on a famous British wet-fly pattern.

What're they taking? yelled some boys overhead.

Cowdung! the fisherman replied.

There was suddenly a long silence from the bridge. *Hey mister!* It was a shrill voice that ended the stillness. *You ever try horse manure?*

It might have happened, but it is unquestionably true that such minor terrestrials all play a surprising role in the diet of the trout. There were several fishermen I knew well in my Michigan summers who fished imitations of several Diptera flies. They liked a spentwing or parachute-tied Adams, using dubbed bodies of several colors from olive to yellowish tan, and sometimes Gerry Queen had me tie him a dozen parachute Adams patterns with spent wings of junglecock eyes. Queen found them particularly effective on the brushy tree-sheltered headwaters of the Pere Marquette in Michigan.

Queen and I were fishing together on the Little South one morning more than twenty-five years ago, and there had been a sparse hatch of Blue-winged Olives not long before breakfast. The hatch was finished before nine o'clock. There was a brief lull in the rise forms, and suddenly the trout were working steadily again. It was getting hotter, and the rises were coming faster, particularly under the willows and trees. But the fish refused our usual dry-fly patterns, including the Blue-winged Olive that had taken them regularly before eight o'clock.

What are they doing? I asked.

Try this. Queen gave me a parachute Adams with spent wings. *It works sometimes in hot weather.*

But I just tried an Adams that size! I protested.

You ever fish a parachute tie? he asked. *Sometimes it makes a difference on these Little South trout.*

I'll give it a try. It seemed doubtful.

It works! Queen smiled.

I clinch-knotted the big parachute dry to my tippet and placed it over a rising fish. The long dark shadow watched as the fly approached its position, dropped back under the line of drift, hung just under the surface, and finally it porpoised and took softly.

Fantastic! I said. *It worked!*

It was the secret that morning, and we waded slowly up the brushy current, casting to alternate fish that we found feeding. We took sixteen trout between eight and fifteen inches, and it was a remarkable example of the importance of light pattern in the surface film. The conventional Adams employed the same colors and materials, yet it had been rejected through a series of perfect drag-free floats. Only the structure of the parachute dressing was different, its brown and grizzly hackles wound on in horizontal fashion, permitting the hackle filaments to ride flat in the surface film. Conventional dry-fly hackles are wound ninety degrees to the hook shank, and only their delicate tips lie in the surface. It was apparently the light pattern, the halo of illumination that surrounds the fibers and filaments, that was the principal difference between the conventional and parachute ties; and it was the subtle variation in light pattern that apparently took the fish. Such considerations are often basic in imitating the terrestrials.

The Hymenoptera include wasps, sawflies, bees and the ubiquitous ants, which are a primary diet form. Such insects can all play a role in the trout diet, and on the limestone streams of Pennsylvania many anglers swear by bee imitations in hot weather. Bee imitations are quite old in angling history, and the famous McGinty and Western bee patterns are familiar to most fishermen. Some skillful fly tiers have worked out close imitations of honey bees, sweat bees, and bumble bees using clipped bodies of dyed deer hair to suggest their coloring and silhouette. Such dressings typically omit hackle, but employ hackle-point wings tied spent, and they have often proved themselves on selective trout. However, it is the ants that are a surprisingly important facet of the trout diet.

Although there had been times in past seasons, both in Europe and the United States, when our fishing had experienced an extensive rise of trout during mating swarms of ants, my first vivid exposure to the daily importance of these insects came on the famous Penns Creek in Pennsylvania. It was hot for early summer, and Charles Wetzel was dressing flies on his porch when we arrived at the dooryard of his farmhouse.

Charles Wetzel! he introduced himself warmly. *We've been expecting you!*

What's hatching? I asked.

Nothing, he smiled. *It's too hot for fly hatches.*

Fishing poor? I frowned unhappily.

Wetzel sat down again and finished a big lacquer-bodied ant that was half-finished in the vise. He touched its gaster and thorax with clear lacquer until the black silk glistened, and then he hooked it into the porch screen to dry with the others.

Fishing's actually good! Wetzel smiled.

There were almost a dozen big ants lightly hooked into the porch-screen sill.

Fishing these? I asked.

Wetzel nodded and grinned knowingly.

Charles Wetzel is one of the living legends among American trout fishermen. Books like *Practical Fly Fishing* established his reputation as a stream tactician and expert on Pennsylvania fly hatches thirty years ago. Wetzel retired to fish the Pennsylvania rivers of his boyhood, and has long been dean emeritus of the Penns Creek country, deep in the rolling ridges of the Appalachians.

Wetzel taught me a lesson that afternoon.

It was still hot and windy as we locked the car and walked down through the woods to the Spinning Wheel Pool. We started fishing below a tiny feeder that mingled its cold flow with the river. The smooth run held the cold tributary water tight against the rocky tree-sheltered bank. The run lasted two hundred feet.

There were still no hatches.

Think I'll fish a big Gray Variant, I said. *It worked last night on the Loyalsock.*

Wetzel smiled and selected one of his ants. There were no fish working anywhere. The strong currents surged and eddied past our waders, milky and rich with the nutrients of its limestone springs. Wetzel chose to fish the spring run under the trees while I fished my big variant upstream. I found no action except for an occasional fly-sliming smallmouth, but Wetzel began catching trout with disturbing regularity.

Finally I swallowed my pride and waded out to his position in the current. Wetzel placed another cast into the cold currents tight against the bank, where the tree branches sheltered the run. His pale English fly line, patiently dried each night and dressed each morning with mucilin on the farmhouse porch, drifted on the current and paused gently as a fish took the ant under the surface and stopped its swing. The old man raised his rod and a fat sixteen-inch brown fought angrily under the trees. Wetzel had taken six fish in a few minutes.

They sure like your ants! I said admiringly.

Bob McCafferty developed them first, Wetzel corrected, *but the trout in Penns Creek really do like them!*

How do you fish an ant? I asked.

Tight against the bank with a dead-drift swing, he answered. *You try it under that big sycamore over there.*

His old Leonard felt smooth, its action sweetened with countless hours of casting on the limestone streams of Pennsylvania, and I dropped his big ant well under the sheltering branches. It settled into its submerged drift along the roots, and suddenly there was a strong pull.

Ha! I said excitedly. *It worked!*

It was a long-remembered lesson about trout fishing in hot weather. Almost twenty years have passed since that experience, but few anglers realize today that ants are a major factor in the trout diet, since most fly-fishermen are preoccupied with mayflies and the other aquatic insects. All anglers have seen trout taking ants in the hot afternoons of late spring and summer, most without knowing what the fish were doing as they bulged and dimpled softly in the surface film. Mating swarms are more obvious examples of ant feeding.

My first experience with flying ants came on a lake in northern

Indiana, when the bass and bluegills disdained their usual diet of hair frogs and popping bugs to cruise the calm surface, taking the spent ants by the thousands.

Some years later on the famous Gunnison in Colorado, our party encountered a blizzardlike swarm of flying ants. The big rainbows went wild, and we went fishless with our conventional dry-fly patterns. There were occasional pale *Heptagenia* hatches, but the trout ignored these fluttering straw-colored mayflies to gorge themselves on ants. Their dietary heresy drove me indoors to the fly vise.

They haven't read Halford! laughed my boyhood friend Frank Klune. *These Gunnison rainbows don't know they're supposed to prefer mayflies!*

Some trout were taken on our hastily dressed ants, but on the whole our attempts were unsuccessful. We first tried bodies of orange silk wound into antlike shapes and soaked in clear lacquer. It made a shiny head and thorax and gaster, but it resulted in bodies better suited to wet-fly fishing than to imitating the spent ants floating awash in the film. It never occurred to us in those years just after the war that bodies dubbed of fur could achieve an antlike sheen when wet, help float our imitations, and look to the fish like a flying ant riding spent in the film.

But these were fishing episodes with mating swarms of flying ants, and it would be another ten years before that afternoon with Wetzel. Still later those wizards who fish the Letort Spring Run, Charles Fox and Vincent Marinaro, demonstrated to me that ants played an almost daily role in the trout diet. Since those experiences on the limestone streams of Pennsylvania, my ant imitations have been dressed with crewel wool bodies for the wet-fly versions and dubbed fur or polypropylene for the dry-fly patterns. The hackles were simply wound on at the midpoint of the hook shank in the conventional manner on both wet and dry versions. However, about six months ago a letter arrived from Wisconsin with several parachute ants dressed in tiny sizes; and the Borger-style ant was born. Gary Borger is a skilled fly dresser from Wausau, and his little parachute-hackled ants have proved themselves widely over difficult trout on several American rivers. It is a style of dressing ants that has completely converted me in a few short months of experimenting, and I now dress most of my imitations parachute-fashion.

Curious fly-fishermen need not study the *Formicidae* with the zeal of the cantankerous Edward Ringwood Hewitt, who actually ate some ants to discover why the trout liked them. Hewitt concluded that it was the tartness of their formic acid content that appealed to the trout, much like people prefer dry wines or dill pickles or green olives. Of course, we cannot know how ants actually taste to trout—even after Hewitt measured their bitterly sharp taste on the human palate. However, the reason why trout like ants is relatively unimportant, since it may only result from their abundance and availability, and it is obvious that trout do take them greedily on widespread rivers.

Since Hewitt performed his famous taste test a half century ago, we have experienced a steady erosion of trout habitat; and that decline has made terrestrial insects increasingly important in the trout-stream scheme of things. Lumbering, thermal pollution, human and industrial wastes, soil erosion and its turbidity, the leaching of surplus fertilizers into trout waters, detergents and phosphates, and the thoughtless mining of streambed aggregates—plus the effect of pesticides and herbicides on aquatic ecosystems—have all had a grinding impact on our familiar fly hatches.

Terrestrial insects like ants have clearly proved themselves a hardier breed, and as our better-known aquatic hatches diminish, the fish have begun to change their feeding habits. Ants particularly form an increasingly important part of their diet equation. The physical configuration of both winged and wingless ants has considerable effect on the way that ants are exposed to trout in various types of water. Like all terrestrial insects, ants are most active in warm weather and are most often found in trout stomachs on hot, windy days. Their morphology and anatomy have an effect on dressing effective imitations, since live ants neither float nor sink well when they fall into the water.

Ants on quiet currents have a ratio between weight and leg-to-body displacement that means they float barely awash and almost pinioned in the surface film. Most trout stream insects either drown or float on the current like mayflies. The familiar insects either trigger clear-cut fishing with wet flies or are easily visible on the surface film, and disappear in the eager rises of the trout. The fact that wingless ants are not seen swarming and ants drifting in the film are difficult to see, make them notably difficult to discover on the water and to imitate.

Monomorium minimum

Two distinct types of ant feeding typically occur. Fish in quiet pools and flats will dimple and bulge softly to tiny *Formicidae* trapped in the surface film. Trout in broken runs and pocket water generally pick up ants that have drowned. Both rise forms will display the character typical of a sipping rise or the lazy, subsurface swirl of a fish capturing something small that cannot escape.

Grasshoppers and crickets are another matter. These active insects are members of the Orthoptera, and any schoolboy knows they are first-rate bait for fish of many species. Trout are no exception, and I caught my first trout with a grasshopper on a tiny meadow creek in Michigan.

Its pool was sheltered under a giant elm, with the trout lying tight in the run along its roots. Our rods were stiff three-piece models of the pale split cane popular in those days. Such tackle was perfectly suited to dapping a live, active grasshopper over the fish. The first trout came on a windy afternoon in August. Our stalk was made on hands and knees through the alfalfa until we were lying belly-flat under the elm, its roots pressing into our ribcages.

The grasshopper dangled about five feet below the agate tip of the bait rod, and I lowered it slowly between the elm and the sluice-culvert fence. Action was immediate, with a quick splash; the rod-tip jerked and I reacted. The trout was derricked violently up into the elm and hung there, struggling feebly among the branches. Finally we extricated it from the tree and sat in the grass admiring its beauty.

Wild twelve-inch brook trout are still treasured in the adult world, but to my boyhood eyes that fish seemed bigger and more beautiful than any other I have ever caught.

The following summer witnessed my baptism in the dry-fly method. June was a good month and its mayfly hatches were heavy. My first dry-fly trout was taken on a spent-wing Adams along the Little Manistee, but it measured only nine inches. There were bigger fish in August, when there were grasshoppers coming off the meadows. My father gave me several Michigan Hoppers, and he told me to try them at midday when the weather got hot. They worked well; and along the river where the coarse grasses trailed in the smooth current, I caught my first good trout.

My casts floated tight against the grass or ticked into the grass until I coaxed them free. One cast came free and dropped nicely along the bank, and the fly teased against the trailing grass. After three feet of float, the down-wing imitation was suddenly intercepted by a sizable shadow. It took with a vicious rise, and I was into a fat seventeen-inch brown. The meadow water was open and undercut along its deep grass-sheltered banks, and I fought the fish over the sandy bottom there. There were no visible snags or deadfalls. It was easy water to fish, and I was able to handle such a trout in spite of my tremble-fingered excitement.

After my triumph with the grasshopper imitation came a week of August doldrums. The trout were sluggish and fed little in the heat. We could see them lying on the pale bottom, gill-panting as they waited for cooler weather. It was too hot for fishing, and we gathered at the local tackle store to join the unhappy porch-talk about the weather.

You be right nice to your boy! The old-timers were still twinkle-eyed over my big trout. *You be right nice!* they laughed. *Maybe he'll tell you how he caught that trout!*

My father always smiled at such jokes.

He might! he was still pleased about my fish. *I've never caught a bigger one, even during the caddis hatch!*

Talk always returned to the hot-weather doldrums. *No decent rise of fish for two weeks now!* observed the town doctor, and the other fishermen nodded in agreement.

What we need is a mackerel sky, said the ice-cream store proprietor. *Clearing storms and cooler weather.*

That's what we need! nodded an old poacher.

We sure do, observed an old logger who fished the marl swamps at night. *Good weather and a grasshopper wind!*

It was an unforgettable summer.

It ended in doldrums that lasted through Labor Day, and there was no grasshopper wind that season. It was during that winter that I learned to tie flies. My father ordered some Michigan Hoppers after Christmas from the late Art Kade in Sheboygan, and I used his elegant dressings as models. My copies were less than perfect, but the originals were exquisitely tied: scarlet hackle tail fibers cocked from a tufted yellow-floss body palmered with a brown multicolored hackle. Brown turkey feather wings held the body hackles flat along the sides. Stiff multicolor hackles completed the dressings, which were tied on elegant English up-eyes. The Kade patterns were so classic in their proportions that his flies still influence the style of my own work today.

There were a number of successful summers with these Michigan patterns in grasshopper time, and there were other grasshopper summers from New Jersey to Colorado and Montana. The grasshoppers produced some large fish, including a twenty-six-inch brown from the Rock Creek meadows in Colorado.

My imitations were no longer exact copies of the Kade grasshopper prototypes. The yellow floss bodies had been abandoned. Their silk fibers turned dark when wet, and the floss bodies were too delicate and slim to suggest the juiciness of the actual grasshoppers. Dubbed yellow wool worked better. It achieved a fat grasshopper silhouette and did not change color when wet. Between the turkey wings was an underwing of fox squirrel to achieve greater buoyancy, counteracting the absorption of the crewel. These versions worked well for several years, particularly on the less-selective fish of western rivers. But the difficult trout of the Pennsylvania limestone streams were another matter. The old grasshopper patterns worked sometimes, but there were also many refusals, particularly with the larger fish.

Anglers on these limestone rivers had long experimented with grasshopper patterns. Many liked the Michigan Hopper or the better-known Joe's Hopper dressings, and some even tried the fore-and-aft style versions. Charles Fox favored a fore-and-aft grasshopper on his difficult fish of the Letort Spring Run, and these flies had been developed and dressed by the late Ray Bergman. But the selective fish of the Fox mileage on the Letort Spring Run seem more difficult every year, and they began refusing these old-time grasshopper imitations with obvious disdain. New variations were clearly needed for such trout.

Our first attempt was a crude experiment of mine dressed in the Turnaround Meadow on the Letort. Western patterns tied with clipped deer hair had worked well in the Slough Creek flats in the Yellowstone and on the big cutthroats of Jackson Hole. Many anglers were reporting good luck with a Muddler fished dry in grasshopper season. Using these clues as our beginning, I tied some lightly dressed little grasshoppers on sixteen long-shanks, with only deer body-hair and yellow nylon-wool bodies. These baby grasshoppers worked surprisingly well, since it was still early in July, and the live grasshoppers in the meadows were relatively small.

Subsequent refusals and lack of success as the grasshoppers grew larger caused us to rethink our theories.

Maybe we should add the old turkey wings inside the roll of deer hair, I suggested. *It might give us a better silhouette.*

Let's try it! Ross Trimmer agreed.

The silhouette of these turkey wings and trailing deer-hair fibers proved important. The absence of hackle permitted the bulk of the imitation grasshopper and its yellowish body to float flush in the surface film. The principal character of a natural grasshopper is rectilinear and slender, while the hackles of conventional imitations are indistinct and caddislike in form. The flaring deer-hair filaments were trimmed away under the throat of the fly to make sure the yellowish dubbing of the body rode awash, just the way the trout observe a live grasshopper. We studied our new imitations, and they looked promising, with an accurate configuration, silhouette, color mix, and light pattern in the surface film.

Looks good! Trimmer observed. *Maybe we should christen it the Letort Hopper!*

The brown trout liked it fine that week.

We used it with good success on Letort Spring Run, and we interested trout that were not visibly feeding, big ghostlike browns that drifted up from deep holding lies in the watercress channels. But there were disconcerting refusals too. We continued to experiment, and our final versions evolved toward the close of that season when the grasshoppers were fully grown.

Tying bigger imitations resulted in the final metamorphosis. When their deer-hair collars were looped and the working nylon pulled tight, the hair butts flared out like stubby, thickly bunched hackles. These butts were scissor-trimmed in a blocky configuration resembling an actual grasshopper thorax and head. Our earlier versions had these deer-hair butts trimmed close and covered with working nylon, like the head of a tiny bucktail. The bulky version was much better. We tested it that following morning on the Letort, and it worked wonders on the most selective fish.

Its success story quickly spread through the limestone country, and the subsequent Letort Cricket pattern was a logical black mutation of its structural concepts. The cricket imitation was also developed on Letort Spring Run, and the following summer Edward Koch took a brown trout with it that scaled slightly more than nine pounds. It was the best dry-fly trout ever recorded from Pennsylvania waters, and a fitting monument to our theories of imitating the Orthoptera flies.

There was a grasshopper wind late that season too, and it eddied in the marshy bottoms and cornfields along the Letort. Ross Trimmer and I met in the Turnaround Meadow early that afternoon, and we walked down to the bench below the Fox house.

It's a great afternoon for hoppers, Trimmer said.

Grasshopper wind! I agreed.

We started walking upstream into the Barnyard Stretch. Ross was in typically high spirits and regularly stained the water with his chewing tobacco. It was an end-of-the-season pilgrimage along the Letort, and it was a fine autumn afternoon.

We should try the Bolter, Trimmer suggested.

It was his name for a heavy brown trout that had foiled several of us when it bolted and broke off. The fish had been estimated at twenty-two inches. It was working quietly along its watercress cover when we approached under the trees. The steady rise forms were methodical and gentle, but several ugly white ducks squatted on the logjam just below the trout. The barnyard ducks were notorious among the Letort regulars for swimming ahead of an angler and spooking his fish, and two of them slipped clumsily into the pool.

Ross Trimmer crouched low and circled above the ducks. *I'll drive 'em downstream from the fish!* he laughed.

The other ducks waddled along the logs and dropped awkwardly into the current. The trout stopped feeding and drifted back under the brushpile. The ducks swam downstream protesting our intrusion noisily. When they were twenty-odd yards below the fish, I slipped into the stream and edged slowly into casting position. Ross sat on the logs and wiped perspiration from his face, and we waited for the trout to start rising. Five minutes later it came up again.

There he is! Trimmer pointed excitedly. *How's that for a ghillying job on a hot afternoon?*

You make a fine ghillie! I grinned.

Well, Trimmer continued tauntingly, *my part's done and I'm waiting!* The fish rose again beside the brushpile.

Okay! I smiled. *I'll try him!*

The cast was difficult and my first two attempts failed, but finally my grasshopper fell right. Its line of drift was not visible from my position as it teased along the watercress, but I heard a sucking rise and saw its rings push gently into the current, and I tightened and set the hook.

There was a heavy splash instead of the usual rapier-quick bolt upstream, and the fish wallowed angrily under the cress. It probed deep along the elodea channels, and I turned it just short of a deadfall. It bored under the watercress again, and I forced it back into open current with lateral pressure, my rod tip deep in the water. It was getting tired now, and my rod pressure held the trout high in the current, well above the trailing elodea. The light was wrong and I could not see the fish. Suddenly it rolled head down, and its broad tail fanned weakly at the surface. The light rod was turned upside down to equalize the strain of the in-fighting, but in a few minutes the fish surrendered.

Looks better than twenty inches, Trimmer observed.

Henfish! I worked the hook free carefully. *She's beautifully shaped and colored!* The trout struggled weakly in the net.

Well, Trimmer said, *let her go!*

We crossed the little river downstream and walked back along the railroad, wading the shallows again at the Barnyard. Some of the regulars were making a cookfire at the bench below the Turnaround Meadow, and the trestle table under the buttonwoods was heavy with food. Other fishermen arrived just before dark to celebrate the end of the season. The chicken and hamburgers and steaks were cooking, and there was cold beer in a wooden tub filled with cracked ice.

The cookfire died slowly, and there were only scraps of talk as the men sat staring into its coals. Finally the fishing talk died too. The soft whisper of the current murmured in the darkness, and it was time to spill water on the ashes. Several regulars started to file up the meadow path and leave, and there is always some sadness that last evening.

I'll take the shadflies any time! somebody was talking about the mayfly hatch on the Penns Creek.

The shadflies only last a few days, Ross Trimmer replied and propelled a stream of tobacco juice into the dying fire. *But the hoppers last more than a month each summer!*

I'll take the grasshoppers too, Charles Fox nodded. *Grasshoppers and meadow water and a grasshopper wind!*

The season was finally over.

6. The Song of
the Little Stream

Every river has its own music, from the tumbling woodwinds and flutes of a Catskill brook in its scarred bed of glacier-smooth granite and polished boulders, to the serpentine beauty of a tinkling cutthroat creek in the wildflowers of some California meadow high above timberline. Fishing such little rivers has a special poetry in itself. Their tiny riffles and pools have all the challenges found on bigger waters, and their shy trout pose all the familiar problems and add a completely fresh dimension in teaching a careless angler the virtues of stealth and patience. The small trout stream is a matchless classroom for the basic truths in all fly-fishing.

Sometimes spring carries high water with its snowmelt and rain, and bigger waters are often unfishable until later. The small trout stream is our salvation then, and its tumbling crystalline riffles and pools are a welcome antidote for the silt-stained currents of the larger rivers downstream.

Yesterday I was fishing the famous Henryville water on the Brodheads. It was a typical morning in early summer, the fresh new leaves moving restlessly against a wine-dark sky. The sun was already hot three hours before noon, and when the sweet wind dropped, the air became strangely heavy. The cotton-bright clouds grew darker now and the western sky behind the soft, wooded ridgeline beyond the river became almost black. The storm gathered swiftly with surprising strength. It became strangely silent.

The churning, ink-colored clouds were rolling a few hundred feet above the river, yet its currents were still. There was no wind where I was fishing, and then there was a terrible crack of lightning. The awesome silence lasted a few moments more, and then there was the drumming sound of heavy rain coming down the thickly forested valley.

It sounds like a freight train, I thought.

The wind struck just before the rain, scattering the fresh buds and bright new leaves into the river like confetti; its ferocity lashed the current. Lightning rattled across the sky, striking the ridgeline behind the mountain, and then it began raining. First it was a heavy rain, drumming into the sullen earth, and then it savaged across the landscape in incredible sheets of driving energy.

The river pearled and darkened, and then, as tumbling freshet tributaries eroded into the clay banks upstream, its swift currents became coffee-colored. Finally the river flowed a dark reddish brown, its musical riffles became surging floods, and its eddying pools became vast cauldrons of seething currents. The fishing was obviously finished.

Miraculously, the storm passed after an hour and the morning seemed almost benign. But the angry river would require more than twenty-four hours to purge itself.

There is a small tributary stream about a mile above where I had been fishing. It drains a small private tract of land which escaped the lumbering that razed these Pocono forests more than a century ago; no giant stumps rise there like rotting tombstones in a tragic epitaph to those years of rapacity. Huge pines shelter its ledgerock pools in deep shadows, dense beds of rhododendron stand on the pine needle benches above the little river, and cold springs dark with *Spirogyna* mosses trickle across the fiddleback ledges into its eddying pools. It is another world locked behind its thickets of alders and willows, and its water joins the main river in a tumbling chute that gives no hint of the poetry hidden a half mile above in the rhododendron.

Many years ago, the owner of the forty-odd acres on the lower reaches of the river built a log-cribbing dam a hundred yards from its mouth. It is silted in with gravel and mud, and its pool is relatively useless. It only succeeds in blocking the autumn runs of spawning brown trout that once used its gravelly shallows.

Sixty feet farther upstream, the little creek has sculptured its own pool below stairsteps of mossy ledges. Its tumbling currents scoured deep into the pale, pea-sized gravel until a foot pool of waist-deep water was formed. Several flat stones slow the currents in the tail shallows into a series of riffling current tongues, and a clump of tag alders shelters the right bank. The pine-needle floor of the forest had absorbed most of the heavy rain that morning, and the little run had pearled slightly. Its smooth currents were noticeably swifter now, and a slight milkiness soiled its usual clarity, but it was still remarkably clear compared to the river.

There was a soft rise in its shallows.

Creeping on my knees where the fiddleback ferns were thick beside the pool, I worked my tiny Henryville Olive under the overhanging limbs until twenty feet of line were out. Sometimes the mere false casting of a pale fly line above a small stream is enough to scatter its trout, and I had changed reels to use a dark brown line that morning. The final cast settled my fly just above the moss-covered stone where the fish had come up, and when it reached the place there was a soft little dimple.

The fifteen-inch brown bolted upstream against the shrill music of the reel, and I let it run against the faint tension of the drag. Forcing it too early could trigger a splashing fight that could disturb the other trout in such a tiny pool. It made several writhing runs the length of the little pool, shuddering and flashing silver in the sunlight at its head, and finally I worked it back.

It came meekly down the pool into the shallows near my feet, until it finally saw me and began to struggle again, but it was too late. The fish surrendered in spite of the cobweb-size tippet, and I turned it gently toward the waiting meshes of the net. It was almost twenty minutes before another trout rose. It took the little Henryville promptly, and there were several others along the tributary creek that morning. The trout were shy and skittish in their minor pools and swift pocket water and riffles, and there was an occasional stream-spawned brook trout too.

It might have been a fishless day without Cranberry Run! I thought.

Years ago the headwater meadows of the Arkansas ran clear and cold, winding through the grassy bottoms between Leadville Junction and the molybdenum mines at Climax. It was one of the finest high-altitude streams in Colorado before a drainage tunnel was constructed to clear the carbonate ore lodes at Leadville and its tailings leached raw into the Arkansas above Leadville. It has run slightly milky since and its fishing is poor, but I can remember some August mornings thirty years ago when it taught me much about brown trout.

It was a treeless meadow of beautiful water with shallow riffles and smooth-flowing little flats, and I fished it regularly through several boyhood summers. It was a stealth-and-cunning river that required staying back from the grassy banks and channels, and sometimes I fished it crouched and kneeling in the slick tail shallows of a pool. It was the kind of small brown-trout river where the knees in a pair of waders will wear out before the seams or felt soles.

It's creep-and-crawl fishing, Frank Klune often observed in those Leadville summers. *You show yourself to those Arkansas Junction browns or make a bad cast and you're finished!*

It is always true of small trout rivers, and it was especially true of those headwaters on the Arkansas. When you started too early after a clear night, the little river was much too cold for good hatches and rises of trout. The stream thermometer could hover at forty-five degrees after a cloudless night at ten thousand feet, and the little Arkansas would seem empty. You could flog its swift little pools from morning until midday without moving anything but the odd six-inch brook trout. Sometimes there were small rainbows and browns too, their parr markings richly mottled on their five-inch lengths, but there was no sign of a decent fish. It was moody fishing on such days.

But some mornings it was hot and windless, with clouds building all day until the Arkansas valley was overcast well before noon, and when the morning was filled with a misting drizzle that lasted only an hour or less, there was a remarkable transformation. The rain often fell for less than a half hour, its silver drops sometimes glittering in the morning sun, and it changed the fishing and everything else.

The swift thigh-deep runs along the undercut banks became alive with hatching mayflies, dark-winged little *Ephemerella* duns that came down the current like tiny slate-colored sailboats. The hatches did not last long. Some came off for only twenty or thirty minutes, and the first mayflies were seldom taken. It was usually some time before a trout actually rose for the fluttering little duns, where they danced beside the grassy banks. It seldom happened until about ten or fifteen minutes had passed, but once the first fish had porpoised, its rises seemed to start the other trout feeding with a quickening rhythm.

Pools that had seemed empty of trout, even when you waded through them just to study their population, were suddenly alive with rising fish. Trout would work steadily along a hummock of collapsed bank or under the solitary bush sheltering the pool. The smallest piece of cover invariably held a fish, and with a well-tied Hendrickson or Red Quill you could catch thirty in a morning. The fish were not large, mostly wild browns from eight to twelve inches, and a fish of sixteen inches was a veritable monster. But you had to fish them with cunning and a workable imitation, and if the trout in a pool saw you before you located them, your chances were finished for an hour.

It's like infantry training all over again! Frank Klune laughed one night over a beer in the Silver Dollar in Leadville. *Belly-flat in the grass or they see you coming and run!*

Ever try casting on your stomach? I asked.

It might help! he admitted.

The most unusual small trout stream I once fished regularly flowed through the colliery town of Sulzbach-Rosenberg in Bavaria. It was a typical German industrial town, with sullen trusswork pit-heads and mining structures everywhere among the houses. Men with coal-blackened faces and goggles returned from work, riding their bicycles or walking through the gritty streets in the shadow of huge pipe systems and ore buckets and expansion loops.

The little stream itself was born in the middle of these colliery structures and conveyor-bucket frames, its limestone springs enclosed in a series of swimming-pool-like excavations lined with tile. It trickled full-blown from the last pool, flowing about five feet wide and two feet deep. Watercress choked the springhead ponds and lined the tiny pools downstream. Its brightly spotted trout held tight against the cress, lying in plain view in most places, and I fished it several times when I was staying at the mill owner's house on the hill.

It was still in the years of the German occupation, and the mill owner had been imprisoned at Ingolstadt by the American military authorities for his political activities before the Second World War. His estate at Sulzbach-Rosenberg had been confiscated, and it served as the billet residence of the American military governor in the Amberg region.

Joseph Hackett was a retired artillery officer who had been seriously wounded in the Italian mountain campaigns that followed Anzio, and in the years we lived in Germany, he was the resident officer in the military government at Amberg. Hackett was primarily a hunter, and he particularly liked the winter drives for roe deer and *Wildschwein* and hares, but the retired major had also liked trout fishing since his boyhood on the coastal rivers above San Francisco. He invited us to fish the Lauterach from his lovely quarters at Sulzbach-Rosenberg, and we arrived in the April darkness after a long drive from Nürnberg over the winding cobblestone roads of northern Bavaria.

Dinner was excellent in the dark paneled dining room above the town, with sweet soups rich with sherry and venison taken from a shooting platform above Schmidsmülen three weeks earlier. The lights of the colliery glittered in the winding little brook below the terrace where we stood with our cognac.

It's got trout, Hackett pointed.

That's remarkable, my father said. *It's not easy to keep a stream clean in the middle of a factory!*

You can if you want it badly enough, Hackett agreed.

Are the fish large? I asked.

No, Hackett answered, *but I've got a problem in Amberg tomorrow morning, and you can fish it yourself before we get started for Schmidsmühlen.*

I'll try it, I said.

It was an unusual little stream, and its trout proved extremely shy. The first few times I tried fishing them, they scurried upstream under the watercress in terror. It was a problem in extra stealth and cunning. The banks were sometimes soft and trembling, and they telegraphed each clumsy step along the trailing grass, flushing the trout from their shadowy lies. Dropping a cast too harshly sent them scuttling under the banks like chickens. The flash of a ferrule in the sunlight frightened them. The bright ballet of a yellow fly line working in the sun was like a warning siren to these trout, and the partial silhouette or shadow of an angler was enough to spook them too. Each tiny pocket was a fresh exercise in shyness and stealth, teaching the ancient lessons about trout that are the heart of small-stream fishing.

There was the tinkling little riffle under the rumbling ore-carrier system, where the fish held tight against thick beds of watercress and chara. The trout could see an angler silhouetted against the sky there, but if the fish were approached carefully from behind the willows it was possible to take them with a well-placed nymph. There was one quiet bend where the fish were lying upstream in a shelving hole, and an angler crouching low could take them easily with the dry-fly method.

It was interesting that neither grazing dairy cattle, nor the daily passing of housewives, workmen on bicycles, and children seemed to bother the fish. The rumbling ore-buckets passed over them steadily without noticeable interruption of their feeding. Yet a careless step along the boggy banks, the brief exposure of a fisherman in a patch of sunlight, or a glimpse of his silhouette would frighten the trout or make them stop working. It was necessary to fish them from behind tree trunks and bushes, stalking each pocket on hands-and-knees in the grass.

It was archetypical of small-stream fishing.

There is no question that all boys who want to become fly-fishermen should spend their apprenticeship on such a small stream. Its lessons are taught gently. The fishing itself is not too difficult, yet it firmly demonstrates what it takes to catch shy trout.

The axioms of small-stream fishing are unmistakable. You must approach each pool and run cautiously. You cannot show yourself to the trout and expect them to keep feeding without alarm. It is amazing how many neophytes fail to realize this basic fact. There is a small pool on Spruce Run in New Jersey that I pass regularly every weekend on my way to fish the Brodheads. It has a concrete weir that blocks the current, and the flow plunges through a hatch. There is a deep, eddying pool below the hatch, about the size of the average living room, and it is regularly stocked by trucks from the rearing ponds at Hackettstown. There are always a few fishermen fishing there on those April mornings, and sometimes as many as ten are found standing on the weir. It is incredible to watch these men fishing for trout in plain view, only a few feet away from fish that can obviously see them. Only a foolish truck fish, with its lifetime of being coddled and fed in a hatchery, would ever accept their wares. Successful trout fishing depends entirely on presenting your fly to the fish before they have detected your presence, and that comes only with a mixture of skill and knowledge thoroughly leavened with patience.

Stealth and cunning are the primary rules. Your approach must be muffled, and you cannot plunge through the streamside willows and alders without alarming the fish. Your final presentation must be gentle, placing your flies softly on the current so the trout will not be frightened. Careful fishermen will most often approach from downstream on a small river, behind skittish trout, and usually conceal themselves behind willows and tree trunks and grass. It is valuable to watch the reaction of the fish, either taking the fly readily or refusing it. Such lessons are not easily learned on larger streams, where you seldom see the trout at close range.

The little stream at Sulzbach-Rosenberg in Germany was a perfect laboratory for such lessons. You could study the fish easily, watching them in the eddying currents beside the watercress, or the smooth runs over ochre-colored gravel. You could watch them wait to intercept a dry fly, or work their fins nervously in anticipation, drifting sideways to take an approaching nymph. Sometimes they inspected the fly and refused it, and sometimes they did not even bother to inspect its drift. The fish were shy and selective, and imitative patterns were usually best. Fly pattern and presentation and leader diameter were all critical; and concealing myself stealthily behind the willows, I once dapped a dry fly in a deep little run below the house and took a fat two-pound brown—an incredible trophy on such a tiny stream.

It was a priceless lesson, like the morning more than thirty-five years ago on the Bear Creek in Michigan. There were several fish in the run below the hatchery there, and I was fishing with live grasshoppers. Although the fish did not scatter in panic when we fished them below the hatchery weirs, we did not catch many either. Above the hatchery there was a zone where fishing was prohibited, and a line of floats marked its boundaries. There was always a school of good fish cruising inside the protected zone above the dam, and these trout never left their sanctuary.

They're pretty smart, my father said.

Must be some way to coax them outside those floats, I said. *Try a grasshopper right beside the barrier!*

The fish were too clever for such tactics. Their schools cruised just short of the barrier of floats, completely ignoring a live grasshopper fished only inches outside their protected zone. They eagerly took one thrown inside the floats, unattached to our tackle, but they refused to come outside even for a grasshopper kicking freely in the surface film.

It's incredible, I laughed. *They'll take a grasshopper two inches inside the floats, but they aren't even tempted by one thrown a few inches outside!*

And they'd probably ignore one on a hook if we fished it ten feet inside the no-fishing area! my father added.

They're smart! I agreed.

It was the same below the hatchery weirs and in the flood channel that protects the hatchery pens from high water. You could feed grasshoppers to the trout and they took them readily, yet they ignored one fished on conventional hooks and leaders. The trout were able to detect which baits were floating free and which were on hooks until we impaled our grasshoppers on small hooks and fished delicate nylon tippets. It was a lesson impossible to learn on bigger streams, yet a brook will reveal such secrets generously to both boys and men, once they have learned stealth and patience and observation.

Small streams and bait are unquestionably the best place to teach a boy about fishing. Success is important in the early years, and grasshoppers and worms will produce results. Fish in the creel are important in the beginning, before the perspective of time swings the pendulum of our attitudes toward the character of our sport and places so little value on the primal instincts in fishing that we prefer to release our catch. Fishing bait in a brook is a perfect genesis for this process, and its techniques are a lexicon of basic truths. The beginner can learn much from his minor triumphs and large frustrations, the lessons we all learned in our early years on small trout streams.

Such lessons wear well in later seasons. You learn that on a small stream it is sometimes better to approach upstream instead of down. The trout always lie facing its currents, and because the blind spot behind their heads lies where the trout's forward-looking eyes cannot focus, you can approach them more easily from below. You quickly learn that freshly stocked hatchery trout are more gullible than their wild cousins, and that stream-bred fish are alarmed at any sudden movement, even the sight of rods and lines moving against the sky. You learn to keep low, creeping and crawling when there are no bushes or tall grass to conceal you on a meadow brook like the one where I began fishing in Michigan. These days on hard-fished waters, it is wise to keep low in fishing over selective trout on any size stream, and I know many men on eastern rivers who wear out the knees in their waders first.

But all the charm of fishing a small stream is not confined to our learning years. There are moods when the cacophony and leg-wearing power of a big river become oppressive. Difficult wading and countless double hauls can erode both body and soul. Big water holds big trout, and there is a period in the maturing in the career of every fisherman when he is addicted to the pursuit of trophy-size fish. Once you have that fever in your blood, it is a passion that drives you beyond good judgment. Your behavior is so irrational that only a turned ankle, the casting arm stiff and aching from big-river casting, or swollen knees hurt in a fall among slippery rocks will help you regain your senses. After such aberrations, it is time for the tranquillity of some unpretentious brook, and its peaceful music will restore your perspective.

It is impossible to define a small stream. It is difficult to establish a yardstick that fully measures character and tells us that a brook becomes a river once its width equals a specified number of yards. It is never a matter of mere physical size, but rather one of temperament.

Some rivers never quite escape the small-stream character of their headwaters. Their character never quite matures, even though they sometimes demand long casting. Our big western spring creeks and the larger limestone streams of our eastern mountains are such waters. Their world is entirely composed of silk-smooth runs and glassy flats, quiet eddies and slow-flowing pools, all with reasonable bottoms of sand, gravel, and small stones. Such streams are intimate and ingratiating, perfect water for a fisherman whose psyche is tired of the abrasive moods of big water. There are also tumbling little mountain streams, and meadow creeks from New England to the high-country parks of our western mountains, that have these friendly moods—while the Henry's Fork of the Snake is perhaps the best example of a large river with a gentle character.

Other small streams are only miniature versions of their bigger relatives. Their currents are surprisingly deep and strong. Although they are relatively minor rivers, their character is marked with heavy water, treacherous ledges, and a bottom butter-slick with algae. Such streams offer the troublesome problems of big water without its big fish.

The techniques and equipment for small-stream fishing are both simple and demanding. Like William Schaldach in his poetic book *Currents and Eddies*, I believe that technique is a shallow word with a cold and disciplined ring, and in our myopic fascination with methods and tackle, we often lose sight of the fishing itself. Yet some technique is necessary in trout fishing, particularly in the world of the small-stream trout.

The rod should be relatively light and short to handle the fine tackle and brushy casting required. Modern rod builders have supplied us with a whole catalog of light fly rods that did not exist when Bergman and Schaldach were writing. Since casts are short, leaders are relatively delicate, flies are rather small, and small streams are so tightly enclosed in foliage, fly rods of five and a half to seven feet are perhaps best. Such rods will weigh from one to three ounces, with the tip calibrations and action suited to fine three- to five-weight double-tapered lines.

Leaders should be no longer than nine feet, since some casts will measure only twelve to fifteen feet, and a little line should extend beyond the tip guide to turn the leader over. Tippets should never exceed 4X, and 6X and 7X diameters are still better.

There are a number of small fly rods on the market which are short and relatively light, but if they are balanced with six- and seven-weight lines, they are not truly light-tackle rods for trout. Their calibrations are not really useful for fine nylon diameters below .007, and such lines fall too hard on thin water over skittish trout. Since we spend a considerable amount of time crawling on our knees in small streams, particularly in meadow water, a slightly longer rod is desirable to keep the backcast free of the weeds behind. Such problems are common on the British chalkstreams and the limestone streams of Ireland and the United States. My experience on such waters indicates that rods of seven to seven and a half feet are best in solving such problems, provided they are matched with three- to five-weight lines.

Casting itself presents difficult problems on small waters. Big rivers provide us with unlimited space and few worries about our backcasts. Fishing a wooded stream is good medicine for everyone at times. Small water will not forgive a careless presentation, and its pools and runs are filled with the pitfalls of streamside grass, bushes, clustered willows, overhanging limbs, alders, trees, and brushpiles. Such waters are a galaxy of obstacles and hazards, and a careless backcast unerringly finds itself in the highest branches.

Avoiding such troubles depends on your casting and the skills implicit in fishing small water. It is surprising how much a small, brushy stream can improve and broaden your casting techniques. The common roll cast, the switch pickup, and the sidearm casts delivered both normally and from the backhand position are all critical in your bag of tricks. These techniques are thoroughly discussed in the earlier chapter on casting, and their methodology is the ticket for brushy little rivers when normal casting simply will not work. However, the entire spectrum of casting skills will not succeed on small rivers unless you develop a special sense of the little stream and its secret rhythms.

It is essential to remember that the closer you approach a pool, the more likely it is that you will be discovered by its fish. Big water itself tends to eliminate this problem. Forty- to sixty-foot casts work at sufficient distance to keep you well outside the trout's cone of vision, but too much time on big water creates some bad habits. Little rivers shrink these distances and demand a better perspective. Coming from big water, it is common to approach a promising run and watch the frightened wake of a twelve-inch brown scuttling for cover. It is humiliating to realize that a stealthy approach might have creeled such a fish, but it is typical of fishing a small stream. Patience and humility are its lessons.

When working a small stream in low water, experienced anglers will use their eyes constantly. Our powers of observation are primary skills. Fish will often be visible at surprising distances in relatively shallow waters. Such foraging trout are dangerously exposed to kingfishers and ospreys and other predators, and are hair-trigger wary. They are extremely difficult to catch without a careful strategy.

Both fly and leader must be chosen carefully, and the leader supple and well soaked. Enough left-hand line should be stripped for a quick shoot, with false casting held to a minimum. The stalk must be executed skillfully. Crouching low, the fisherman creeps into range. The cast must be perfect, because a poor presentation will frighten the fish. It must be focused on the trout lying farthest downstream toward the angler, and if it is hooked after a successful cast, it should be played gently to coax it away from the others. Sometimes a hooked fish can be led downstream with enough subtlety that its fellow trout remain unfrightened, and after resting the pool briefly, the angler can try the next one upstream. When several such fish are captured, any angler can be justly proud. His skills are clearly demonstrated, and his hunting instincts have not been entirely dulled by the cacophony of city life.

Surprisingly small places can shelter trout in midsummer, and the angler must remain alert. He can never permit his powers of observation to wane. The smallest holding lie beside a stone or log, the tiny spine of darker water in a brief riffle, and the shadowy place along the bank can always shelter a trout. Deadfalls, small ledges, undercut grassy banks, overhanging trees, and sunken roots are all potential holding places. Small tributaries and springholes entering the stream are obvious lies for a small-stream trout. Hot-weather fish often gather in surprising numbers where such cold water trickles in among the fiddlebacks and moss. Their water is crystal clear and cold. Properly mined, such springholes and tributary flows can prove a rich lode of trout in late summer, and I can think of at least fifty such places from the Adirondacks to Maryland, and in the dog days they can salvage a session that might have proved fishless.

There are countless memories of small-stream fishing. Some I have written about in books like *Remembrances of Rivers Past*, and there are other memories from New England to the Rocky Mountains. Sometimes these little rivers produce surprisingly large trout, like the big rainbow taken on

Blacktail Spring Creek in Jackson Hole, or the big browns that had entered Fairy Creek in the Yellowstone in late September. There was the huge brown that Frank Klune once took along tiny Busk Creek, above Turquoise Lake in Colorado, and another I once captured at the tumbling mouth of Stiles Brook in the Adirondacks. Big fish were also discovered on several spring creeks in Montana, and I once took a fine four-pound rainbow on the Wise farther west in the Big Hole country. Although big fish are rare on small waters, they are not impossible.

Some memories are filled with mixed emotions. Shortly after the Second World War we were staying in the beautiful little hotel at Hintersee in the Bavarian Alps. It was not a fishing holiday, but I had stowed some tackle in our luggage, and one morning I tried the swift little tributary that feeds the lake.

It was a quiet meadow stream that flowed from a mountain valley on the alpine threshold of Austria. Its meadows were bright with snow buttercups. The village on the Austrian border had a charming onion-topped church and white stucco houses with steep, sheltering roofs of thick sod, their balconies bright with geraniums. The little stream flowed over pale gravel, and I took several fish in its upper meadows near the border crossing. There was a deeper pool where the meadows ended, and the stream wound into the dense pines. It surrendered a lovely wild brown of fifteen inches, which carried its fight into the weedy shallows downstream. The trout came to the net grudgingly, and I was admiring its beauty in the morning sun when I discovered a grisly echo of the war.

My God! My heart thudded wildly.

The bright gravel shallows concealed a rotting gasmask and the corrugated canister of the German army, and downstream in a bed of watercress was a corroded *Wehrmacht* helmet just above a silt-covered skull. These grim artifacts of the war were a threnodic climax on that pastoral morning in Bavaria.

But there were other mornings on other streams when their pianissimo moods remained untarnished, and I have memories with the melodic perfection of a flute solo. There was a hot morning years ago, that I fished down John's Brook when the unseasonable weather had reduced the Ausable flats to shimmering panfish ponds. It was cool hiking up the mountain just after daylight, and there was dew in the cobwebs across the trail. The brook danced and plunged below in its bed of giant glacier-polished boulders, its roar surprisingly large where it echoed among the rocks. High on the shoulder of the mountain, I finally climbed down and fished back to Keene Valley, working the swift runs and churning little pools. The trout were eager, taking pale little Cahills readily when an angler remained hidden, and I took forty or fifty small brook trout in a morning. They were beautiful, brightly jeweled little fish that I released, and just above the village I took a fine thirteen-inch brown from a dark pocket between the boulders. It was hot when I finally reached Keene Valley, and I walked proudly toward the Spreadeagle with the brown trout in my wicker creel.

Good morning? Jeffrey Norton was waiting.

It was beautiful! I wiped my forehead sweatily. *How about an ice-cold beer before lunch?*

Perfect! Norton nodded happily.

You know, I sipped my beer thirstily, *there's something special about fishing a small stream like John's Brook.*

You're right! he agreed. *It's like getting out of the city—it really strips the fat off your soul!*

Norton was right.

7. Field Problems
in Fishing Lakes,
Ponds, and Reservoirs

It was getting colder when we finally reached Tarryall, and climbed past the half-rotted buildings of the ghost town into the sprawling foothill basin beyond. The Colorado trout season was only a few days old. Spring weather is unpredictable in those altitudes and the sky was an ominous ink blue beyond the 10,000-foot saddle of Kenosha Pass. The sky seemed to promise fresh snow, and its sullen clouds obscured the mountains.

The road climbed past the south shoulder of the Tarryall Dam, and wound back toward the rocky shoreline of the reservoir.

Blizzard coming! Dick Coffee growled. *Just our luck!*

The squall was still fifteen miles away.

Doesn't look good, I agreed unhappily, *but we might as well stay and try the fishing anyway!*

You're probably right. Coffee set the brake.

The raw wind gusted around the station wagon now, scattering sand across the windshield.

Must be forty degrees out there now! I shivered.

Several bait fishermen had been scouring the bottom with night crawlers and canned corn. Two of them had several small hatchery rainbows on a bass stringer, with one good brown trout.

Think flies will work in a blizzard?

Let's find out what they've been eating, I suggested. *Maybe they'll let me check the stomach of that brown.*

Might tell us something at that, Coffee said.

We walked down to the bait fishermen with the stringer.

You will probably think I'm crazy, I began an awkward preamble. *But I'd like to clean your brown trout for you.*

136

Must be crazy! one laughed.

Why'd you want to clean that brown? the other fisherman parried suspiciously. *What's in it for you?*

Simple, I explained. *I get to check his stomach.*

Check his stomach? he said warily.

See what he's been eating, Dick Coffee explained.

The bait fishermen looked at each other and shrugged.

Okay, they said, *but we still think you're crazy!*

He is crazy, Coffee growled.

My knife sliced easily from the ventral fin toward the gill structure, and I stripped the entrails free, cutting away the pectorals. Carefully incising the stomach membranes, I forced its contents into my hand.

What's he been taking? Coffee asked.

Dragonfly nymphs, I replied. *Don't have anything like them in my fly books—have to make some!*

You tie flies, Coffee laughed. *I'm going fishing!*

Good luck! I rummaged in my gear.

It was getting darker before I finished the first nymph, and the meadow basin above the reservoir was already ink-colored with the advancing snow squalls. Three fat muskrat-bodied nymphs lay on the car seat. The big flies were weighted with soft fuse wire, and the rod was strung with a fast sinking line. The first big snowflakes hit the windows when I left the station wagon and walked shivering toward the reservoir.

It was snowing fiercely now. The far shoreline was obscured in the swirling flakes. Dick Coffee became a shadowy figure standing in the water, and the thick flakes covered the ground quickly. The snow hit us wetly in the face and encrusted my shooting glasses.

You want one of these nymphs? I yelled.

Coffee laughed through the falling snow. *You really think it'll make a difference in this blizzard?*

Might! I waded out into the shallows.

They're not going to take anything in this weather! he grumbled. *They won't take what I'm using either!*

That fish I checked was full of nymphs, I said.

The other fishermen were leaving, their parkas covered with snow.

Winter takes a spring vacation, Coffee growled unhappily through the driving flakes. *Summer is two weeks of bad skiing!*

It's not snowing where the fish are, I laughed.

That's real comforting! Coffee shot a long cast angrily into the snow. *Maybe we should join 'em!*

My first cast worked out and virtually disappeared into the snow squall, and I let it sink twenty counts before starting the retrieve. The fly came back clean and I did not feel it touch bottom. The next cast was permitted to sink twenty-five counts, and when I retrieved, it ticked into the gravel twice and there was a wisp of algae trailing from the hook. It had come back a little too deep.

Let it sink twenty-three, I thought.

The laborious hand-twist retrieve had worked the nymph back only six or seven turns when there was a sudden pull, and I was into a good rainbow. It bolted deep into the lake and jumped, falling heavily in the swirling snowflakes.

Can hear him, Coffee laughed, *but can't see him!*

It was a sleek eighteen-inch rainbow, and I took several more around a pound while the squalls covered us with their wet, swirling flakes. When the snow stopped and it started clearing, the trout stopped taking too.

Well, Coffee said, *that was pretty strange.*

The sun came out behind the Mosquito Range, and the fresh snow glittered with a terrible brightness. *They sure liked the dragonfly nymphs*, I laughed, *and they took in the worst of the squalls.*

Let's get back before we're snowbound, he said.

You're right, I agreed.

It was not unique on our western reservoirs, particularly at about 9,000 feet, where the water temperatures stay cold and a fish would starve if it waited for the optimal feeding temperatures of sixty-odd degrees. We had fished a shoreline partially sheltered from the wind, and the trout were bottom-feeding on a shelf between the steep gravel banks and the dropoff into the deep water of the reservoir. Since most of the food in a lake or impoundment is found in its shallows, and the inlet acreages and weedy shallows along the north shore were torn with surf and whitecaps, we had chosen the only feeding grounds left that morning.

There was a similar morning years ago on San Cristobal Reservoir in southern Colorado. It is an enlarged lake, with a dam to raise its water level, and its outlet flowage is the source of the storied Lake Fork of the Gunnison.

Jim MacKenzie, Evert Tom, and Dick Coffee were camping with me on the west shore of the reservoir one opening weekend, and we went out early in two rowboats from the livery below our campsite. The inlet shallows enter the lake through thickets of half-drowned scrub oaks and willows, and the water was slightly roiled with snowmelt. However, these shallows were the first to warm on those cold spring mornings, and MacKenzie and I rowed to fish them first. Coffee and Tom rowed east to fish below the cliffs, where there was a big shelf about fifteen feet down. The underwater shelf was still in the morning shadows.

The reservoir was a little high with snowmelt and the brushy inlet shallows were like a mangrove swamp.

Let's row into those brushy lagoons, I suggested. *The sun's been warming them for several hours.*

What about the cliffs? MacKenzie asked.

No. I shook my head. *It was pretty cold last night, and it'll take another two or three hours before the water warms up enough for the fish to work that deep.*

You're the boss, he said.

We fished among the drowned willows and scrub oaks with big

dragonfly nymphs, and the results were remarkable. My cast cropped a fat muskrat-bodied nymph along the roots of some willows. It had barely started to sink when a two-pound rainbow darted out from the shadows and took my nymph savagely. We located thirty-odd fish that morning, and landed more than twenty. It was almost noon when we stopped and worked down the east shore to the shelf under the cliffs where Coffee and Tom were fishing. Their boat was anchored a good backcast from the cliff face, and they were fishing deep on the bottom shelf with the cast-and-countdown method and fast sinking lines.

Any luck? MacKenzie yelled.

We've got ten or twelve, Coffee answered, *but they only started taking an hour or two ago—it was perfectly slow in the beginning!*

After the sun had been on the water a while, I said, *and it finally got warm enough for them to feed.*

That's about it, Tom said.

Well I'll be damned, MacKenzie laughed. *It went just like you said it would!*

Sometimes it does, I smiled.

The inlet and outlet flowages of most lakes and impoundments are prime fishing areas. Their currents carry food and oxygen. The shallow waters are primary nurseries in the diet chain of the trout, sustaining both still-water and current-loving insects. Usually the fish in the outlet flowages are larger than the others in a lake, and the outlets are a prime area for prospecting unknown waters. Both beaver ponds and man-made impoundments still have their original streambeds relatively intact in their bottoms. These are the prime holding zones in such waters, except when the fish are foraging out across the shallows, and the cast-and-countdown method is common practice in such places. Ray Bergman wrote about such wet-fly tactics in his book *Trout*, and they are common from Cranberry Lake on the Oswegatchie in New York to weedy Henry's Lake and the sprawling Crane Prairie Reservoir in our western mountains. It is a basic lake-fishing technique.

Other prime fishing in the inlet shallows can often come from mayfly and caddis hatches endemic to their ecology. Several times on big western reservoirs, like Tarryall in Colorado and Hebgen in Montana, there has been superb fishing with imitations of tiny midge pupae. Such rises of fish are often distinguished by small rise forms coming in a steady rhythm from cruising trout, and no visible insects on the surface. There are also fine hatches of *Tricorythodes* and *Callibaetis* flies, as well as larger still-water mayflies, like the big *Siphlonurus* drakes that hatch in August and September. Sometimes there are huge hatches of the little, many-brooded mayflies, drifting like seeds on the surface or herded against a downwind shore by the breeze. The fish take them greedily at such times.

They take them so steadily that they seldom pause between rises, Bud Lilly explained in West Yellowstone last August. *The boys who fish Hebgen regularly call them the gulpers.*

They're gluttons! I agreed.

Such fishing is much better when there is a light wind riffle on the water, since the fish cannot see the boat or the leader easily. The fish cruise boldly, taking the naturals in a steady, sequential rhythm. Sometimes a fish will put five or six rises together in a line, and then abruptly change direction or return along its original feeding path.

Since the water levels in reservoirs can fluctuate widely, their draw-down and high-storage levels can strongly affect our fishing. Reduced levels of water can concentrate both fish and their diet forms, but too rapid a draw-down cycle can decimate fly life as the water recedes. More water can pose other problems and opportunities.

During the years when I was involved in the design and construction of the Air Force Academy in Colorado, we regularly fished Eleven-Mile Reservoir on the South Platte. One spring there was an unusually large accumulation of snow in the mountains, and the water officials at Denver decided on extensive water storage at Eleven-Mile. The sagebrush flats became vast shallows with the snowmelt flooding behind the dam, and one day in those flood bottoms Evert Tom and I had a picnic with big rainbows that had come in from deep water to feed on the hatching *Poecillus* beetles. We took them with dry-fly beetle imitations in the Letort style, with a light riffling wind putting delicate patterns on the water, and it was tricky fighting a big rainbow on light tackle in the brush.

Terrestrial hatches and mating swarms are often a factor in lake and reservoir fishing. Jenny Lake in the Jackson Hole country gets a big swarm of mating carpenter ants each spring, and its cutthroats and hybrid cutthroat-rainbows come to the surface to feed on the winged-ant swarms. Bob Carmichael once operated the little tackle shop at Moose Crossing on the Snake, and he loved the carpenter-ant season in Jackson Hole for its exceptional dry-fly sport.

Fantastic! He rumbled good-naturedly. *Big fish working on top when the wind's down on Jenny, really big fish of six to ten pounds.*

Sounds good! I said.

Several years later I witnessed these mating swarms, and on a still evening in a quiet bay I located several big cutthroats. Hundreds of winged ants struggled helplessly in the surface film, and the big fish patrolled the flat water, sipping them in leisurely fashion as they swam. There would be a series of rises in a lazy sequence, establishing the direction of a swimming fish, and I would place my big ant imitation slightly ahead of where I thought the fish would show next. Sometimes a fish would change direction and disappear in a porpoise roll. Several of these fish went eighteen to twenty inches, and the trophy-size trout were a hybrid of five pounds and a magnificent cutthroat that scaled eight.

Beaver ponds pose all of the problems found on man-made reservoirs in miniature. The old stream channel lies in the bed of the impounded water, and the fish use it for shelter, foraging out at times in the flooded shallows for food. New beaver ponds often prove quite fertile. The fish trapped in their flooding find their world suddenly multiplied, and the rotting vegetation fertilizes the water chemistry. Fishing is often unusually good in the early months of a beaver pond, before the decaying deadfalls and willow roots tip the scale, leaching their acidity into the ecosystem. Fishing declines as the pond becomes more acid, and a similar life cycle obtains on newly completed reservoirs.

Fishing beaver ponds is relatively simple. Unless there is an obvious fly hatch, dry flies are secondary to wet flies and nymphs. Sunk flies are usually best in a lake since they are retrieved and cover more water. Staying out of sight is still perhaps the cardinal rule. It is often possible to fish a small beaver pond from below its stick-tangle dam, keeping totally out of sight behind the barrier itself. It is seldom advisable to wade into a beaver pond unless it is quite large. Both the detritus stirred free during wading and the disturbance of the wading itself can frighten the trout. You should also be wary of their bottom quality, since it is possible to sink into the muck and become trapped. Bright weather will usually find the trout hiding in the drowned channel of the pond, or working along its deadfalls and willows. Cloudy weather and twilight coax the trout to cruise and forage more boldly, and the fisherman can find them anywhere.

Beaver pond fishing is pretty much the same from New England to the Pacific, although the country changes character. Sometimes high water forces us to return to the beaver-pond fishing of our boyhood, and we rediscover its rewards.

There are many memories of beaver ponds, from Maine to the Pacific Coast, and the mind returns to them from time to time. There were tiny cutthroat ponds in the Wasatch Mountains of Utah, and the superb fishery for brook trout and Wyoming natives high in the headwaters of the Gros Ventre, on the remote Darwin Ranch. There were huge brookies in the beaver-pond bottoms of the Snake in Jackson Hole that Bob Carmichael would tell you about if you passed muster, drawing a scraggly treasure map on the back of an envelope. Colorado boyhood summers were rich with beaver-pond fishing, and I remember their jewellike beauty along Rock Creek, Tennessee Creek, Willow Creek, and Empire Creek in the Leadville country. Sometimes these little ponds were generous, and I remember the time that Frank Klune and I caught such creelsful of big brook trout from the beaver ponds on Empire Creek that we were arrested and accused of poaching a lake belonging to the mayor of Leadville. No one believed such fat brook trout were found anywhere in the valley except his private preserve at O'Brien's Lake.

There are other western memories too, like the great blue heron on a Montana beaver pond in the Big Hole country, and the trumpeter swans nesting in another beaver-stick sanctuary in the Yellowstone. Beaver-pond fishing is good in the cutthroat headwaters of the Frying Pan, and I once had superb sport on a nameless pond in the Lime Creek country.

But there is beaver-pond fishing farther east, too. There have been some fine evenings on the headwaters of the Brule and the Namekagon and the Wolf in Wisconsin. Robert Traver has eloquently described his love for beaver-pond country in the Upper Peninsula of Michigan, in books like *Trout Madness* and *The Anatomy of a Fisherman*, and I have had some good sport in such ponds on the watersheds of the Tahquemenon and the Two-Hearted and the Fox. The late Paul Young used to tell me about the big trout in some beaver ponds on the Driggs, but he died before he provided the map he had promised. Some men refuse to make maps or reveal beaver ponds as priceless as a secret woodcock cover, and even brush out their jeep tracks on logging roads and trails leading into their favorite brook trout places.

Our eastern mountains have beaver-pond fishing too. There are good ponds in the Allegheny country, especially in the trout streams tributary to the Susquehanna, and I once had fine sport on the little Sawkill near Milford, fishing a reach of water that had belonged to the late Gifford Pinchot. There are sometimes fresh ponds on other Pocono streams, like the Wallenpaupack, Buck Hill, Blooming Grove, and the Shohola. Such acid swamp-dark waters produce brook trout with such bright coloring that their mottled flanks look like a jeweler's tray lined with rubies and turquoise and opals.

There are similar secrets in the Catskills and Adirondacks, and I particularly remember the bright coloring of the brook trout in a beaver pond on the Bouquet. Vermont and New Hampshire and Massachusetts have their beaver-pond secrets too, and I once fished a pond in Maine just after daylight. Its fish were dimpling the still surface and mist still lingered over the deadfall bogs at its inlet. The scrub pines were almost black against a flame-colored dawn, and it lingers in the mind like the exquisite watercolors that Winslow Homer painted at Mink Pond in his Adirondack summers.

There are other axioms worth remembering in fishing lakes, ponds, and reservoirs. Sometimes a lake has two distinct parts connected by a shallow neck of water, and sometimes it has little-known reefs and shallows lying well out from its shoreline. Such places are both spawning grounds and rich larders of baitfish and fly hatches. Fish cruising between deeper sections must pass through such connecting shallows, and fish from those pelagic zones come there to feed in morning and evening. Perhaps the most classic example that comes to mind is the channel connecting Lewis Lake and Shoshone Lake in the Yellowstone, and the crocodile-size browns that migrate into its lagoons and riffling shallows in early October.

Other examples are more typical, and years ago I made fine catches of brook trout at Maroon Lake, near Aspen, in Colorado, hiking up from the tourist area at its outlet to the narrow arm that connects the lower lake with its upper acreages. Its water was icy in late spring, but you could wade out waist-deep into the connecting shallows and cast across to the immense rockslide that had come down from the shoulder of Pyramid Mountain over the centuries. Fishing a weighted nymph, it was possible to move a fish on virtually every cast when they were coming well, and for several evenings I supplied an entire seminar group at the Aspen Institute with fresh trout. It was a contribution valued far beyond my participation in the panel discussions during that conference at Aspen.

Reefs and shallows well out in a lake are a priceless discovery, and their location should be marked carefully in the mind. Landmarks on the shoreline can be used, lining up a tree or house on the east and west boundaries of the lake, and two other bench marks on the north and south. The intersection of these axes clearly defines the location of such shallows in midlake, and it is a method familiar to men who troll deep for lake trout and landlocked salmon in New England. Such knowledge is extremely valuable. Perhaps the most striking example of such fishing in my experience did not come on American waters, but occurred this past spring while I was sea-trout fishing on Lough Currane in Ireland.

Paddy Donnelly was my boatman, and his weathered face echoed the character of the Killarney mountains above the lake, dour and brooding except for his bright eyes and a smile as welcome as a brief few minutes of Irish sunshine between squalls of misting rain at Ballinskelligs. Lough Currane looked as dour as a lead-sheathed coffin when we pushed off in his boat from the rocky landing below his thatch-roofed cottage.

Fine morning! Paddy said.

With this rainy weather? We shook hands warmly.

Paddy nodded happily. *'Tis a fine soft morning we'll be having, with good hatches of Bibio flies and olives, and just enough wind for a crust on the water.*

Where do we fish? I asked.

Donnelly pointed across the water toward the middle of the lake, where the ruins of a tenth-century structure stood dark against the water and the barren mountains beyond.

We'll be starting along the Church Island, he said. *We'll be fishing the shoals and skerries and smaller islands, drifting along with the wind.*

Okay, I smiled, *let's try it!*

The old boatman took us across the lake, his leather-wrapped oars creaking in their wooden locks, and finally he turned the boat broadside into the light wind. It riffled the water and took us gradually down the shoreline of the Church Island.

What flies should I fish? I asked.

Donnelly searched my fly-books thoughtfully. *You may fish as you like, but for these Kerry sea-trout in Lough Currane we like a three-fly cast—with the Watson's Fancy on the point, and the Bibio and Black Pennel on the droppers.*

We'll try them! I said.

My experience with multiple casts and dropper flies on brown trout has not been noticeably successful except in strong, boulder-strewn rivers, and I had little faith in fishing three flies on waters as popular and hard-fished as Lough Currane. However, there was a quiet competence about Paddy Donnelly with none of the poetic exaggeration I had sometimes found in other Irish ghillies, and I quickly trusted his judgment. The three flies were rigged and waiting.

Should I start? I asked.

Donnelly studied the western shoreline across the lake, and then swivelled his head to look back toward the ruined church. *No,* he shook his head quietly. *Just a few yards more.*

We drifted farther down the lake, the boat holding broadside into the wind. *Start your fishing now,* Donnelly suggested.

The first two casts produced nothing, but I began fishing them out methodically, laying successive casts in a clockwise fan pattern as we drifted along the island and stripping them back quickly. The third cast went out on the wind and settled, and I had just started to strip it back when there was a huge splash well out in the waves.

Fish! I yelled excitedly.

The reel protested as it surrendered about fifty yards of line, and a large sea trout cartwheeled wildly across the water.

Four pounds, Donnelly watched with a practiced eye, and finally reached for the net.

The fish jumped several times before I worked it back, and fought its deep circling below the boat until we netted it. The boatman killed it with a quick rap of the priest, unhooked the fly carefully, and patiently untangled the dropper flies. Eager to start fishing again, I worked the line out with a quick series of lengthening false casts. Donnelly smiled and studied the shorelines.

Wait, he said. *Too deep here.*

The old boatman rowed briefly and studied a beehive cairn of rocks on the island, glancing back to check its alignment with his cottage across the water. Finally he nodded with satisfaction, and I started into another fan pattern of casts. Less than a dozen casts had been fished out when there was a wrenching strike and the reel shrieked again, drowning the cries of the foraging gulls. This fish did not jump and it felt stronger, and it was a long time before it surrendered.

Eight pounds! Donnelly exclaimed when it came over the gunwale, wrenching and twisting in the boat net. *'Tis the finest sea-trout of the season!*

He cradled his oars and pumped my hand warmly.

The fishing lasted about two hours, with the old boatman navigating to each reef and shallow in Lough Currane expertly, telling me with a series of nods and gestures when to start and stop fishing. It was an impressive performance, demonstrating his exact knowledge of the shape and position and depth of each shoal and outcropping, and its precise relationship to several landmarks on shore. We caught another half-dozen fish between three and four pounds before they finally stopped rising, and when we reached the boat landing below his cottage I rummaged through my duffel for the silver flask of Tullamore whisky.

The boatman accepted the dram cup gratefully.

Paddy! I raised the flask in the misting rain. *We'll drink to you and your skills—that was the best display of knowledge I've seen on any lake in the world!*

Donnelly smiled and drained his Irish whisky.

8. Tactics in Fishing
the Tail Waters

I t is a surprisingly large region, encompassing almost 60,000 square
miles in Arkansas and Missouri. It is a forested plateau of ancient
mountains, the only extensive uplands between the Rocky Mountains
and the Appalachians farther east. Its valleys are deeply carved into
limestone and sandstone formations laid across the bottoms of vast
Paleozoic seas, its geology honeycombed with caverns and flowing springs.
Its rivers flow alkaline and rich toward the Arkansas, Missouri, and the
sprawling Mississippi itself. It is a region filled with paradox and surprise.

Its boundaries are defined in terms of both climate and geography. Its
cool spring-fed rivers have evolved thirteen species of fish unique to the
Ozarks, species that have never migrated into the tepid silt-laden streams at
lower altitudes. Ozark rivers like the Buffalo and Current and White were
once among the finest free-flowing rivers in America, teeming with
smallmouth bass.

The White has been dammed in the gargantuan reservoirs at Table
Rock and Bull Shoals and Norfolk, but the Buffalo and the Current still
run free through their forests of white oak and hickory. Both flora and
fauna in these valleys are unusual. The Ozark Plateau marks the western
limits of the great forests that once covered the eastern United States. Its
western foothills are a threshold for the prairies that rise steadily toward the
Rocky Mountain escarpment. The Missouri flows along its northern
borders, the southern limits of the Pleistocene glaciers that chilled the
prehistoric climate of the Ozarks without sculpturing their hills, and the
semitropical alluvial bottoms of the Mississippi lie toward the southeast.
Such factors play a surprising role in the Ozark country.

Their hills provide a sanctuary for a community of plants and animals

145

that no longer survive in adjacent regions. The birches found much farther north still thrive in the cool hollows along their rivers and spring-fed creeks. Beech trees have their primary range in our eastern forests, yet they are plentiful in the moist river bottoms of the Ozarks. Lichens commonly found in the subarctic tundra and caribou barrens around Hudson Bay are also found on the north-facing escarpments. Water tupelo and buttonbush, plants more common in the bayous of Mississippi and Louisiana, are found in Ozark swamps and sinkhole bogs. Scorpions are common in the parched barrens of Texas and Oklahoma, but populations are surprisingly found in the Ozark plateau, particularly where rocky formations are exposed to the strong summer sun.

The Ozarks have been a paradise for hunting and fishing since the Osage tribe lived in its western foothills during the hot months of midsummer. French traders penetrated the Ozarks from both the Missouri and the Mississippi, leaving their heritage in the names of many places. Zebulon Pike explored its northern drainages enroute to the Rocky Mountains, but it was Henry Schoolcraft who first explored the Ozark Plateau in 1818, barely fifteen years after the Louisiana Purchase.

There are still wild turkeys and whitetail deer in the Ozarks, and ruffed grouse fill the April woods with their drumming. The spring is a time of flowering redbud, wild azalea, dogwood, may apples, and bloodroot. Baitfish like the duskystripe shiners and mottled darters and bleeding shiners are spawning. Mock orange and blue lobelia and fragrant verbena bloom among the thickets of rhododendron and buckthorn in the river bottoms. Strange subarctic species like false bugbane, northern bedstraw, delicate white camas, arctic harebells, and *Phytidium* mosses are also found in the northern foothills; and farther west the Ozarks are a prelude to the high plains. The bunchgrass glades are bright with prairie species like purple beardtongue, slender liatrus, Missouri primrose, puffball brier, sunflower, prairie rose, Indian paintbrush, tickseed, and most surprisingly —spiny clusters of prickly-pear cactus, with their incredibly yellow flowers in springtime.

Although the Ozark Plateau remains remarkably wild, it too has suffered over the past century. French trappers and fur traders encouraged the Osage tribes to exploit the colonies of muskrats and beavers, and began the iron and lead mining that continues today. Hunters from Tennessee thinned out the turkey and deer, and eradicated the buffalo and elk. There are still a few bears, and sometimes there is the report of a puma in the high brush country in the headwaters of Archey's Fork or the Buffalo.

Farmers came too, crossing the Mississippi from Kentucky and Tennessee. Their methods were tragically primitive. Some girdled the trees to kill and clear them for growing corn. Others believed that the rich humus of decaying leaves and pine needles on the forest floor prevented the growth of grass, which it unquestionably did, and they burned it off each spring. Burning-off is an agricultural practice still found among the primitive Araucan populations in Chile, and the cultivation found among the hill tribesmen of India and Nepal, but it is surprising to learn that such foolish theories were still found on the American frontier in the nineteenth century. Burning the humus destroyed the principal source of organic matter sustaining the flinty soil of the Ozark Plateau, and when their farms failed to prosper, these men soon turned to lumbering in the hills.

The first timber cutting took place on the northern drainages, because rivers like the Gasconnade and Osage and Big Piney could transport the logs to the Missouri and Saint Louis. The cutters took the shortleaf pine first, moving steadily south as the mature trees fell before their gleaming axes. Once the conifers were exhausted, the lumbermen turned to the stands of white and black oak, hickory, and black walnut. These trees were used in mansions from Saint Louis to New Orleans.

When the railroads pushed west from Chicago and Saint Louis and Kansas City, timber from the Ozarks was used for ties and trestles. Tie whacking became the principal industry. The gandy dancers needed timber for thousands of miles of trackage, and although no one has tried to calculate how many railroad ties cut from the Ozark forests went into construction of the Santa Fe or Union Pacific, tie whacking remains a major industry in the region. Between poor farming technology and the rapacity of the timber cutting, the Ozarks suffered badly from erosion in the last century, and its clear rivers often ran milky with each rain.

But Ozark ecology reached its perigee on the threshold of this century. Logging had reduced the primeval forests to ragged stands of scrub timber. Spring burning had finally transformed the hillside farms into gravelly wastelands where little grew except weeds and blackjack oak and sumac. Game was growing scarce and the fishing was poor in the Ozarks, completely unlike the centuries when the Osage tribes migrated there to hunt and fish and escape the summer heat of the Oklahoma prairies.

But the last half century has seen the stubborn renaissance of the Ozarks, starting with the creation of the national forest system by Theodore Roosevelt and Gifford Pinchot. The Ozark National Scenic Riverways Act of 1964 has ended the depredations and dam building of the Corps of Engineers. Farming and population have both declined.

Most of the Ozark rivers are flowing clear again, and their waters are the true glory of the region. Fishermen will forgive the flat Ozark summits and relatively sparse forests their monotony, understanding it is that very monotony that makes the remarkable rivers and limestone springs possible. The precipitation these forests need to flourish, but can no longer retain after the timbering and humus burning, is quickly absorbed into the porous limestone and sandstone formations. It trickles deep into the sinks and fissures, gathering in enormous water-filled caves. Ozark springs are so spectacular, and so uniform in their steady outpouring of flow, that the region abounds in old wives' tales about the origins of their waters.

Some natives believe the water comes from the Great Lakes through labyrinthine channels in the earth itself, while others believe that seepages from the Mississippi are the source. Some even believe that the Ozark springs come from the snowmelt of the Rocky Mountains, and I once met an old man at Big Spring who believed its flow actually came from the icy depths of Hudson's Bay.

What about the salt water? I smiled.

Don't care about things like that! The old man stood watching its turbulent currents boiling up at the bottom of a dolomite bluff. *It comes underground from Hudson's Bay!*

Perhaps you're right, I said.

Big Spring feeds the Current in Missouri with the incredible volume of one billion gallons each day, almost enough water to supply the entire daily needs of New York, and its remarkable flow is almost equalled at Mammoth and Greer Springs.

Although exotic explanations seem equal to such dramatic outpourings of water, these remarkable Ozark springs are fed by nothing more exotic than slowly collected rainfall and snowmelt. Although annual precipitation is only a moderately heavy forty to fifty inches, the hydrology of the region is remarkable. Springs are relatively simple things, but their simplicity removes none of their mystery. Precipitation gradually soaks into the decaying humus, soil, sand or gravel that covers the surface topography. Below these surface materials lies a porous geology, generally composed of sandstone or dolomite or limestone in the Ozarks. The seepage first gathers in the aerated layers, where the porous rock holds both air and water. It finally collects in the zone of saturation, where the rock pores are completely filled. Between these two levels lies the water table, which generally follows surface formations. But when the water table lies above the surface, lakes and marshy acreages are formed; and where erosion or fissures in the bedrock intersect the table, the birth of a flowing spring is the result.

The total number of Ozark springheads is unknown, but it is agreed that the region is one of the most prolific aquifers in the world. Literally hundreds of Ozark springs produce between five and ten million gallons a day, and there are ten springs in the region that flow at the rate of more than fifty million gallons. It perhaps was Ward Dorrance, in his book *Three Ozark Streams*, who perfectly described the poetry of these Ozark springheads:

> It is a world of springs and swift rivers. Everywhere there is a leafy sound of rising, running, bright waters flowing. If we should place our ears to the ground we might hear the fertile pulsing of a giant subterranean heart.

These remarkable springheads feed a network of equally remarkable rivers, carving their courses deep into the layers of sedimentary dolomite and limestone. These rivers have been famous for their float trips and smallmouth bass since writers like Jack London, and the equally celebrated Ozark Ripley, described them in the decade just after the First World War. Missouri rivers with exceptional smallmouth fishing include the Meramec,

Gasconnade, Black, Big Piney, Roaring Spring, Jack's Fork, Elk, Eleven Point, Spring, Pomme de Terre, Osage, and the remarkable Current, which is perhaps the most famous bass river in America.

Arkansas has a series of equally famous smallmouth streams, like the Little Osage, Mulberry, Ouachita, Caddo, Strawberry, Crooked, and the Middle Fork of the Saline. But it is the wild little Buffalo that remains the most famous of these Arkansas bass streams, particularly since the Corps of Engineers completed three major dams on the sprawling watershed of the White.

It was the crystalline White that started the traditional Ozark float trips, ranging from day trips lasting a few miles to floats lasting several days. The guides prepare superb lunches on the day trips, with cookfires on the gravel bars, and the commissary boats travel ahead on the longer journeys to set up the overnight camps. The White is remarkably clear, flowing swiftly in its narrow shallows and lingering in placid half-mile flats with every pebble showing on the bottom. The floats start at daylight, with night mists still hanging over the current, shrouding the weathered bluffs above the river. The cold springs that enter the river leave their fingerprints of watercress along the bank, chilling the main currents downstream. The river is always surprisingly cold even on the hottest days, and its chill is quickly felt when the sun leaves the river in late afternoon. Darkness gathers swiftly in the narrow valleys, and the warmth of a dying cookfire is welcome after the supper dishes are scoured in the sand.

The White runs much colder now, and its smallmouth bass are scarce until the river reaches Calico Rock, almost fifty miles below the dam at Bull Shoals. The Corps of Engineers dammed the White in 1951, adding the Table Rock Dam upstream seven years later. The Norfolk impoundment on the north fork of the White had already been completed in 1944, and the icy tail waters of these dams have changed the character of the White completely. Its temperatures seldom reach sixty degrees, and average about fifty-two degrees through the year. The native smallmouths have migrated downstream in search of warmer currents, and trout have largely displaced them. Trout hatcheries have subsequently been built below the Norfolk and Greer's Ferry impoundments, and almost 500,000 browns and rainbows are stocked each season. Records show that the fishery is averaging more than four hundred trout better than four pounds each season, and its record fish is a full seventeen pounds.

Similar man-made fisheries have evolved in the cold discharges of the Greer's Ferry reservoir on the Little Red River, the Greeson reservoir on the Little Missouri, and the Ouachita impoundment on the Ouachita fifty miles southwest of Little Rock. But the crystalline White below the Norfolk and Bull Shoals dams remains the principal trout water in the Ozarks, perhaps the finest tail-water fishery in the world.

Our earlier chapter on the ecology of dams discussed their interruption of rivers and their impact on their community of life, both in the impounded waters behind the dam and in the tail waters downstream.

Spillways tend to warm a river too much for trout, and penstocks that release their effluents too deep in the lake can make its tail waters too cold for good fly hatches and trout growth. Many years ago, I took a half-dozen browns in the icy tail waters of the Taylor Dam in Colorado, and found them as emaciated as poorly conditioned pickerel. Some impoundments vary their discharges so much that the temperatures vary radically downstream, offering high winter-cold currents one week and midsummer conditions only a few days later.

One twilight along the White, with the river running swift and full, Dave Whitlock and I fished the shallow edges and quiet eddies behind the deadfalls and snags. There were no fly hatches emerging, and we fished the shelving edges where the currents dropped off into the deeper holes. The fish were holding on the edges of the strongest flows, away from their usual lies in the primary current tongues, and we fished our Muddlers on fast-sinking lines.

It's a little like worm-fishing in a spate, I laughed. *The fish leave their usual holding places, and you find them lying along the edges and behind things that break the flow.* We hooked fish simultaneously.

Just like we're kids again! Whitlock laughed.

The fish continued to take our flies until dark, intercepting the deep bellying swing along the bottom gravel. Each fish took with a sullen pull, like a spring smallmouth taking a crayfish, and when they stopped taking we walked back happily toward the cookfire.

It was different just after daylight. The river flowed low and clear with the penstocks closed, its currents as smooth as a chalkstream. The night mist drifted on the downstream wind, and the silken flow was disturbed by dozens of dimpling trout. The river was warmer with less water coming through the dam, and the trout were rising steadily to the tiny *Tricorythodes* flies in the shallow flats.

Muddler time is over, Whitlock said.

You're right, I agreed. *Last night it was big flies fished on the bottom, and this morning its tiny stuff on 6X!*

It's not unusual! Whitlock nodded.

We fished over highly selective trout until it was time for breakfast and the next day's float, taking several sixteen- to eighteen-inch rainbows on our tiny hen-winged spinners.

That's great fishing, Whitlock said.

We walked back up the gravelbar to breakfast.

It's some change of pace, I agreed happily. *Bottom dredging on big water at nightfall and midging on a shallow flat only twelve hours later—over the same fish on the same pool!*

Tail-water fishing is like that, Whitlock shook his head. *You can get early-season conditions or low-water problems of midsummer any time of year.*

Or time of day! I laughed.

That's right, Whitlock agreed. *It all depends on whether they're storing or releasing water.*

It's tough to switch tactics like that, I said.

You mean big Montana nymphs and bucktails in the morning, Whitlock grinned, *and English chalkstream problems that afternoon?*

Exactly, I laughed.

Such radical variations in flow are a common problem in fishing our tail waters, both in terms of their changed temperatures and their changes in current and depth. Tail-water anglers with experience are always prepared to fish on the bottom, like big-water fishermen from the Klamath to the Yellowstone, or cope with smutting trout on a river that has suddenly dropped when the floodgates of an upstream dam are closed.

Closing the hatches can also affect fly hatches, since a reduction of flow can increase river temperatures enough to trigger a fine rise of fish. There was one afternoon on the White when the river was a swift torrent of water chilled in the depths of Bull Shoals. There were no rises and nothing worked, even the productive sowbug imitations.

But toward evening, the flow lessened imperceptibly and it felt slightly warmer against my legs. My stream thermometer read fifty-seven, six degrees warmer than it had registered an hour before lunch. The river dropped steadily until riffles and pockets emerged from its swift, poker-faced current. It still seemed empty of trout until I saw the first porpoising rise along a deadfall. There was another rise a few feet downstream, and still another quickly followed.

There was a strong swirl in the shallows, and a hatching sedge barely escaped the splash. Soon there were other caddisflies fluttering along the smooth current, and the fish were working steadily to the *Rhyacophila* hatch. We collected a few and found they were a species commonly found in Pennsylvania and Michigan, another relict population the glaciers have isolated in the Ozarks. The solution was a sparsely-dressed Woodcock and Green fished upstream to rising fish, and I took a dozen fine trout before dark. The following night the steady midday flow of the river was not reduced, and we waited in vain for the hatch.

Looks like it's no cigar, I said finally.

Afraid you're right, Whitlock agreed. *Why do you think we had good hatches last night and nothing now?*

Don't know, I waded ashore. *Maybe the dropping water and slightly warming temperatures caused the hatch last night.*

And the high water turned them off? he suggested.

It's possible, I said.

Another effect that impoundments may have is to magnify the relative acidity or alkalinity of their tail waters. New dams often have a short-term fertilizing effect on otherwise acid habitats, improving the fertility of the water downstream. However, decaying vegetation and accumulating silts and detritus in a reservoir will eventually reverse this fertility with their acids. Building dams on alkaline rivers like the Ozark streams can magnify their alkalinity below the dams, gathering minute particles of silt rich in carbonates and bicarbonates and phosphates in their depths. Such accumulations can enrich a tail-water river beyond its original water chemistry, resulting in improved fly life and fish populations, and the Island Park reservoir on the Henry's Fork is a singular example of such alkaline magnification. Another factor is increasing population of slow-water insect life, particularly the minute Diptera larvae and pupae, which often pass through the penstocks unharmed.

Twice I have seen exceptional rises of trout to these diminutive insects on the South Platte in Colorado. There are four reservoirs of the Denver water system on the river: impoundments like Cheeseman, Eleven Mile and Antero dams on the South Platte itself, and the Tarryall impoundment on Tarryall Creek. These reservoirs are known for their rich midge populations, and my experiences with midge pupae coming through the penstocks occurred in both Deckers and Eleven Mile canyons.

Beno Walker, Jim Wallace and I were fishing the Deckers Canyon below the Cheeseman Dam one afternoon, with the reservoir low and the river at minimum flow. Its pools were pondlike and still when we came down the canyon trail to the river. When the evening shadows began to reach across the river, the currents quickened imperceptibly with a slightly increased discharge from the dam, and suddenly the fish were dimpling everywhere.

What are they doing? Beno Walker yelled.

I'm not sure, I shouted back. *Whatever they're taking, it's something small and there's a lot of it.*

You think it's terrestrials?

No, I yelled. *Flying ants can cause this kind of steady feeding, but we could see a swarm of ants.*

What is it then? Walker waded upstream.

Well, I watched several fish dimpling in a lazy rhythm. *It could be midge pupae coming through the dam.*

What should work? Beno asked.

It won't be Humpies or Renegades, I laughed. *Maybe something black on a twenty or twenty-two hook.*

Lets me out, Beno shook his head.

The solution was a black midge pupa on a twenty-two hook, fished in the surface film on a .005 tippet, and I took almost thirty fish before the gathering darkness forced us back up the canyon trail to the car. Similar patterns of cause-and-effect occurred a few weeks later on the South Platte below Eleven Mile Reservoir. However, on that day the river was running high and cold with discharges from the dam, and no fish were working anywhere. The water was perfect for chilling a picnic bottle of Piesporter, and after an hour of fishing along the bottom with nymphs, I gave up and walked back for lunch. The wine was cold and good, perfect for washing down the freshly cut wedges of Gouda and cold sandwiches, and I finally sat watching the current with a cup of coffee freshly brewed over a fire of dried beaver cuttings.

There's a rise! I thought aloud.

The river had dropped slightly during lunch, and although no hatching flies were visible on the water, the number of rises increased steadily. The current continued to fall, and it ebbed slightly while the trout settled into a steady pattern of gentle rise forms. It soon became a fine rise of fish that covered the pool.

Time to try them, I whispered to myself.

It was a productive afternoon, and I took almost forty decent fish before it was time to drive back to Colorado Springs. It was a little like the rise of fish in the Deckers Canyon, yet it was different too. The Deckers water had been extremely low, and the partial release of water had carried thousands and thousands of tiny Diptera through the floodgates. The heavy discharge through the Eleven Mile Dam had been saturated with tiny pupal forms all day, but its temperatures were too cold for the fish to take them. When the gates were partially closed, the river dropped and grew warm enough to accelerate their metabolic rhythms, and the trout fed greedily on the tiny flies.

Another intriguing effect of dams on our trout streams is also found on the South Platte above Eleven Mile. Its large population of big rainbows cannot migrate downstream to spawn, and they run upstream into the serpentine headwaters of the South Platte at Hartsel. The spawning run occurs in April and May, delayed by the altitude of 7,000 feet, and it would normally occur during unfishable water levels except for the impoundment at Antero Junction.

The spring thaw usually discolors these headwaters with snowmelt, but the Antero Reservoir acts as a huge stilling basin for the first weeks of the runoff. It collects the turbid snow water behind its earthworks, permitting the South Platte to flow clear and surprisingly low during its spring spawning run of rainbows. Fishing them is a little like stalking, since they are often clearly visible in the shallows, and expert Colorado fishermen like James Poor and Peter Van Gytenbeek find weighted nymphs are best. The Platte is still cold at those altitudes in late spring, and working a fly slowly along the bottom is deadly. Poor likes a pair of stonefly nymphs of his own design, imitating the big *Pteronarcys* flies at two stages of their nymphal growth. Van Gytenbeek likes a roughly dubbed shrimp imitation, heavily weighted and dressed on ten and twelve hooks.

It was on the South Platte tail waters that I took a lucky trophy-size brown one spring, and the fish was the result of a good natured challenge delivered at lunch in the Hartsel Hotel. We had finished a morning's fishing on the Big Ranch below town, and had left our gear at the main house. The challenge was delivered by my old friend Philip Wright, and his badgering began when we ordered our hamburgers. Donald Zahner and Charles Myers, the fishing writer for the *Denver Post,* had happily joined the fun before we ordered dessert.

It's a real test of skill, Wright explained teasingly. *It's a big brown that lives right here in Hartsel.*

He holds under a log below the bridge, somebody added.

Breaks them off! another voice said.

You have to accept a challenge like that! Myers laughed and drained his Coors. *Remember the Code of the West.*

That's right! Zahner insisted.

The waitress arrived with apple pie and coffee. *Ridiculous!* I shook my head. *The fish is probably gone!*

No, Myers said. *Somebody lost him just last week.*

You're chicken, Zahner chided.

But I've left all my gear at the ranch, I parried their joking helplessly. *My waders and everything!*

You've got your flies! Wright said gleefully. *Your fishing vest is still in my car!*

And you don't need waders in the meadow! Myers added.

But I don't have my rod! I said.

No problem, Zahner finished his pie with a flourish and ignored the check. *You can use one of my rods.*

That's some handicap! I grumbled.

You can't chicken out now, Wright cackled. *We've got everything you need for this fish—you can't back off!*

Zahner paid my check and pushed me outside. *Zahner,* I protested weakly, *how did I get into this?*

You're the fastest gun in town! Myers grinned.

Code of the West! Zahner laughed.

We walked down to the bridge with a surprising crowd from the hotel bar, and I rigged Zahner's rod with a fresh twelve foot leader tapered to 6X.

Your rod's handicap enough, I handed Zahner his tangled leader, *without giving me that mine-shaft cable for a tippet!*

He knows how to hurt a guy! Zahner winced.

The river winds down a gravel shallows from the highway bridge, carving a deep hole in the bend downstream. There was a huge deadfall wedged in the deepest currents, its silvery branches throbbing in the flow. The open meadow offered no cover, and a standing fisherman is clearly silhouetted against the sky. It was impossible to get close enough to cast without an infantry-style approach, and I crawled stealthily through the bunchgrass. The best cast was across the grass, angled slightly upstream to get the maximum fly swing along the fallen tree. The river flowed deep and smooth along undercut banks.

You sure there's a big fish here? I asked them.

It's true, Myers nodded.

The odds of moving the fish seemed astronomical, but I rose to one knee and started false casting, once the nymph and leader were properly soaked and sinking. The fly worked out and settled well above the log, the belly of the line falling in the grass, and the current worked it deep along the shelving gravel.

It stopped its swing under the deadfall. *Well,* I thought wryly, *that does it for today—it's snagged on the log!*

But there was a huge splash, and a spade-size tail broke water along the deadfall as a heavy fish forced the straining rod into a tight circle. It bolted upstream into the shallows, and I worried it with a nagging pressure from below. The fish chose to fight both me and the riffling current for several minutes, and its strength had weakened when it turned back to its holding lie under the log. It was a fatal mistake, and I turned it short of the snags, working it back with the current.

The remaining few minutes of the fight were routine, although we had forgotten a landing net. The crowd gathered behind me when the big brown finally surrendered in the gravelly shallows, and I lifted it briefly from the water before releasing it.

That's a good fish! somebody said.

He'll go twenty-two or twenty-three inches, Charles Myers shook his head in amazement. *He's huge!*

Never thought you had a prayer, Wright laughed.

Makes two of us! I sighed.

Putah Creek is a tail-water fishery sixty miles north of San Francisco. It was created after the construction of the Berryessa Reservoir. Its currents are like a wine-country chalkstream, rich in weeds and fly hatches and trout. Its trout are hard-fished and selective, and each season it surrenders a few rainbows between six and eight pounds on flies. There are also some fine brown trout, sleek and a little silvery on a rich diet of scuds and sowbugs, but these fish are caught less frequently.

Last fall I fished the little Putah with Hal Janssen and David Inks, since a week of heavy rains had forced the steelhead rivers over their banks and into the vineyards. The runoff was being stored behind the Berryessa Dam, and although the creek was a little milky, it was surprisingly low and fishable. The current was so imperceptible that the first big pool below the dam was a still mirror surrounded by weeds, its flow suppressed in the thick beds of coontail. During normal water levels, several channels left the pool, with good trout holding normally in the flowages between the weeds. The pool itself was a smooth strong-flowing reach of water with its fish facing the current.

Well, Janssen laughed. *It's fishable enough.*

It used to be stream fishing, Inks shook his head in agreement, *but tonight it's almost like a lake.*

How do you fish it in higher water? I asked.

It has heavy hatches of small mayflies and caddis, Janssen replied, *and we let our little imitations swing with the current to suggest their swimming nymphs and pupae.*

What about damselfly nymphs?

When they're gathering to hatch along the weeds, Janssen said, *it's one of the best big flies we fish.* He searched his fly books and gave me one of his pale green damselfly nymphs.

What have they been taking? I asked.

We've been getting them on Pheasant Tail nymphs, Inks said, *and on the little Puyans' Hare's Ear patterns.*

They're still hatching, Janssen pointed.

Let's try them, I said.

It was difficult wading out through the densely matted weeds, and we took up positions slightly back from the open water of the pondlike channel. Janssen watched me shiver with a sudden chill when I reached a casting point waist-deep in the weeds.

It's pretty cold for a sunfish creek, he laughed.

The evening wind eddied down the valley, riffling the surface of the stream and carrying the muffled roar of tailrace water from the dam.

It's cold enough all right, my teeth almost chattered as the icy chill penetrated through my waders. *It's amazing how a dam tail water can turn a warm sunfish creek into an ice box!*

Hal Janssen dropped his nymph upstream along the weeds, let it settle a few seconds, and started a slow hand-twist retrieve. Its left-hand rhythms had barely started when I saw Janssen raise his rod, and a good rainbow cartwheeled out in a series of jumps.

That didn't take long! I yelled.

It's always like that on Putah, Inks laughed. *Janssen fishes it just like a vacuum cleaner!*

Good thing he releases them! I said.

Their predictions were correct, in terms of both fly patterns and tactics. We fished the little Pheasant Tail nymphs, their bodies weighted with copper wire, and Puyans' Hare's Ear imitations over a foundation of delicate fuse wire. The flies were tiny, dressed on eighteen and twenty wet-fly hooks, and they sank readily after our leaders were wet enough. Our tactics were simple enough. We merely fished a series of clockwise and counterclockwise casts from each position, letting the nymphs sink and fishing them back slowly.

David Inks took a fish on his third cast, working his nymph in the outlet channel below an immense tangle of fallen trees, and on my third cast I hooked a fifteen-inch brown.

Didn't take him long to get the drill, Janssen shouted.

The fish was superbly conditioned, and it fought me stubbornly until it finally surrendered, and I could skate it toward me across the surface of the weeds.

Okay, I protested. *I've got this fish, but how do I release it from this nightmare of weeds?*

Throw it! Janssen laughed.

You can't throw a fish back! I shouted back. *You're supposed to let them go gently.* Inks was laughing across the lagoon.

That works when you can reach the water, he interjected, *but you're ten feet away and up to your scuppers in weeds!*

So what now? I groaned. The trout hung limp in my left hand.

It's an old Putah Creek method, Janssen explained. *It's a little like a lateral!*

Football lateral? I choked back my laughter.

But gently! Inks advised.

We took twenty or thirty fish between us that evening, fishing our tiny nymphs in a patient fan pattern, and letting them sink a few seconds before starting a retrieve. It looked easy when you had the problems solved, but we met another fisherman on the path who had gone fishless.

You guys get your limits? he asked.

We did pretty well, Janssen admitted, *but we put them all back.* The other fisherman looked puzzled and frowned.

What did you use? he asked. *Salmon eggs?*

No, Inks smiled, *flies.*

That's funny, the fisherman shook his head. *I tried a Royal Coachman and Rio Grande King, and it didn't work.*

Better luck next time, Janssen smiled.

It was Russell MacGregor who first introduced me to the Lackawaxen, which was a fine smallmouth stream when Zane Grey lived near its junction with the Delaware. The Wallenpaupack Reservoir a few miles upstream from the Lackawaxen, which dammed the Wallenpaupack Creek into a sizable lake, completely changed the Lackawaxen and its ecology. It has become a fine trout stream over the past thirty years, with a large population of rainbows in its fast-water mileage, and some huge browns in its pools. MacGregor introduced me to the superb reach of water where the tumbling little Blooming Grove reaches the Lackawaxen. We fished it each evening from his cottage at the Forest Lake Club, working Forest Lake in the mornings with bass bugs, and we had fine sport with both trout and smallmouths. MacGregor has fished and loved the lower Lackawaxen for many years.

It's a moody river, MacGregor explained one afternoon on his porch, looking north toward the Catskills on the horizon. *Its flow and temperature are pretty erratic.*

What times seem best? I asked.

Depends on the time of year, MacGregor took my glass back inside to the bar. *The fish come pretty well in the spring, when the water from the dam is flowing much warmer than the stream itself.*

Starts them feeding?

That's right! MacGregor continued. *When river levels and temperatures in the Lackawaxen are just right for trout—between fifty and sixty-five degrees—the cold water from the Wallenpaupack can turn the fish off!*

But the discharges can keep the Lackawaxen fishing well through July and August, MacGregor returned with my scotch-and-soda, *when the other streams are too low and warm.*

That's right, MacGregor agreed.

When do the fish feed best? I watched a pileated woodpecker working on a dead oak. *When the water is rising or falling?*

The woodpecker hammered noisily. *That varies too,* MacGregor said thoughtfully. *When the river itself is right, the temperature gets better when they close the dam—and when it's too low and warm in August, a little cold water coming down starts the fish moving again.*

That's worth remembering. I took a long sip of scotch. *Where do the fish lie in high and low water?*

When the Lackawaxen is high and cold, he said, *the fish lie well down the pools and hold on the bottom—and some are found along the sides, in the eddies and behind boulders where the flow is reduced.*

What about low water? I asked.

The fish are looking for both food and oxygen then, MacGregor finished. *You find them in the fast shallows.*

And right up in the throats of the pools? I asked.

Right! MacGregor nodded.

Later that month, MacGregor introduced me to the finest tail-water fishery in our eastern states, the big water on the Delaware between Hancock and Long Eddy. It is a river of swift half-mile riffles and mile-long pools, and only twenty-five years ago it held a population of smallmouths and walleyed pike. There were always a few trout in the cool flowages of tributaries like the Lackawaxen and Callicoon. But after the completion of the Peapacton Reservoir above Shinhopple, on the East Branch of the Delaware, the river ran cold and strong from the dam tail waters to the spreading riffles above Port Jervis.

That evening we fished a sweeping waist-deep riffle that surged past our waders in the twilight, and when a heavy hatch of big *Isonychia* drakes came off in the shallows, the big rainbows started rolling and slashing on top. It was easier to find rising trout than to find a way to reach them. The current was swift and strong, with treacherous holes that have trapped a lot of anglers over the years, but I took a pair of three-pound rainbows.

It was fifteen years ago that we fished the big riffles at Narrowsburg and Barryville, and trout have come to dominate the fishery since then. Since the Cannonsville Dam was filled on the West Branch of the Delaware above Deposit, the main river below Hancock and Fish Eddy receives another source of cold dam tailings. Its population of big rainbows is remarkable, and there are fly hatches of incredible diversity and numbers. During hot weather, big trout abandon the lower Beaverkill for the colder East Branch of the Delaware, and trout migrating into winter holes in the Delaware often decide to remain there, particularly since the Beaverkill itself often becomes warm enough for smallmouths, between Cook's Falls and Baxters.

It's so rich with fly life, Harry Darbee explains wryly, *the stocked rainbows migrate through on their way to salt water and decide to stay—maybe it's the raw sewage from all those little towns.*

Beautiful! Gardner Grant winced.

Gardner Grant is the energetic president of the Theodore Gordon Flyfishers, but he spends so much time fishing the Delaware and talking about its rainbows that he sounds like a public relations man for the region. Grant worked as a canoe-trip guide in Maine during his college vacations from Yale, and his skills in travelling a swift river are perfectly suited to fishing the Delaware.

Grant likes the big flats on bends away from the highway, like the five-mile bend above Callicoon, or the fifteen miles of river between Hancock and Long Eddy.

It's another world on those bends away from the road, Grant sighs happily, *it's a wilderness only two hours from New York.*

We fished one of those mile-long flats one evening in late summer, hooking a half-dozen fat rainbows that accelerated downstream on blistering runs that spooled deep into the backing. It is not easy fishing. It calls for a willingness to wade deep; and the double haul is almost mandatory. The favorite pattern for Grant and most of the other regulars, who call themselves the Delaware Navy, is the familiar Adams dry-fly dressing in relatively small sizes. Leaders are usually 4X or 5X, since a free-wheeling Delaware rainbow will often strip enough fly line and backing from the reel that its dragging in the current will break a finer tippet. But when the river is running clear and right for wading, and the hatches are good enough to coax the big rainbows to surface feed, the Delaware can provide exceptional sport.

Is it really that good? somebody asked.

It's a good thing George Washington didn't fish, Gardner Grant laughed over a late supper in the Antrim Lodge.

What's that got to do with anything? I interrupted.

Never get him across the Delaware to Trenton with all these big rainbows around! he explained wryly and sipped his Chivas.

Funny, I grumbled.

Several years ago, my good friend David Rose was trapped by rising waters from the dam on the Housatonic in Connecticut. Rose was a beginning fisherman then, and he failed to hear the warning siren or respond to the river clues when they came. The first clue is always a change in the sound of a river when it starts to rise. Its rising level of sound is quickly followed with visual clues, like a deadfall starting to throb in a gathering current, or a shallow riffle deepening into a swift-flowing run. Dam tailings often reveal a slight milkiness too, perhaps from silts displaced by the rising water.

Experienced fishermen can feel a rising current in the subtle change of pressure against their legs, but a beginner can miss these warnings. David Rose scrambled to a jumble of big rocks nearby, but he quickly realized that the river was still rising, and that there was no safety there. The current was already dangerously swift, but he floundered ashore with only a bad soaking.

Fishing can be dangerous, Rose laughs today. *But there were moments out there when I thought I wouldn't make it back!*

Rising water in a scheduled release from a dam can be dangerous, but a knowledgeable fisherman can learn to use it to his advantage too. Water released from a dam does not flood an entire river at once, and its crest travels rather slowly downstream. This past spring I learned some interesting lessons about tail-waters on the Au Sable in Michigan.

The big rainbows from Lake Huron come into the Au Sable on a fine spawning run in late April, travelling like salmon in small schools of three- to twenty-pound fish. These fish enter the estuary at Oscoda, ascending the lower river slowly until they are finally stopped below the Foote Dam only six miles above the lake. The engineers at Foote Dam store water during the night, when the power demand is relatively low, and start releasing it through their turbines early in the morning. When the tail waters are low just after daylight, you can wade clear across the river in the shallows, and you can see the fish clearly from the parking area fifty feet above the tailrace gravelbars.

That morning I was meeting Gary Schnicke, who is the chief state biologist on the Au Sable, for a session on Michigan steelheads. It was cold and clear at daylight when I left the Fellows cottage on the North Branch, driving east through the Michigan timber country toward Oscoda. There are several reservoirs on the Au Sable below Mio, storing and releasing water until it finally comes through the powerhouse at Foote Dam. We stopped in a diner at Mio for breakfast, and after daylight we drove east on the Guennie Road. It was bright red along the horizon, and there were dozens of deer browsing along the shoulders.

The deer smell rain coming, Schnicke said, *and they're out foraging to get their bellies full before the weather turns sour.*

Then it's changing! I said.

We reached the dam and rigged our tackle.

Look down there, Schnicke pointed to the tailrace shallows. *Those wakes are spawning rainbows, and when you see angry swirls and splashes, it's the cockfish chasing away a smaller male or an egg-stealing sucker or bass!*

There were surprisingly large swirls and restless wakes of big fish showing everywhere below the dam.

You mean those rolling fish are all big steelhead trout? I asked.

That's right, Schnicke laughed, *and big steelheads too!*

Why are we standing around up here? I asked.

Gary Schnicke chuckled and led the way down the steep clay banks to the river.

It's a man-made fishery, he explained. *We plant the steelhead smolts at the dam and harvest them when they finally come back from Lake Huron.*

What about all this spawning activity?

The fish sure try, he acknowledged. *But they're not very successful with these cycles of rising and falling water.*

Hard on fly life too? I asked.

You bet! he said.

We'd better get fishing! I pointed to a school of big rainbows lying in the shallows. *How much time before they open the gates?*

We've got about an hour, Schnicke replied.

And we get more fishing time by driving downstream to stay ahead of the high water? I asked. *How much?*

About two more hours, he said.

The men who know their local tail-water fishing understand both the cycles of storage and discharge at the dam itself, and the time it takes a surge of released water to reach the better riffles and pools. That morning I took a small three-pound steelhead on a big streamer in the tailrace, and Schnicke lost a larger fish in the bend downstream. When the siren finally sounded at the powerhouse, we fished another twenty minutes before Schnicke came briskly up the bank.

Time to head downstream! he yelled.

We drove down the Oscoda road until Schnicke turned into the trees toward the river. There were several cars and campers where we parked, and the young biologist swiftly locked his car and started down the trail at a brisk dog trot.

The Au Sable comes down through the trees in a sweeping bend, flowing deep and strong against a high clay bank. We walked the high gravel bank looking for fish, until Schnicke finally spotted several big rainbows over a shoal of pea gravel.

You stay here and fish these, he pointed out five steelheads, *and I'll find another bunch upstream.*

The river flowed smooth and relatively shallow, with no trace of the turbidity generated when the flow quickened in the tailrace below the dam. The rainbows below me were big, and I could see them clearly as I worked my big nymph in front of them on the gravelbar. Although we both hooked big steelheads that came off on the second or third jumps, we failed to land a single trout that morning. But we had two full hours of casting time before the river finally rose and became unfishable, and I learned an important lesson about fishing tail waters.

Since the simple demand of future populations for potable water will unquestionably require more and more reservoirs to store seasonal rains and spring runoffs, we will probably see many more tail-water fisheries created in years to come. Some will restore rivers that supported trout a century ago, while others will transform warm-water fisheries into prime trout water. It is even possible that reservoirs could create trout habitat of whole cloth, like the Amawalk Outlet which connects two reservoirs in the New York water system.

It's remarkable! Gardner Grant describes the Amawalk enthusiastically. *It's less than an hour from Broadway and Times Square, but with fly-only and no-killing, it provides surprisingly good fishing over a lot of good trout.*

It's perhaps our oldest tail-water fishery, I said, *and tail waters may be a prelude to the future—particularly near major cities.*

Absolutely! Grant agreed.

9. Field Problems in Fishing the High-Lake Country

It is sagebrush foothill country south of Colorado Springs, with ponderosa and pinon trees on the boulder-strewn ridges. The parched, gravelly soil is broken with rattlesnake outcroppings above the river, and the road drops down toward the bridge over the swift-flowing Arkansas.

The village lies across the bridge in the distance, and the Sangre de Cristo Mountains lie beyond their arid foothill ranges. There are alpine lakes there, hidden in the lodgepole shoulders and basins at high altitude. The dirt county road climbs toward the south from the village, through the cottonwood and scrub-oak bottoms beyond the Arkansas, past the tidy houses and abandoned coke kilns at Florence.

The county road winds and switchbacks almost lazily toward the sagebrush foothills, working into the sandy arroyos and their pale chalk-colored bluffs. The sagebrush hills are honeycombed and scarred with the sulphur-colored tailings of abandoned silver mines, and the sculptured cliffs are polished by the wind. Twenty-five miles later, the dusty hills drop behind and the county road reaches straight across the valley floor. Its prairie is pale bunchgrass there, sprawling almost fifty miles from Cotopaxi on the Arkansas to the high-basin headwaters of the Huerfano. Its wind-swept emptiness is starkly beautiful.

The rotting skeleton of the mining pit-head is silhouetted against the morning light beyond the empty town. Its houses lie ahead across the buffalo grass flats of the valley floor. Past the weathered tombstones of the cemetery, its intricate wrought-iron fencework choked with tumbleweeds, lies the half-deserted mining camp at Silvercliff.

It's a fascinating town, said Beno Walker.

We passed the first rough-sawed outbuildings of the town. Its streets and decaying houses are solitary echoes of the silver boom almost a century ago in this barren wind-swept valley. The county road reaches west toward the serrated parapets of the high Sangre de Cristo Mountains. Their crenellated summits were almost ruby-colored with the rising sun.

They deserve their name, I said softly.

Beno Walker was staring absently into the dusty streets. *What's that?* he asked. *What deserves what name?*

Sangre de Cristo, I replied. *The Blood of Christ.*

You're right, he agreed.

The blood-colored sunrise on the high mountains faded as quickly as it had formed. The morning wind stirred in the prairie bottoms. Two mallards exploded from an irrigation canal, flew swiftly toward the north in a climbing turn, and wheeled back on the wind. Magpies were quarreling over a dead jackrabbit in the road ahead, and they rose awkwardly from their carrion. The magpies watched sullenly from the fence line and settled again when we had passed.

The simple houses and skeletal false-front buildings of Silvercliff are like gravestones. The school and courthouse buildings are solemn bench marks from the past, and the abandoned adobe-walled saloons are empty too. The dusty boardwalks and hitching rails have been weathered silver in the wind. The streetscape looks like a moody Burchfield painting, empty of people and filled with a strange melancholia.

Lonely country, I thought.

Two cowboys were walking their ponies in the dusty street, their sweat-stained hats and sheepskin jackets turned against the wind. It is a long, cold ride that starts before daylight from the outlying ranches, even in the midsummer months.

Beno waved and one cowboy nodded back.

Beyond the outbuildings of the town, willows line the meandering course of Grape Creek, and the road starts climbing slowly toward the mountains. Creek willows and cottonwoods on the valley floor gradually change to ponderosas on the lower slopes. The jeep road switchbacks steeply along the shoulder of the mountain, climbing through the quaking aspens into the first stands of lodgepole pines. Hermit Creek tumbles far below the road, and where it plunges and falls down a steep outcropping of granite, the jeep road finally becomes deeply rutted and impassable, and the foot trail begins.

Last stop, I laughed. *Everybody out!*

Fishing the high-lake country is a horseback or backpacking sport at timberline altitudes where summer is a brief three-week season between ice-out and the first hard frosts in late August. Many high lakes are not entirely free of winter in late July, and there are still snowbanks where a fisherman can chill his trout like a refrigerator. August is the best month for the high-lake country, and even then the nights are cold above 10,000 feet. Our western mountains are full of such lakes.

There are superb back-country lakes throughout the entire system of mountains along the Pacific coast, with the golden-trout waters of the Sierra Nevada perhaps the most famous. The Rocky Mountain escarpment offers countless high lakes too, from the foothill ranges of New Mexico all the way to the Brooks Range in Alaska. Some of the best high-country lakes are in Colorado, particularly in the Sangre de Cristo Mountains and the plateau wilderness above Rifle and Trapper's Lake and Meeker. Other fine high lakes in Colorado are found in the Grand Mesa country west of Gunnison, the beautiful Elk Mountain wilderness areas southwest of Aspen, the Flattops wilderness, and the timberline backcountry that surrounds the Mount of the Holy Cross.

Wyoming offers some fine high-lake fishing in the Snowy Range behind Laramie, and particularly in the majestic Wind River Mountains southeast of Jackson Hole. The Wind River Country is accessible to fishermen only with horseback or backpacking, and there are a number of reliable outfitters in foothill towns like Dubois and Pinedale and Lander who know its high-lake secrets. Montana and Idaho offer other timberline fishing too, in the Anaconda country and the Sawtooth headwaters of the Salmon wilderness, and in the towering Bitterroot and Beartooth mountains farther north.

The high-country is still a remote, unspoiled world for a fisherman willing to work for his sport, since hiking into its alpine lakes is never easy, and there are saddle sores for the less hardy souls who join the pack trains. Weather at timberline is fickle at best, and even a midsummer day can turn subarctic and stormy without warning. Fishing at these altitudes can test your character, particularly in the party that is ill-equipped for bad weather and cold temperatures, and the lakes themselves are changeable and moody.

Some of the best are in the Sangre de Cristo country of Colorado, and it was getting warmer when we finally left the car. It is a steep climb into Hermit Lake, the first of a three-lake chain that stairsteps up a series of timberline basins. The foot trail works up the first escarpment into a mountain park thick with silver-bark aspens, their pale leaves fluttering in the early morning wind.

Two mule deer were drinking in the creek that morning, and they melted into the aspen thickets. The lakes were still two miles and another 1,000 feet higher, and although they do not offer memorable sport, each has a singular character typical of high lakes everywhere.

Hermit Lake lies at about 11,000 feet, surrounded with tall coniferous trees except along its south shore, where a huge rockslide reaches deep into the water. Horseshoe is a crescent-shaped lake at almost 12,000 feet in the treeless crater of an extinct volcano, and little Shelf Lake lies still higher, on a barren shoulder of the ridge above Hermit.

The trail crosses a series of high benches. Its steep climb is gentler once its first half mile is covered, crossing a partially timbered meadow, and then it climbs higher into the second basin beyond. It winds upward through narrow pathways in the boulders until it reaches a grove of firs and Engelmann spruce. There are immense deadfalls beside the trail there, weathered the color of fine pewter.

Beno Walker stopped to catch his wind. *You bring up the rear and collect the gear I drop,* he grinned.

Great! I sighed. *Who picks up behind me?*

It's a problem, he laughed.

The way my legs feel now we could starve and freeze with what we're still carrying when we finally get to Hermit! My mouth tasted like a pocketful of old copper pennies. *This load could make a pack mule quit.*

Well, Beno said, *let's saddle up!*

Steep rockslides lie across the valley, echoing the primordial earthquakes that originally shaped these lakes. Hermit Lake lay ahead now, glittering through its dense veil of spruce and pines. Chipmunks and marmots scurried among the outcroppings and rockfalls to reach their hiding places as we approached, and a red-tailed hawk circled lazily on the warming wind that stirred and rose from the valley floor.

The sun was higher now.

It is best to make your camp first in the backcountry and fish later. It is a matter of self-discipline. When you know your flaws of character, you also know that the fishing will mesmerize you well into the twilight hours, until it is too dark to make a proper camp and gather enough wood for cooking and a night fire. The understandable urge to start fishing after the climb must be check-reined.

We staked out the Bauer tension-tents in a sheltering copse of tall spruce trees, where the Hermit outlet gathered and spilled its currents through a jackstraw tangle of logs. We checked the trees for signs of decay and sited our camp some distance from a large dead spruce, for safety in case it fell in a sudden high-country storm.

There was still a single large snowbank in a hollow sheltered from the sun, and I shaped a cooling hole for our food with my belt knife. We stripped the big deadfalls of three nights' worth of firewood, and racked it carefully between two trees. Beno dug a firepit and lined it with stones, making sure they were not taken from the creek, and picked a site that would carry the cooking smoke away from our tents—both on the morning winds that always rose from the valley floor, and the cool evening winds that eddied back down the mountain.

Hermit is a typical mountain lake slightly below timberline, formed in some ancient rockslide that dammed the flow of its inlets to form a small depression that gathered the glacial melt. Its waters are slightly acid with the detritus of pine needles and rotting deadfalls and the silts of centuries. Like all mountain lakes, its best fishing is generally found at the inlets and outlets, where the population of still-water insects is augmented with current-loving species. Spawning undoubtedly occurs in the shoal that spreads its miniature alluvial fan of pea-gravel below the main inlet, which lies near the northwest extremity of the lake. The south shoreline is a steep rockslide, its submerged boulders dark with algal growth and bright *Dichelyma* mosses. It is a rocky shore too deep for good photosynthesis and heavy insect populations. The remaining shoreline from the toe of the rockslide, and around past the outlet along the eastern and northern shallows to the principal inlet is densely lined with trees. These tree-sheltered shallows receive the most warmth from the midday and afternoon sunlight, and shelter the most nymphs and crustaceans. The brook trout prefer its slightly acid waters, although the lack of fertility results in a somewhat stunted population of eight- to twelve-inch fish. Hermit is also deep enough to prevent excessive winterkill, but it lacks sufficient shallows and alkalinity to sustain a really first-rate trout fishery.

The principal diet forms in a timberline lake like Hermit are the slow-water nymphs, larvae and pupal forms of the aquatic insects. Its waters are too acid for heavy populations of the little *Gammarus* and *Hyalella* shrimps. Minor populations of the current-loving aquatic insects are also found in the inlet and outlet flowages. Although they are minute, the larval threadworms and surface-film pupae of the Diptera midges are perhaps the most common high-country diet of the trout, and the wind can carry such pupae from the shallows into the lake itself.

My best sport on the timberline lakes has invariably come with nymphs or larval and pupal imitations fished just under the surface. Sometimes a big weighted pattern like a Fledermaus is very effective, fished with a sinking line and a slow hand-twist retrieve along the dark detritus of the bottom. Freshwater shrimps are also found at these lower depths, and the swimming nymphs of various mayflies, damselflies, and dragonflies are also common in our mountain waters. Beetle larvae and caddisflies are relatively common subaquatic forms in our still-water biosystems, and during a hatching period, properly tied nymphs fished just under the surface can be deadly. Midge pupae should be fished dead drift just under the film, casting your imitations with a greased leader well ahead of a cruising fish. Perhaps the single most effective high-lake pattern in my fly books is the western Gray Nymph, tied in both weighted types for working deep and light-wire versions for fishing in the film, and in hook sizes four through twenty-four. Its larger sizes can suggest a fat Anisoptera nymph clambering along the bottom, and its tiny versions can serve as a workable midge pupa.

Hatching caddisfly pupae are another diet form extremely important in the high country, and dark little wet flies with mottled body hackles are effective then. Patterns like the traditional Partridge and Orange, Woodcock and Hare's Mask, Grouse and Green, and Partridge and Olive can prove deadly at such times. Trichoptera imitations should be fished under the surface with a slow, teasing retrieve during a sedge hatch.

Dry-fly fishing can prove effective when there is a hatch of sedges or *Chironomus* midges or speckle-winged mayflies, and when the fish are taking them visibly, but usually a high lake can be fished more effectively with wet flies and nymphs.

There were many experiences on Hermit in the years we lived in Colorado Springs, but the afternoon that is most memorable occurred on my backpacking trip with Beno Walker. Once our camp was ready, the wind dropped down until the surface of the lake was still and mirror smooth.

Look over there! Beno pointed suddenly. *They've started rising along those fallen trees!* The rises became more frequent, and dozens of trout were working along the deadfalls.

No rises in open water, I thought aloud.

You're right, Beno agreed. *The rises are all right there in the fallen tree trunks—what're the fish doing?*

Let's study them and find out, I said.

We walked down toward the shallows, where a tangle of dead trees lay in the outlet. Two fish bolted into deep water when our shadows touched the lake, and I squatted on my heels to study the shallows. The smooth trunks of the fallen trees were covered with pale green algae, and about five minutes passed before the lake revealed its secrets.

Look at these logs, I said suddenly.

Mixed with the bright tufts of pale algae along the rotting trunks were hundreds of olive green damselfly nymphs, climbing imperceptibly toward the waterline or simply waiting for their final cycle of emergence. The slender nymphs hung so motionless along the trees that only the delicate sculling motions of their abdominal gills betrayed them. Their protective coloring was so subtle and effective that only when a hatching nymph had crawled into the surface film to split its subaquatic skin was its presence revealed. There were literally hundreds of them.

What's there? Beno asked.

Green damselfly nymphs! I pointed. *Hundreds there on the logs, and they're getting ready to hatch!*

No wonder all the fish are there! he said.

Using a bright apple green imitation, we took dozens of hungry brook trout that afternoon and evening, although none exceeded fifteen inches. Brook trout thrive in such habitat, their population outstripping their surroundings until there are too many fish for the forage, and their average size is small. The heavy damselfly hatch lasted only a day.

We started early on our third morning for Horseshoe Lake, high in the extinct crater above Hermit. The trail is gentle enough in the beginning, climbing a little through the thick-trunked spruce forest until it suddenly turns north, and switchbacks up a steep shoulder of the mountain. The trees are thinner there. The trail seems to drop down again beyond the treeline, where it traverses the hogback saddle of a ridge that leads toward the final rim that conceals the lake.

The climb is hard work in the thinning air above 11,000 feet, and both Hermit and its sheltering trees lay far below in the first real basin above the valley floor. The trail works along the last sheltering rim, through rocky meadows filled with tiny wildflowers. It was still early morning, with the rising sun touching only the barren summit ridges another 2,000 feet above the trail, and the forest-rimmed shoreline of Hermit was still in darkness 1,000 feet behind.

There are many stories about the big rainbows in Horseshoe. It lies in the remains of an extinct crater, its glittering water in a ragged half-moon shape covering several acres. It has no inlets once the early summer snowmelt is finished, and in August there is barely an outlet trickle. Its lack of autumn spawning habitat means that brook trout were never stocked there from the federal hatcheries during the Depression years, and its ecology has all the components necessary for trophy-size fish.

The lake is deep in its center, and in the narrowing bay below the mountain wall that rises toward the summit. The outlet corner is relatively shallow, and the north shore has a rich shelf of marl that drops suddenly into ink-blue depths in the middle of the lake. The shoreline and its surrounding basin are treeless. The rocky meadows rise in ragged terraces, boggy with snowmelt and seepage along the north side. It was barren and beautiful, and we stood on the rim above the lake, watching the first morning wind stir and riffle its smooth surface.

Horseshoe may have limited spawning conditions, but it has everything else to support big fish. It has deep water to minimize winterkill when its thickly frozen surface is buried under snow, completely shutting out sunlight and photosynthesis. It has sufficient shallows to support extensive forage populations for its trout, and its heavy deposits of marl provide rich fertility along its north side.

Should've seen it! The old man had told me one winter morning at Saguache, when we had been jump shooting mallards in the San Luis country beyond the Sangre de Cristo range. *My mules crossed the last ridge just before noon, and Horseshoe was like a mirror—riding down from the rim you could see every pebble and stone in the shallows, and suddenly I saw them—rainbows like crocodiles in schools of five or six fish.*

Really big rainbows? we asked excitedly.

Big rainbows! the old prospector cackled. *Ain't many brutes like them Horseshoe rainbows left!*

We hiked down into the crater and shouldered off our packs and fishing gear in a sheltered place among the rocks. The wind was lightly riffling the lake, obscuring its depths and its fish from our scrutiny. Twice I saw strong rise forms well out in the choppy surface of the lake, but a high-density sinking line made more sense than a dry fly.

I strung my rod with a fast-sinking Dacron line and walked around the rocky outlet shoreline to stalk the marl shallows along the north side of the lake. It was impossible to discern a cruising fish, and I began to cast a clockwise fan pattern, prospecting geometrically with my weighted nymphs at random. Each cast worked out some eighty feet and dropped a big nymph beyond the marl shelf, where the water looked deep and swimming-pool green. There was nothing for a half hour, and then there came a strong pull that telegraphed back into the rod. The big trout gave a wrenching wallow just under the surface, showed its spade-size tail in a huge splash, and bored deep off the marl shallows. It angrily stripped line into the backing, and then the line suddenly went slack.

Damn! I shouted unhappily. *Broke me off!*

Twenty minutes later I hooked another rainbow of about four pounds that cartwheeled high into the air and bolted laterally along the shelf, the backing making a high-pitched tearing vibration where it sliced sideways through the water. Suddenly there was a guitar-string sound as the singing leader touched a sharp-edged piece of fractured lava, and the big rainbow was suddenly gone.

Lost him too! I yelled in exasperation.

Let's try the third lake, Beno suggested. *We can give these brutes a rest and fish them again on our way down.*

Good, I agreed. *Let's try it!*

Shelf Lake was a longer climb than it looked, over a saddle and ridge of broken outcroppings, and into the strange balconylike hollow that held the relatively shallow lake. Two fishermen were coming back down the trail, and we met them on the rocky little rim above the basin that sheltered Horseshoe.

It's no good! they said.

Have you been fishing it? I asked.

We hiked up directly from Hermit yesterday, and it's no use to climb up there this year! added the second angler unhappily.

What's wrong? asked Beno.

It's too shallow! the first man replied. *The snow covered the ice so thickly that it shut out the light—and the trout were all winterkilled.*

How could you tell? I asked.

It's dead! they explained sadly. *There are dead brook trout lying all over the shallows!*

Back to Horseshoe! Beno suggested.

We fished it carefully for another three hours, finally hiking back to Hermit when a rain squall lashed across the lake. Its icy, needle-sharp raindrops quickly drove us to seek shelter among the rocks. There were no more rises after the rain and the early evening wind felt raw when the squalls moved on past.

Several weeks later I talked with a pair of confirmed high-lake addicts who lived for the few brief weeks between ice-out in early summer and the first high-country storms of early September. Over the years, they had made the climb into Horseshoe more than a dozen times without taking one of its big rainbows.

It's a fickle lake, one explained. *It's high and ice-cold and its weather can change every fifteen minutes, but it's beautiful!*

You're stubborn men, I laughed.

Maybe, the second fisherman agreed, *but you can't make up your mind too quickly on a good high lake—when it's got shallows and deep water and reasonable fly hatches, it must have big fish!*

Yes, I agreed, *plus good spawning flowages.*

You're right, the first man continued excitedly, *but it's strange when you're really hooked on fishing the high country—it's so fickle that just when you give up on a lake, it gets generous for somebody else!*

It's a little crazy, his friend nodded. *The first time I ever fished the Pierre Lakes above Snowmass we caught big fish like there was no tomorrow—but I've never taken a good trout from those lakes since.*

You have to have faith! I agreed.

What's that? the first man asked absently. *I was daydreaming about the third time I climbed into Horseshoe, and found its big rainbows cruising for a good hatch of flies—it was terrific!*

I've seen your malady before, I smiled.

10. Fly-Fishing Problems
in Our Western Mountains

I t has been almost forty years. Daylight came slowly across the sun-bleached prairies, and we had left the ranch south of Grainfield two hours after midnight to avoid the August heat. It was my first trip to Colorado, and that morning my head was so filled with stories of frontier days that it was impossible to sleep when the first grayish light filled the sky.

It looked like the rest of the high-plains country, ranches tucked into sheltered places under the flint-colored bluffs, hiding in groves of cotton-woods originally planted as timber claims. The muddy creeks were almost dry, and the cloudless sky forecast another day of dry heat and no rain. Windmills creaked high on their wooden frames, pumping cool water into the cattle tanks, and the shrinking creeks wound in serpentine chalk-colored channels lined with wild plums and hackberries.

My mother had told me the stories from her girlhood in this hard country, and that August morning some of their settings came alive. She told about the Roubidoux family, and its trading post at Fort Wallace, and about the years before the Little Big Horn when the Seventh Cavalry was stationed there. My father left the highway at Fort Wallace, following the county road south toward the river, and my mother pointed to the sandstone ruins of the military buildings. Below the town on an open buffalo-grass ridge was the military cemetery, with the graves of fallen cavalry troopers on dry depressions in the gravelly soil, and there were sunflowers growing in one corner where the soft sandstone wall that enclosed the cemetery held the rainfall in a low place. Tumbleweeds were caught in the iron fence that surrounded a pale prairie-stone obelisk.

It's a lonely place to be buried, my father said.

My mother walked along the gravel path toward the grillwork.

Come look at the obelisk, she called.

What's it say? I asked.

It was a memorial for cavalry troopers who had been killed on patrols, and at the Beecher's Island fight on the Arikaree farther north, when the cavalry rescued a camp of buffalo hunters that had been besieged for days by a sizable war party. The soldiers whose names were carved into the butter-soft rock had never been recovered for burial, and the obelisk was their sole memorial.

The first light was getting stronger now. It was soft across the flint hills toward the south, where the headwaters of the Smoky Hill wound east toward Russell Springs and Ellsworth, where Wyatt Earp had worn his first marshal's star. The prairie wind whispered in the bunchgrass below the cemetery, where a herd of cattle moved restlessly down toward the river, and it stirred and grew until it carried the gritty soil against our faces. It rattled against the stone obelisk when we turned to leave, and a tumbleweed crossed the path.

Blowing sand, said my father absently. *It won't be many years before it erases the names on these stones.*

We started west again, passing through the crossroads towns at Wallace and Sharon Springs. Arapahoe and Cheyenne Wells were ahead, and beyond lies the prairie ridge that divides the watersheds of the Smokey Hill and the Big Sandy. The pale-grass prairies reached for miles, and in the gathering daylight the oiled road stretched west like a surveyor's line toward the distant horizon.

Look! said my mother. *You can see them!*

The far horizon seemed empty and I stared.

See what? I answered unhappily. *There's nothing there.*

Look again! she said. *It's the Rockies!*

The treeless prairies reached one hundred miles west, and the cool wind sighed across the road. There had been stories of sighting the Rocky Mountains for the first time, stories I had heard about mountain men like Jim Bridger and Kit Carson and Captain Zebulon Pike—who discovered the mountain that bears his name at Colorado Springs.

Can't you see them? she laughed.

No! I said unhappily. *I don't see anything except some blue-colored clouds right on the horizon.*

Those clouds are the mountains! she said, ruffling my hair.

It was true, and suddenly the distant peaks caught the first light of sunrise, looking like pink smoke across one hundred miles of prairie. It must have been the same for Pike and his expeditionary force, watching the same cloud on the horizon for days while they picked their painfully slow route through stirrup-deep grass and dry washes, until they finally realized it was an escarpment of 14,000-foot mountains. Standing on that barren ridge beyond Cheyenne Wells that morning almost forty years ago is indelibly recorded in my memory, and I stood there shivering a little, partially from the wind and more from delicious excitement. Forty-odd years later, I still feel the same about the Colorado mountains.

The region is a vast area of majestic peaks, foothill basins, and sagebrush plateaus, reaching north from the *piñon* buttes on its southern borders, all the way to the forest-rimmed lakes of British Columbia. Its spinal cord is the mountains themselves, the towering range that trappers and buffalo hunters and cavalry troopers called the Rockies. Early history in the region is visible in the canvases of frontier painters like George Catlin, Alfred Jacob Miller, and Albert Bierstadt. The later events that occurred before barbed wire fenced off the high-plains country are found in the work of cowboy artists like Frederic Remington.

South-flowing watersheds in the region still echo the centuries-old tradition of the Spanish horse soldiers who explored and briefly conquered their valleys. The heritage of Spain lies in rivers with names such as Chama, Cucharas, Conejos, Huerfano, Las Animas, Los Pinos, and the storied Rio Grande itself.

There are still secrets in these mountains.

The 8,000-foot-high headwaters of the Gila, only one hundred miles above Mexico, hold a rare species of black-spotted trout that is protected in our time. Montana grayling are still abundant in the icy headwaters of the Beaverhead and the Big Hole. There are rare golden trout in some of the high lakes in the Wind River country of Wyoming, and the forest-rimmed lakes of British Columbia, like Stump and Peterhope and Shuswap shelter a unique subspecies of rainbow trout—the acrobatic, pole-vaulting Kamloops as bright as freshly minted coins.

Thousands of rivers and reservoirs and high lakes lie between. Fly-fishermen will find a cornucopia of native cutthroats, and introduced species like rainbows, goldens, browns, and brook trout. The Rocky Mountains dominate a world so vast and varied that its people—the lumberjacks, ranchers, miners, and their descendants in fast-growing foothill cities like Denver and Salt Lake—often forget that the region is virtually a continent in itself.

It sprawls more than 1,500 miles from Mexico to British Columbia, far more than the distance between the Macedonian river where fly-fishing for trout was born 2,000 years ago, and the north-flowing rivers of Scotland where the continent of Europe projects westward into the Atlantic.

Fly-fishing in our western mountains is as varied as the magnificent country. There are literally all types of water in the Rockies. Some fishermen prefer the relatively small streams and beaver ponds, perhaps because their character is intimate and comprehensible. Others spend most of their time on big western reservoirs. Fishing wilderness lakes high in the mountains offers still another set of problems. The sprawling big-water rivers offer difficult wading, but also trophy-size fish for anglers willing to challenge their intimidating size. The final surprise is the western spring creeks, small weed-rich streams that emerge full-blown in limestone upwellings and geothermal basins—and offer fishing with minute flies and cobweb-thin leaders over trout as selective as any on the legendary rivers of Europe.

These western waters are changing under the pressure of increasing population, and their fish are more wary and demanding than they were as recently as ten or fifteen years ago. The immense numbers of wilderness fish described in the chronicles of Lewis and Clark have been gone for a century, although some high lakes in remote areas are still filled with eager and gullible trout. Such fishing is found in pack-trip and hiking country, but fish in the foothill rivers behind Denver and Salt Lake and Colorado Springs are as shy as their cousins in streams two hours outside Boston and Philadelphia and New York.

Such varied conditions demand skills in the full spectrum of fly-fishing techniques, and both eastern and western anglers are going to need some homework in the years ahead. Eastern fishermen are accustomed to small-scale rivers that are relatively easy to read and fish. Their trout are soon discovered in the dark run under the overhanging buttonwoods, beside the only boulder in the pool, and in the narrow current tongue that tumbles into a fifty-yard flat. Such skilled eastern fishermen are often baffled on a river like the Snake or the Yellowstone or the Gunnison, and they find its stadium-size pools and half-mile flats a little disconcerting.

Western fishermen often remember the relatively easy fishing of the past, when the fish would take almost anything they cast, and they too are a little unsettled by the more recent shyness and selective-feeding behavior appearing on their rivers. Modern fishing in the Rocky Mountains requires delicate tactics and a growing knowledge of fly hatches, as well as big-water techniques with a sinking line. There is room for both the chalkstream methods required on the crystalline spring creeks, and the bottom-scouring muddler on the half-mile riffles of the Yellowstone. The man who really masters fly-fishing in the Rockies must handle the polarities of both methods well, particularly in a future that promises more and more fishing pressure, if he wishes to become a complete angler.

Since fishing all the types of water in the Rocky Mountains demands both stamina and refinement, it is difficult to recommend a single rod-and-reel combination that can handle the full spectrum of problems. Anglers who want to focus on small rivers, beaver ponds, and the spring creeks will probably lean toward a relatively light rod of seven to eight feet. Such rods would be balanced with five- to six-weight fly lines, and since fishing such waters often involves an infantry approach in high grass, a slightly longer rod still capable of fishing a delicate tippet is the ticket. Both floating and sinking double tapers are needed, although most forward-taper designs deliver too harshly for the skittish trout of smaller waters.

Such rods weigh about two and one-half to three and one-half ounces in fiberglass, and two and three-quarters to four and a quarter ounces in split bamboo. Reels for light-tippet fishing should have a smooth click system that will not shear an 8X nylon when a good fish bolts and strips off line. Matching reels for the rods described above should measure three to three and a half inches in diameter, and should weigh between three and a half and four and a half ounces. Their capacity should be about one hundred yards of twenty- to thirty-pound Dacron backing behind the ninety feet of fly lines. Dacron is better than other synthetic materials for such backing line, because it does not stretch as radically under tension. Too much elasticity in the backing can tighten and cause a reel machined from the lightweight modern alloys to warp and bind, when an angler recovers his stretched backing from a big fish. The relatively heavy backing is recommended because its diameter tends not to bite into the remaining line, jamming under the stress of a bolting fish.

Fishing heavy water demands other gear. Big rivers and reservoirs involve both distance casting and sinking weight forward lines. Rods designed for such tactics vary between eight and eight and a half feet, balanced with seven- and eight-weight lines. Glass equipment of this length and power will weigh from three and three-quarters to four and three-quarters ounces, and four and a quarter to five and a half ounces in split cane. Balanced reels should hold 100 to 150 yards of thirty-pound Dacron backing. Both double-taper and torpedo-taper lines are useful. Reels for such tackle will measure from three and a half to three and three-quarters inches, and weigh between five and six and a quarter ounces. Thirty-pound backing has sufficient diameter to prevent its biting into the remaining line, and binding when a trophy-size trout makes its strong downstream run. It is a lesson in acceleration learned painfully from big rainbows and salmon over the years.

There are many times on big western reservoirs and lakes when the fish rise avidly to a hatch, or porpoise to emerging nymphs and pupae just under the surface. Dry flies, wets, and nymphs must be chosen then to match the color, size, configuration, and behavior of the naturals. Bucktails and streamers should imitate the baitfish indigenous to the water being covered, and suggest their unique swimming motions.

The fish of lakes and impoundments have a singular pattern of behavior important to a western fisherman: they cruise together in search of food, each fish stringing together several rises in a sequence. Unlike stream fishing, a fisherman must not cast to the rise forms that are showing. Experienced lake fishermen have learned to observe a series of rises, and cast to the place where such a cruising trout is likely to rise next.

Fishermen on big lakes and reservoirs should remember a few other simple rules, particularly when the fish are not revealing themselves with surface rises. Most food in lakes and beaver ponds and impoundments is found in the relatively shallow waters, rather than in the depths. The inlet channels are especially good feeding places. Shallow outlets of big lakes often hold some of the largest trout. The shallow acreages with inlet and outlet currents are particularly rich areas, because their currents mean higher oxygen levels, and a wider range of slow-water and current-loving natural foods.

Two basic methods of presentation are important on the western lakes and reservoirs. Both utilize a fan pattern of covering the water, one horizontal in a clock-face technique, and the other vertical, working the fly back at various depths.

The clock-face method involves covering the surface around the angler in a disciplined manner, rather than casting at random. The pattern begins at approximately nine o'clock, working the fly out as far as possible and fishing it back. The succeeding casts are placed in a clockwise pattern past twelve, until the final cast is retrieved from three o'clock. When the fan pattern is complete, the fisherman should move a step along the shoreline, and repeat the whole clock-face exercise again. It can also be repeated again without moving, and the pattern of casts is more likely to intercept a cruising fish that mere random casting might miss.

The vertical fan patterns of retrieves at various depths have a similar logic. The fisherman simply employs a countdown technique. Each successive cast is permitted to sink a few seconds deeper, until either feeding trout are located, or the bottom is reached. This is indicated by the retrieve ticking against the bottom ledges and gravel or the fly picking up some moss.

When the sink count of twenty-five works into the weeds or touches bottom, the fisherman should reduce the count slightly. The short count works the fly back just above the bottom, where the nymphs and diving-beetle larvae and tiny crustaceans are most abundant. Such countdown tactics are a primary factor in fishing lakes, impoundments, and deep currents on our western rivers, and they are the secret on famous lakes like Wade and Cliff in Montana—and the rich weed-filled shallows of Henry's Lake in Idaho.

Some of the best fly-fishing reservoirs in the Rockies are found at Antero and Eleven Mile and San Cristobal in Colorado. Wyoming has Grassy Lake near Yellowstone Park, and Flaming Gorge on the lower watershed of the Green, and Montana has superb sport on large impoundments like Georgetown and Hebgen. High lakes offer similar problems of technique in locating fish and covering the water; and casting ahead of a cruising trout to anticipate its next rise is critical too. High-altitude waters are also best in the shallow acreages where aquatic foods are concentrated, particularly the inlets and outlets. The temperatures of high lakes are typically cold, and the best sport is usually found when the surface warms during the day. Evenings that follow a hot, sunny day are often good. The warming water has accelerated both the metabolism and the hunger of the fish, and in the twilight they forage more boldly.

Sometimes a light surface-riffling wind on a lake or beaver pond or reservoir can make the fish less aware of clumsy casting and relatively crude tippets. Trout cruise under the broken surface, unafraid of feeding openly in bright weather. Under such conditions, still-water fishing is easier.

Productive high lakes are usually distinguished by four key factors in their biosystems: there must be sufficient volume and depth of water so the fish have enough oxygen to prevent winterkill when snow covers the ice. Heavy drifts shut out the light, and end the photosynthesis that normally replenishes oxygen in the water. The best high lakes often have natural deposits of phosphates or lime marl or other sources of alkalinity, often from geothermal or volcanic origins. The nutrients sustain both a rich food chain and a rapid growth potential for the trout. Sufficient outlet and inlet currents are important for the spring-spawning cutthroats and rainbows, and the introduced populations of fall-spawning brookies. Such currents vary considerably from lake to lake, and they do not always provide spawning-size gravel. Aquatic foods do not thrive in the alkaline waters unless the lake also provides adequate acreages of shallow water. It is such forage-shallows that hold the organisms which grow and sustain large trout.

High lakes are also characterized by moodiness. Weather is fickle at such altitudes. When you find a lake that does not winterkill, has relatively alkaline waters, sustains natural spawning, and also provides food-rich shallows, fish it several times to test its character before you finally judge its fishing qualities.

Big western rivers offer completely different fishing. Sweeping riffles and half-mile flats provide a few visible clues to their holding places, and a man familiar only with the tactics of fishing a small stream is lost. There are few undercut banks, logjams, or boulders to scour out sheltered taking lies. The smooth currents have a poker-faced façade that conceals most of their secrets. Many western rivers have large whitefish populations, and they prefer the tail shallows and quiet currents. Whitefish often hold in places that brown trout would like on a smaller eastern stream. Western trout are usually in the stronger currents feeding into a pool—particularly wild cutthroats and muscular rainbows—and an eastern fisherman can waste precious time working places that hold no trout until he discovers this particular secret of our western rivers.

There are times when heavy fly hatches bring the fish up on even the biggest rivers. Their rises and porpoise rolls clearly reveal their feeding stations at such times. Famous hatches like the big stoneflies that emerge in early summer on the great fast-water rivers like the Madison and Gunnison and Snake, the large olive-bodied mayflies that come off slower streams like the Henry's Fork of the Snake, and the pupal migrations of tiny *Chironomus* flies can all trigger impressive rises of fish. Such hatches can make the fish both greedy and selective on the biggest rivers.

Gene Anderegg and I were waist-deep in the sprawling Big Hole fifteen years ago, frustrated by fifty-odd trout rising all around us. Their swirls barely disturbed the smooth current.

It's something minute, Anderegg yelled. *Can't see anything on the surface, and they're sure lazy rise forms!*

Two browns porpoised like sleepy cats.

Might be tiny ants, he continued. *Tiny ants or jassids or midges in the film—maybe I'll try ants on them.*

Good! I answered. *I'll try midge pupae in the film.*

Petri heil! he laughed.

Big Hole fish are supposed to scoff at refinements like matching the hatch and light tackle. Its trout are expected to fall all over themselves to take big Muddlers and Wooly Worms and weighted nymphs like the improbably-named Girdlebug fished deep along the bottom, but these fish had obviously failed to read the script. The big western flies all failed, and the fish dimpled and swirled everywhere.

Nothing! Anderegg laughed.

We've tried everything on them! I answered. *They don't know they're supposed to take Humpies and Muddlers.*

You're right! he shook his head and waded upstream.

The common solution for such rise forms is a tiny ant or jassid imitation, and sometimes a minute nymph or midge pupa. We tried dozens of tiny patterns without moving a fish, while they continued to work everywhere down the flat.

They're laughing at us, I said.

Finally I noticed a rhythm in their feeding. The light wind riffled the current slightly, stirring in the cottonwoods above the pool. The rises increased each time the wind moved in the trees; it was blowing tiny insects into the river.

It must be terrestrials! I said.

But we tried every terrestrial in the box! Anderegg replied. *The fish didn't even bother to look at them!*

Beetles! I suggested suddenly.

Anderegg reeled in his line and waded toward me.

Okay, he laughed. *We forgot to try beetles!*

Tiny cottonwood beetles, I continued eagerly. *Sometimes the wind blows the tiny bark beetles from the trees this time of year!*

Let's try one, he suggested.

The only beetle imitations in my boxes had been dressed from ringneck pheasant feathers, lacquering a pair of greenish black throat feathers together in a pattern that Ross Trimmer and I had developed for Japanese beetles on Letort Spring Run. Their ovoid wing silhouettes were set jassid-style above a trimmed black hackle, tied to lie flat in the film. But they were on sixteen hooks, much too large for a tiny cottonwood beetle less than a quarter inch in length, and I hastily trimmed the wing smaller with the scissors on my trout-knife.

Okay, I said. *We're ready now.*

The modified beetle dropped softly above a good fish, and when it reached its feeding station, the fly disappeared in a quiet dimple. The little reel protested shrilly as the two-pound brown felt the hook and bolted.

It worked! I yelled.

Anderegg came wading upstream while I played the fish on the delicate one-pound tippet. *Fantastic!* He shook his head. *Never would have believed that kind of selectivity here!*

It happens, I agreed.

Such choosiness is relatively rare on large western rivers like the Big Hole, but days like that are happening more and more each summer. It is precisely the kind of minute-fly-fishing a good Catskill or Appalachian fly-fisherman understands—tactics that were developed and perfected on the Letort in Pennsylvania—and western anglers will need such techniques more often in the future.

However, few eastern anglers have worked enough really big water to understand the basic methods of fishing it. When a river is a series of half-mile riffles and waist-deep flats, casting to a single rising fish is seldom practicable. The fisherman must execute fairly long casts, covering as much water as possible in a precise pattern. His most effective techniques are similar to those used on steelhead and salmon, and involve both geometry and discipline.

Big western rivers have few actual pools where their currents are constrained by outcroppings and ledges and canyon walls, although such places exist. The really large rivers are formed of tumbling riffles and deep flats with swelling currents. The swiftest water often consists of brief chutes where the gravel shelves off abruptly between a flat and the riffling throat of the next flat downstream. It is open water, almost without distinguishing character, like a pond with a current. It reveals virtually nothing of its bottom to the eye, although it is probably punctuated with outcroppings of bedrock, undercut ledges, and partially-buried boulders where the scouring currents have deepened the river. Such secrets may offer only subtle hints of their presence, in eddying currents that scarcely disturb the surface.

You've got to cover a lot of river in a day, Bob Carmichael used to growl good-naturedly in his shop at Jackson Hole years ago. *And you've got to cover it carefully.*

Carmichael loved and understood big water, with the skills sharpened in many seasons on sprawling flats of the Snake and Gros Ventre and the Buffalo. Although poor health denied him access to heavy water in the years before his death, his advice was sound for those who listened. His rivers were a world of strong many-channeled currents, mixed with tumbling chutes and flats and half-mile riffles that have baffled many visiting anglers—and swift currents that have drowned more than a few who took them lightly.

Covering such water is discipline and hard work. It involves starting where a heavy riffle or chute shelves off and slows, meeting the deeper currents of the flat. Trout can hold well in these chutes, even where the current is choppy and swift, because bottom friction causes a cushion of slower water deep along the stones and gravel.

Start pretty far up, Carmichael explained. *Sometimes the biggest fish lie right along the chutes—especially our Jackson Hole cutthroats—in heavy water that seems impossible to stay in easily.*

Carmichael was right about that.

We took heavy rainbows and cutthroats right in the chutes, fishing across the current tongues with a sinking line and big weighted nymphs and muddlers. Letting them sink deep over the shelving bottom, we teased them enticingly with a lazy rhythm of the rod. The heavy currents worked our flies, and we waited until they hung directly downstream before we stripped in line. Several casts should be made into any obvious holding lie, making sure it has been adequately covered.

Otherwise, the fisherman should simply fish out the entire flat with discipline and geometry. Each time a cast is completed, with the big nymphs or muddler finishing its current swing, the angler retrieves his line with a few slow strips directly upstream. Then it should be stripped back fast, and a step taken downstream while the line works out again. The next cast should drop about two feet farther downstream, well out across the current tongues, so it swings back in a deep arc along the bottom.

Such tactics cover the pool with a series of concentric quarter-circles, making sure every fish has seen the fly. Mere random casting from various points could miss a good trout in a mood to take the fly.

Pocket-water fishing is easier. It simply involves casting to the likely looking eddies and smooth runs and pockets among the rocks. The fish are holding in such cushions in the current. They lie beside the stones and boulders, in a swelling current just upstream, and in the reverse eddies below. There are others in the darker currents along the edges of the tumbling white water, and in the slicks between the swift current tongues. It is fishing that requires accurate casting to such places, and a quick strike in response to a rise, since the agile pocket-water trout must decide and take its food quickly.

Charles Fothergill is a well-known guide on the swift Roaring Fork in Colorado, particularly in the famous Slaughter House water below Aspen.

Pocket fishing isn't often a problem in selectivity, Fothergill believes. *Any fish in currents like that makes his mind up fast—or goes hungry!*

Good holding water lies in many places. Pools form below waterfalls, logjams and deadfalls, boulders, dams, ledges, and undercut banks where a river changes its direction. Pools can lie at the bottom of any narrow defile or canyon, where bedrock ledges block the flow of the river, and where primary gravel bars cause upwelling currents. Bridge abutments can form holding pools too.

Such pools invariably shelter big fish. Their depth offers protection, while the currents bring oxygen and food that can be ingested at leisure. Unlike riffles and pocket water and runs, pools have a quiet tempo. However, there are always places in a pool where an unexpected fish might hold and feed outside the shelter of the deeper lies. Sometimes the fish drop back toward the tail shallows, depending on the prey they are seeking, and can forage in surprisingly shallow water.

Anglers should never wade into the tail or lower reaches of any pool without studying it carefully for fish. Spooked trout will bolt upstream through the shallows, and their panic is contagious.

Since a small fish is usually fleeing to hiding places not far above the shallows, his panic is less a problem than a bigger trout bolting toward his lie in the primary depths of the pool. Study the shallows carefully, and try to catch any good fish holding there. Hooking such fish, and forcing them downstream from the others lying in the lower reaches of the pool will prevent the chain reaction of panic that can be triggered when a large trout bolts upstream from the tail shallows.

Cover it all! the late Joe Brooks always suggested. *Sometimes you'll find a real dinosaur in the riffles, lying in water hardly deep enough to cover its dorsal fin!*

However, most big trout will dominate the best feeding places along the primary current tongues. Such currents are carrying food, particularly the nymphs and fly hatches from the riffles upstream. Since the primary feeding stations for a big trout involve both cover and food supply, any pocket that offers good protection beside a primary current can shelter a trophy fish. Their holding lies will be found along sheltering ledges, deadfalls and logjams, cribbings, timbers, and willow-shaded undercut banks. What method an angler should use varies with the moods of both the fish and their rivers. Obvious surface rises to hatching insects call for dry flies, of colors and sizes that imitate the naturals. Porpoising swirls or deep rolls, flashing along the bottom, usually require imitations of nymphs and larvae. Skittering baitfish mean a big trout is in a meat-and-potatoes mood and is chasing minnows. The fisherman must learn to observe the behavior of the trout and understand the clues in that behavior before he can catch them consistently.

Lacking such obvious clues, an angler on big western rivers should know what principal nymphs and baitfish are found on the water he is fishing. Such foods have well-known imitations that should be fished along the bottom with a sinking line.

There are days when nothing is showing, Dan Bailey said a few years ago in his fly shop at Livingston on the Yellowstone. *You've got to use a big nymph or bucktail—and you've got to scratch gravel to get them!*

But the icy little spring creeks and geyser-basin rivers like the Gibbon and the Firehole are another challenge altogether. There are big springs that rise as full-blown little rivers from the earth in many western valleys. These little streams are rich with weeds and fly life, carrying the alkalinity of phosphates, lime marl, and hot springs. The ecological result of such alkalinity is identical—optimal feeding temperatures throughout the year, rich weed growth, heavy fly hatches of tiny caddis and mayflies and midges, plus terrestrials in the summer, and trout as wary and selective as any in the world. Skilled western anglers who enjoy the challenge of stalking these fish, sometimes belly-flat in the grass, can name these famous spring creeks on their fingers.

Colorado has the weedy meadows and watercress headwaters of the South Platte and the Tarryall, plus the artesian-fed network in the San Luis Valley. Wyoming has little rivers like Flat Creek and Fish Creek and a handful of spring creeks at Jackson Hole. Yellowstone Park has the Firehole and the Gibbon. California has its famous Hot Creek on the arid eastern slopes of the Sierras and Hat Creek, a cornucopia of fly hatches born in the hot springs of Lassen Volcanic Park. Montana has many famous spring creeks. The best are probably the Big Spring Creek at Lewistown, the superb pair on the Armstrong and Nelson ranches above Livingston, and the smaller spring creeks at Twin Bridges on the Big Hole and Ennis on the Madison. The Gallatin alone has a handful of fine little spring creeks in its watershed above Bozeman. Idaho has its great ones too, particularly the Henry's Fork of the Snake, probably the biggest spring creek in the world, its Teton River tributary and the little-known spring creek at Swan Valley; and perhaps the most famous of the western chalkstreams—the serpentine meadow reaches of Silver Creek at Picabo.

Fishing such waters well is not easy. *It's a good yardstick!* Bud Lilly observed thoughtfully at his West Yellowstone shop a few seasons back. *You've got to be better than good!*

The fish are shy enough to demand delicate leaders tapered to 7X and 8X tippets. Nymphs tied to imitate freshwater shrimps and scuds are a good choice fished in the weedy channels when the fish are not visibly feeding, although these spring creeks are known for their free-rising trout. Many hatches of tiny Sulphurs and Blue-winged Olives and *Callibaetis* flies are common throughout the season, since these are many-brooded mayfly species that thrive in the western spring-creek habitats. Experienced anglers fish dry with diminutive Blue Quills and Blue-winged Olives and Light Cahills on eighteen to twenty-four hooks. Such minutiae ride the smooth current like tiny sailboats, and rises to them are lazy almost-sipping swirls.

Rise forms when there is nothing visible floating on the current pose another problem in tactics. Such rises usually mean tiny ants and leafhoppers and beetles, but they can also be focused on the larval and pupal forms of midges, and tiny wet flies dressed with black, olive, or dark-grayish bodies are often the solution. There are also times when tiny hatching mayfly nymphs and caddis pupae are just under the surface, and the trout take so closely under the film that they disturb the water with dramatic rises and porpoise rolls. It is a time for small wet flies and nymphs on light tackle.

Spring-creek fishing is never easy. The trout are shy and selective on most days, cocking under a floating dry fly to inspect it before refusing it disdainfully. Such wariness is light years away from working a fat Muddler or Wooly Worm along the bottom of some half-mile flat, floating a big Humpy or Hair-wing Wulff on broken pockets, or catching foolish trout in some wilderness lake or beaver pond.

My first experience with difficult spring-creek fishing came on the Yellowstone above Livingston, and its frustrations have proved typical over the years. The fish sipped and porpoise-rolled and dimpled in the weedy channels for hours that morning; and we never touched them.

Well, Dan Bailey asked with a twinkle in his pale eyes, *you've fished those British chalkstreams—what do you think?*

These fish are tough, I admitted sheepishly.

Amen! said Bailey.

11. Streamside Experiences in Matching the Hatch

Matching the hatch was not a major factor on my boyhood rivers but there were baffling days even then when it mattered. Searching my memory for obvious examples, I find one morning on the upper Pere Marquette that stands out vividly for its impact on my early thinking. It was an experience that taught me several basic lessons in matching a fly hatch of naturals, both in terms of observation and streamside fly tying.

It was a surprisingly cold morning in early June and mist still drifted above the spring-fed swamps along the Middle Branch when I left the car at the Forks Pool. It was chilly enough for me to see my breath in spite of the calendar, and my fingers were a little clumsy when I threaded the fly line through the guides. The river flowed smooth and strong, where the swift currents of the Middle Branch riffled under the bridge to join the darker tea-colored water of the Little South. The river felt warmer than the air, and I studied it for rising fish before rummaging in my fishing coat pockets for a fly book.

I'll fish a pair of wet flies down to Noble's Bend, I decided and studied the patterns in my fly book. *Maybe a pair of Cahills.*

The Cahills were firmly attached to the tippet and a dropper about eighteen inches up the leader. Roll casting steadily, I worked down the riffling current tongue of the Forks Pool without moving a fish.

It's still too cold, I thought.

The river winds toward the north from the Forks, flowing waist-deep and smooth and sliding laterally across its stony bottom to work against the deadfalls below. Its currents are dark with the promise of big fish under the trees before they turn back toward the still water downstream. The sweeping bend downstream was a productive reach of water in those summer months, with many good trout holding over its open gravel and some heavy fish in the shade of the trees. The current narrows below, gathering its strength into a strong, leg-wearying flow that shelves off deeply under a dense jackstraw tangle of logs. There was a single towering snag rising through the deadfalls, and that summer it was home to a pair of nesting woodducks. The still water at Noble's lies downstream.

Although I fished the familiar water carefully, nothing responded to my little Cahills until I covered the sheltering alders below the logjam. The fish that struck was not large; it followed my swinging flies lethargically in the cold current, taking the dropper with a half-hearted pull.

Well, I thought, *it's something!*

The sun worked higher and a few flies were hatching when I changed reels to fish back with a floating fly. There were a few brownish gray sedges egg laying along the willows when the first trout started feeding, and I selected a spent-wing Adams. It took one fish, but the others refused it completely.

That's strange. I shook my head.

Selective feeding in those years was seldom a serious problem, but I finally stopped fishing to study the hatching flies. Mixed with the fluttering caddisflies were a few dark little hatching duns, and although I was unable to catch a specimen, it seemed likely that a small Blue Quill would work. It had been the solution during a similar hatch a few weeks earlier, and I changed flies with confidence, clinch-knotting a sixteen Blue Quill to my leader tippet.

The fluttering little duns came down the current, and I watched the fish take them readily. It was definitely the little mayflies, and I placed my imitation above a fish that was working below the logs. The dry fly settled, flirted in the currents over the trout, and was casually refused.

Must be drag, I thought.

Several casts came down over the fish, and although it inspected one dragless float briefly, it continued to refuse the fly. My Blue Quill was obviously not the solution, and I waded over into the primary current tongue to catch one of the naturals.

It came fluttering toward me, and I cupped my hand and lowered it to intercept the hatching dun. The river eddied past my fingers, and the little mayfly darted past on the flow, disappearing in the tumbling currents around my waders. Several flies escaped me before I finally picked one off the water by its upright wings, and I placed it carefully in a plastic fly box. It hung upside down on the lid, and its colors seemed strange. Its wings were dark bluish-gray, its legs and three delicate tails somewhat paler, its eyes were large and rust colored, and its body was a bright olive. There was nothing like it in my fly boxes.

When I had tried every pattern with dun-colored hackles without taking a fish, I waded back upstream to the car and the fly tying box in its trunk. There was no body material of the proper color, but there was a small cellophane package of olive-dyed hackles in my kit, and I stripped the fibers with my fingers. The color of the hackle was a pale olive except for the dyed edge of its quill, and it looked like the bodies of the naturals when I wound it on the hook. Dun-colored tails and hackles with sparsely dressed wings of woodduck completed the fly. When there were two patterns finished, lying face down on their hackles on the glove compartment door, it was time to try the river again.

The hatch was almost over when I finally reached the flat. There were still a few olives coming down the riffles below the Forks Pool, and wading slowly downstream, I discovered three good fish still working along the deadfalls. The fish rose busily along the far bank, preoccupied enough with the hatching flies that I slipped past without alarming them.

Wonder if they'll still refuse a Blue Quill? I thought.

It was an interesting question, and I swallowed my impatience to try the little olive patterns I had tied. The fish rose in irregular rhythms, now coming to the dwindling hatch along the mossy logs. One inspected a Blue Quill momentarily, turned back to its feeding station, and softly took another natural. The other two fish refused the Blue Quill without interrupting their feeding.

They're still picky! I shook my head.

The little olive imitation was knotted to my tippet and anointed with a mixture of paraffin and carbon tetrachloride. Several drops blossomed in brief oil-film flowers on the current below my waders, and I blew on the hackles before drying them with false casting.

The fly dropped above the first trout, teasing down past the current-polished logs until it disappeared in a satisfied rise. It was a fat fourteen-inch brown, and it threshed with surprise.

It worked! I thought happily.

The fish was netted after I coaxed it downstream from the others, and I rinsed and dried the fly. The second fish had not bothered with my little Blue Quill earlier, but it took the Olive without hesitation.

Well, I thought, *that's two of them.*

The third fish was bigger. It was working along a mossy stump that lay in dappled patterns of bright sunlight and shadow, and my first casts dragged slightly. It followed one float with interest and finally refused. It was a difficult fish, and I waded deep to get below its position, dropping both line and leader in the same currents to get a better float. The fly drifted properly on a slack leader and the fish took quietly, shaking angrily and bolting upstream when I tightened.

Three! I said aloud.

The fish was about two pounds, and I lost it when the brittle tippet sheared in the roots upstream. But it was a trout that had rejected the other patterns, and finding a fly it wanted was unforgettably intriguing. It was an important lesson in selectivity, and matching the hatch was firmly etched in my memory.

Another incident occurred on the Au Sable. It was a mellow afternoon in early summer, in a sweeping bend of the North Branch below Lovells. Only a few fish were showing until the late shadows reached well across the current. The wind was warm, drifting upriver and smelling of pines and cedar swamps.

The birds were the first symptom of change, darting and wheeling high in the sun above the river. It was the prelude to a mating swarm of mayflies and more and more insects soon gathered from the trees. The flies were small straw-colored *Ephemerellas*, rising and falling rhythmically over the current. The birds were frantic now as their dancing flight came lower. The mating swarm was heavier, the males holding twenty-odd feet above the river. In a timeless mating dance, the females rose to meet the males and fluttered back toward the water. Finally the fertilized females dipped closer and closer to the smooth current, until their bodies were tipped with tiny butter-colored egg sacs.

The twilight was quickly filled with countless flies. When the females began dropping to oviposit their egg sacs in the water, the waiting trout began taking them eagerly. The mating spinners had been swarming above the river, and the fish did not start to work until the females started laying their eggs.

Ginger Quill, I thought.

The fish were working steadily now. There were both parachute spentwings and conventional Ginger Quills in my fly box and I tried them both without success. Both the male and female naturals resembled these dry flies, with their hackle quill bodies and pale ginger hackles.

That's strange, I thought.

The light Cahills in my boxes were tied with chalky fur bodies, and I did not really expect them to work, but the failure of the Ginger Quills was a surprise. Their dressings looked right to me, but the fish thought otherwise. Trout after trout rejected them at a time when the evening was so filled with egg-sac spinners that the fish went crazy.

There were so many rising now that I searched my fly boxes frantically.

Maybe it's the egg sacs they're looking for, I thought aloud.

The Female Beaverkill is a popular pattern in Michigan, and I often carried them dressed with somewhat paler hackles than the commercial patterns one finds in the shops. There were a few tied on sixteen hooks, with pale ginger hackles and delicate little woodduck tails and bodies of yellow rayon floss. Their egg sacs were bright yellow wool tied full and fat at the root of the tails.

Try one! I thought.

The results were immediate. The little egg-sac Beaverkill settled above a nearby fish and was engulfed in an eager splash. Six or eight more took just as eagerly once the fly was dried and floating again, and then they stopped taking.

Funny! I shook my head. *What the devil's wrong?*

The fish were still working, although their rise forms were quieter now.

There were still a few egg-sac spinners coming down, but it was the smaller males that filled the twilight now. Bending down to study the current in the waning light, I discovered it was covered with spent males and females, their egg sacs fully extruded and gone.

It could explain the quiet rises, I thought eagerly. *Maybe I should try those parachute spentwings again.*

The egg-sac spinners had expended their eggs, and when I tried a pale spentwing with parachute hackles, a trout took it without hesitation. It was the first time I had consciously observed trout changing their feeding preferences during a single evening, looking first for the rich egg-filled spinners, and finally turning to the spent flies when their mating was finally done. The Ginger Quills had failed when the egg-sac spinners were available, because the fish found the egg-filled females more attractive. The effectiveness of the Female Beaverkills ended when the egg laying was virtually complete, and most of the spinners had fallen spent in the surface film. Their eggs had been expended and the fish turned eagerly to the parachute Ginger Quill. The egg-laying spinners were fluttering above the current, and the trout made splashy rises in an effort to capture them. The spent flies were easy to catch; once they became the principal diet form on the water, the trout took them with quiet, dimpling rises.

It was a second indelible lesson in selectivity.

This past October I observed a striking example of similar behavior on the Henry's Fork of the Snake. The trout began rising steadily an hour before twilight, feeding greedily on a hatch of minute *Pseudocloëon* flies, and I took a dozen good rainbows on a tiny Gray-winged Olive dressed on a twenty-six hook. The little pattern worked wonders while the little duns were hatching, but suddenly the fish started refusing it.

René Harrop was fishing a hundred yards upstream, and I looked up to see how he was doing. Harrop was studying the water intently and not fishing, and it was obvious that his trout had also turned selective.

What are they doing now? I shouted.

I'm not sure, Harrop answered, *but I've got a big swarm of tiny spinners up here.* The fish were working steadily again.

Think it could be spinners? I asked.

Might be, Harrop said. *These little spinners are the same species as the duns we've been fishing.*

You really think these rainbows are that picky?

Sometimes they are, he laughed.

René Harrop is one of the finest fishermen I know, and is one of the best fly dressers anywhere, particularly on the tiny hatches. Harrop and his wife tie thousands and thousands of minute flies each winter, and his knowledge of the Henry's Fork and its hatches is remarkable.

The tiny spinners of the *Pseudocloëon* flies are exactly the same colors as the duns that precede them, except that their wings lie spent in the surface film. Imitations are dressed on twenty-six and twenty-eight hooks, and it seems unlikely that only the silhouette of the spentwings lying in the film could make a difference with such tiny flies, since color and size are identical in both duns and spinners.

You think a spent no-hackle will work? I yelled. *My fish down here just won't take the dun!*

Give it a try! Harrop insisted.

There were a half dozen pale spent-wing olive spinners in my fly boxes and I changed flies. Several good fish were dimpling softly in the smooth current downstream, and I was looking into the waning light when my first cast settled on the water. There was a delicate sucking swirl and a sixteen-inch rainbow exploded when it felt the tiny hook. More than a dozen fish took the tiny spentwing before I hooked an acrobatic four-pounder that stripped my light reel into its backing.

They like that little spinner! Harrop shouted.

It's amazing! I yelled back. *I've never seen such a clear case of selectivity to nothing more than silhouette and light pattern in the film!*

And in such tiny sizes! he laughed.

Another spring some years before, the fish on the main Au Sable below Stephan's Bridge taught me a variation on this same theme of changing fly preferences in mid-hatch. We were floating the river downstream to Wakeley Bridge, starting in the late morning. It was cold and the morning was clear, filled with the promise of hatches and a good day's sport.

Two bait fishermen were cleaning their fifteen-fish limits at the Gates canoe landing, and the crayfish were already working on the entrails in the shallows downstream. The current whispered past the cribbing where we moored the canoe as we loaded it carefully with tackle duffels and lunch baskets and a pair of thermos bottles.

Soup, Gerry Queen explained with a conspiratorial grin, *and this other one's got the Old Fashioneds for later!*

Nobody's perfect! I replied.

We pushed off into the smooth current, moving noiselessly except for the soft music of the river through the deadfalls and sweepers, and the counterpoint of our paddles. The river was still less than fifty degrees and our nymphs were ignored.

Below the landing at Stephan's Bridge, with its bustling activity and racks of rental canoes, the river became wilder and less pastoral. There were swift shallows over mottled bottoms of pale sand and gravel, dark runs under the deadfalls and willows, and deep eddying bends where the river looped back on itself. It was now late morning, and it was getting almost warm in the places where the river was sheltered from the chill wind. Redwinged blackbirds were building nests in a marshy stand of willows, where the April currents had worked back into the cedars.

Okra-lee-o! the birds cried sweetly.

Some dark mayflies started hatching in a quiet backwater where the sun had warmed the river. They were rather large, with slate gray wings and lead-colored bodies, and the smaller males were almost black, riding the current in the bright sunlight. It was a hatch of big *Leptophlebias,* although it would be years before I learned to identify these clumsily hatching flies. A few trout started to feed, and we backed our canoe out of the main currents, while I slipped over the side to fish them. The fish were small, but I took two or three on a dark Hendrickson tied with rusty, slate-dun hackles.

Well, Gerry said, *that's a start.*

Hooking the Hendrickson in the keeper ring, I clambered back into the canoe and we pushed off into the current. Our early breakfast was wearing off when we reached a sunny bank sheltered from the wind, and we stopped for lunch.

Before we had finished our hot bean soup, there was a good hatch of flies coming off the smooth run above the canoe. The fish were soon feeding steadily. We both waded out into the flat, working out line to cover the fish with the dark Hendricksons that had taken the fish before lunch. The trout refused them.

They've changed brands, I muttered.

You're right, Queen agreed.

The hatch had changed since morning. These flies were less dark, and had pale grayish tan bodies with brownish dorsal markings. Light Hendricksons tied with bronze blue-dun hackles and grayish cream fox dubbing worked perfectly, and we caught and released a dozen fish between us from the run.

That's more like it, I said.

These flies started about two o'clock, Queen looked at his watch, *and it's almost three-thirty.*

We'd better start down. I nodded.

We launched the canoe and loaded it, pushing off as the shadows lengthened across the river. Downstream a mile, the Au Sable gathered its currents at the bottom of a long waist-deep flat into a stretch of swifter water lined with sweepers.

Hatch is still heavy here. Queen stopped paddling. *Look at all the rising fish!* We drifted silently past the cedars.

Let's stop and fish awhile, I suggested.

We wrestled the canoe into the willows and moored it. Several good fish were working in the swift run, and we waded out into position to try them with our flies.

Let's take a couple for breakfast, Gerry yelled.

It was not so easy. The flies looked the same on the water, but our Hendricksons were rejected. *These fish down here won't take my fly,* I complained. *Wonder what's wrong?*

Maybe the hatch has changed?

It was possible, and I waded across into a primary current to check the naturals. There were still good numbers of the dark-winged *Ephemerella* flies coming down, although the hatch was almost finished. It was five minutes before I caught one of the mayflies. It had dark slate-colored wings and darkly ringed rust-colored body. The hatch had changed.

They're different, I yelled.

That explains why the fish ignored our flies, Queen said. *What're these flies like that are hatching now?*

Darker, I answered. *Reddish brown bodies.*

Red Quill? Queen asked.

Exactly, I said.

We took several fish with Red Quills before the hatch became sporadic and finally ended. Here was a prime example of the serial problems in matching the hatch across a single day, in which three overlapping species emerged. Rather than matching the emergence of a single natural, sometimes two or three hatches must be matched over several hours of fishing. It is a lesson I have had to learn many times over the years. It also was an example of the impossibility of matching the hatch by merely observing the flies on the water. More than twenty-five years ago on the Au Sable, the fish had proved twice in a single afternoon how foolish such laziness can be.

It is equally impossible to match the hatch by observing naturals fluttering in the air, particularly in sunlight. Any insect observed against the light always looks much paler than it actually is, and it is not unusual to hear fishermen talking about picking fly patterns from the look of a hatching insect in flight. It is the kind of mistake you can observe often on trout waters from Maine to California.

What's hatching? It is a familiar cry.

Don't know! The answer is equally familiar. *They look like Light Cahills, but the fish just won't take the Cahills!*

You actually catch one of the flies? somebody asks.

No, comes the sheepish reply.

Such exchanges are typical on almost every river, and except for failing to respect the shyness and cunning of the trout, matching the hatch without capturing a specimen is perhaps the single most basic mistake in stream tactics. It is a mistake often made with caddisflies, since their pale rear wings are visible in flight, but are folded underneath the darker forewings when they are on the water. Most insects look paler in flight, but the whitish rear wings of most Trichoptera exaggerate this effect even more. Sedge hatches gave me trouble for years, because I invariably misjudged their color and size in the air. Many caddis hatches rise to memory, from early experiences with *Cheumatopsyche* flies on the Frying Pan in Colorado and *Rhyacophila* hatches on the Little South Pere Marquette in Michigan to similar problems on European rivers like the Pegnitz and Leizach in Bavaria. Such difficulties in matching caddis hatches are found on back country rivers too, like the Quilquihue and Collón Curá and Caleufu in the foothill pampas of Patagonia.

One evening on the lower Quilquihue comes instantly to mind for its remarkable hatch of sedges. We were camping on the river not far from its junction with the Chimehuin, and the late Guy Dawson had fished his favorite pools with me on the Quilquihue the first afternoon. Dawson was particularly attracted to the last major pool above the Chimehuin, although it surrendered only two eighteen-inch rainbows that day.

It's a fine pool, Dawson insisted. *It's provided two fish over eight pounds this summer, and the season lasts another two months.*

Browns or rainbows? I asked.

Both! he smiled.

It was a pool that formed where two channels of the river came together at the head of a right-angle bend. The primary channel shelved off steeply at the bottom of a one-hundred-yard chute. It deepened to some ten feet of water there, with a long current tongue working two hundred yards down a curving, undercut bank. The pool ended in a smooth knee-deep flat, where the fish dropped back to feed just before dark.

Two days later, I was fishing the pool in late afternoon when a hatch of big sedges emerged. The flies looked straw-colored and as large as size eight or ten, and they hopscotched and fluttered busily down the current. The fish suddenly were working on the surface, taking them greedily.

My fly books were filled with big bucktails and streamers, and one was layered with inch-long wet flies and nymphs. Matching the hatch was not a problem I had expected to find on the little-fished rivers of Argentina. There was a box of big western dry flies in my wading vest, and I rummaged through it for something that resembled the big Trichopteras that filled the twilight like a blizzard. There were three or four Donnelly Variants in one compartment, three dressed in dark brown hackles mixed with grizzly, and two mixed with pale ginger. Bob Carmichael had sold them to me years before, for fishing the tumbling Gros Ventre and Snake in Jackson Hole.

The Light Donnelly Variant looked just like the hatching flies, and I put it over the half-dozen big rainbows that were busily taking the naturals. It was completely rejected.

Funny, I thought. *It looks perfect!*

The big dry fly came down among the fluttering naturals and the feeding trout. One fat rainbow took a big caddis, ignored my imitation, and took another natural the moment my fly floated past. The clear pattern of rejection was repeated several times, and I stood there watching the fish gorge themselves.

It was a frustrating sight.

Suddenly I noticed a pair of big sedges clinging to my dark waders on the downwind side. Their wings and antennae were darkly mottled brown, totally unlike their pale yellowish appearance in the evening sunlight.

Maybe that's it. I reached inside my vest for the fly box. *Maybe the darker version will work!*

The dark pattern did not look yellow enough to match the hatching flies that fluttered along the surface in the wind, but it looked right to the fish. The pool yielded the best evening of dry-fly sport I have ever experienced anywhere. It was simply a matter of getting the fly floating again after each trout drowned it, and then putting it above another fish.

The pool was filled with good rainbows running eighteen to twenty inches, and I caught them until my arm and wrist were exhausted. The best fish went twenty-three inches, and took the dry fly with a tantalizingly slow head-and-tail rise that sent my pulse racing.

It's fantastic! I thought when the hatch was finished and the pool flowed silent again. *Twenty-nine fish over two pounds with dry flies—imagine the score if I'd picked the right fly when these sedges started!*

It was a unique experience, and it has never happened again in several trips into the Argentine, although that pool on the Quilquihue has always been productive. This past season it surrendered an eight-pound brown to a Muddler worked deep along the bottom, and it has become one of my favorites. It will always be Dawson's Pool in my mind.

Several years later on the Chimehuin, we were fishing the famous Black Bridge Pool a few miles below its junction with the Quilquihue. It is big-fish water, wide and smooth flowing below a place where the river batters and churns through a series of earthquake faults in the lava. It was late afternoon and the barren cinder cone of the Cerro de los Pinos rose in the east above the foothills across the two rivers, its ragged summits reflected in the currents.

When a similar hatch of big sedges started coming off the mile-long flat below the bridge, I laughed happily and started rooting through my fly vest for the Donnelly Variants.

It's going to be some evening! I thought.

But I was wrong again. The big rainbows started rolling and swirling everywhere, and I waded eagerly into the heavy current. The big variant worked rhythmically back and forth while I lengthened line, and I laid it expectantly over a good fish. It floated down its feeding lane unmolested, and I watched it drift through and start to drag badly.

Damn! I said.

Every fish within casting distance let it pass, and my excitement quickly ebbed. It was a fairly good hatch, and the trout were showing well, but several dry flies that seemed like good imitations were rejected completely.

Maybe they're not feeding on top, I thought.

I stopped fishing and watched the fish working only thirty feet out in the current. The bulging rises were strong, indicating that the fish really wanted what they were taking, and that what they were feeding on was relatively difficult to capture. The rises were not splashy, although an occasional fish did break the surface after a fluttering sedge.

Suddenly I realized that a fish had slashed eagerly across the current, and that a sedge came leapfrogging out of the splash. But that sedge had not been visible coming down the current before the rise.

It was hatching! I thought eagerly. *That fish missed it just before it hatched, and tried again!*

Several minutes of watching confirmed that diagnosis. The rises were not to the fluttering adults, although in my excitement I had just assumed the fish were taking the sedges that were everywhere. Two or three fish broke the steady rhythm of their feeding when a hatching fly escaped their swirling rises, and they splashed clumsily after the freshly hatched sedges. The fish were taking the hatching pupae.

Something with soft mottled hackles. I frowned. *Soft partridge or woodcock with a dubbed body of hare's mask.*

It was time for a simple Yorkshire-type wet, but the closest thing in my fly books was a darkly-hackled March Brown dressed in the British pattern. There were a half-dozen on size eight hooks. Their wings were too prominent, and I trimmed them down with the scissors in my fishing knife, clipping off the tails and picking out the dubbing with the stiletto.

Looks buggy enough, I concluded.

The rainbows were still working steadily. My first cast dropped quartering downstream above a good fish, and I teased its swing with the rod tip. It worked through the trout's position and there was a strong pull as the fish hooked itself, tailwalking explosively across the swift current. It was the solution that other long-ago afternoon on the Chimehuin.

There was a similar experience on the incomparable Firehole in the Yellowstone in late September. The Firehole is famous for its hatches and its surface-feeding trout, and Bergman's *Trout* is filled with praise for its marvellous dry-fly sport. His praise has led many fishermen to forget using their wet flies and nymphs on the Firehole, and it once led me to miss the solution to matching one of its hatches during several days of typically good feeding activity.

Gene Anderegg and I were fishing the Firehole that September, and it was more moody and difficult than usual. Our first morning in the Nez Percé meadows, the trout rose steadily in the pools, in the weedy channels, and along the sheltering banks.

The rises were strong, dramatic boils that occasionally erupted into a splash. It was a type of feeding behavior atypical of the Firehole trout and the quiet dimples usually visible everywhere on its currents. We took a number of small fish between six and twelve inches, using tiny spent-wing Adams and Whitcraft patterns tied on eighteen and twenty hooks. Two fish in a shallow flat succumbed to the jassid, but the larger trout kept feeding strongly in the main currents. There was one good fish working in a channel where the thick weeds had forced the current to scour deep under a grassy meadow bank.

I'm going to fish a bigger fly! Anderegg shook his head unhappily. *I'm going to fish a sixteen Adams!*

Try a really big fly—try a fourteen!

That's next! he yelled.

His bigger Adams was not the answer either, at least floated on the surface as its dressing intended, but a strange clue occurred while he was fishing it. The deep channel in the weeds, where a series of eddying currents undulated rhythmically, held the big trout that consistently refused the little dry fly. Once it rose splashily to a natural, drowning the artificial in the disturbance of its rise form, and another fish took the Adams swinging wet across the current.

We'll take anything we can get! Gene laughed.

It was a clue we ignored then, but it was the solution to the riddle of matching the hatch that morning.

There were several buffalo in the straw-grass meadows above Ojo Caliente, which spews thousands of gallons of scalding water every few minutes across the barren ledges into the Firehold. We sat in the warm grass, enjoying our sandwiches and watching the huge animals work down toward the river, grazing slowly on the rich forage. Finally they crossed the Firehole below Sentinel Creek, the swift current pushing heavily against their heavy legs and shoulders, and disappeared in the meadow bottoms beyond the river.

That season found the cold flow of Sentinel Creek forced against the far bank of the river, held between its buffalo grass and dense beds of weeds. Good fish were holding in this channel, both for its colder temperatures, and in anticipation of ascending Sentinel to spawn in a few weeks.

One good trout was working regularly, lying tight against the trailing grass, but it refused my little Whitcraft several times. Bad floats seemed like a possibility, and I moved slightly upstream to try another angle. The fish was feeding in a steady rhythm, and I studied it briefly before making another cast. My fly caught in the grass, pulled free suddenly, and was instantly drowned by the bellying leader. It was such a still current that I decided to let the Whitcraft ride through without picking up. Too early a pickup might send the fish scurrying upstream.

Easy does it, I whispered.

Suddenly there was a bulging swirl, the leader paused and darted upstream, and the fish was hooked. It bolted upstream along the channel, and held heavily along the bottom gravel. The fish surrendered stubbornly, its eighteen inches threshing in the net until I worked the hook free and released it.

Good fish? Anderegg yelled.

Couple of pounds, I answered. *You have any good fish working up there?* Several fish were rising above me.

Two or three up here, he said.

This fish was just like your fish before lunch, I yelled back. *Took my dry fly when it drowned.*

Maybe they're trying to tell us something!

Could be, I agreed.

The fish were obviously concentrating on hatching-sedge pupae, splashing at the odd pupal form that escaped to become an adult insect. Fishing wet seemed a solution. Certainly the effectiveness of a drowned dry fly is a telltale clue of such behavior. There were a dozen small partridge and brown wet flies in my wading vest, dressings that I use to imitate hatching caddisflies on the Brodheads each season, and I walked upstream to give several to Gene Anderegg.

Seems like sacrilege to fish wet on the Firehole! Anderegg grinned. *But it's probably the answer.*

Let's both try it, I said.

Anderegg changed flies, and I was still wading quietly toward the shallows when he hooked a fish.

Got one! he laughed. *That fish's been ignoring me for an hour!*

Good sign, I yelled back.

Anderegg hooked a larger trout before I started downstream to resume fishing, and it was a wild brown that chose to cartwheel like a rainbow down the current. Fishing wet to rising trout was the solution that September afternoon, with the geysers in the distance.

Another example of such offbeat behavior occurred one day on the Rolling Rock, when I was fishing with Bill Oliver of Pittsburgh. It was late April and there were heavy hatches of big *Ephemerella* flies coming down. We fished in late morning with the frost thick on the laurel and fiddleback ferns. The river was still cold from a cloudless night, registering only forty-six degrees on my Hardy thermometer. There were a few small stoneflies emerging before lunch, and I took some fish before we ate.

We had our lunch on the terrace at Rolling Rock, watching the freshly budded branches swaying against the April skies, and the green fairways of the golf course reaching toward the hills in the distance. It was a lunch filled with good talk about fishing books and Bill's fine collection of angling literature, since he is even more serious about the history of fly-fishing than about fishing itself.

It's two o'clock! Bill Oliver looked at his watch. *Your books predict Hendricksons today!*

They're not infallible! I laughed.

We drew another beat that afternoon, and I waded in along a reach of broken water below a cribbing dam, where a thin lacework of water fell smoothly from the logs. Trout were starting to work in the pockets, and although I took a few with a dry-fly imitation, most of the better fish refused it. The feeding rhythms increased.

It's not right, I said.

Most of those refusals are brown trout, Oliver said. *The brookies seem to like your Hendrickson just fine!*

That's what's wrong, I laughed.

Those brookies are from our hatchery, Oliver continued, *but some of those browns are wild carry-over fish.*

Exactly, I said.

The Hendrickson is a mayfly species that splits its thoracic skin and starts to pop its wings well before reaching the surface, and an emerging nymph pattern is often deadly. The hatching flies were clearly Hendricksons, yet the fish were letting most of the naturals float past, and kept rising regularly in the tail shallows.

I think they're on the hatching nymphs, I said.

Oliver smiled. *Give it a try!*

The preceding winter I had experimented extensively with the Rogowski-type hatching nymphs, which used rolled sections of nylon stockings to suggest emerging wing structure. They were roughly tied with dubbing and partridge legs and delicate woodduck tails. There was a fifteen-inch brown lying in a small pocket upstream, clearly visible in a patch of sunlight.

It was rising intermittently, and when I dropped my nymph slightly above its holding lie, the fish drifted toward the left and took it hard. The tempo of the hatch increased steadily, and I took fish after fish with my hatching nymph pattern. The fish strangely ignored the adult flies all afternoon, staying with the nymphs just under the surface—and fishing my imitation upstream to visibly rising trout produced almost a hundred trout between us.

Sometimes minor differences in color are important in matching the hatch, and my memory holds many examples of times when trout reacted to such subtle differences. Perhaps my first experience with subtle color phenomena occurred in earlier years on the headwaters of the Arkansas above Leadville Junction. The river was finally clear of high-country snowmelt, and the hatches were constant. We had good late-morning sport with dark blue-winged mayflies having heavily ringed and grayish-cream bodies, and on several days there were occasional specimens of *Ephemerella hecuba* that always started the big fish working. Frank Klune and I fished the Arkansas meadows every morning, and we could have filled our creels any time we wished. We took the fish regularly with three eastern patterns that matched these hatches: darkly hackled little Gordon Quills, Hendricksons, and Red Quills. These flies worked for three weeks, until another hatch came off in a swift little pool about a mile above the Leadville Junction Bridge.

They look like Red Quills, I guessed.

They're darker, Klune yelled upstream, *and they're a size or two smaller!* He walked toward me.

See if you can catch one! I shouted.

The naturals were extremely dark, with iron-blue wings and deep purplish red coloring on the belly segments of their bodies. These insects were too purplish for a normal Red Quill pattern to imitate them properly, and that night I dyed a bleached peacock eye a rich purple. The quills were wrapped over light brown underbodies, combined with iron blue hackles and tails. We used woodduck wings, perhaps imitating the Catskill style of fly dressing without thinking, and they took trout well. Dark hackle-point wings would probably have worked better. It was an interesting example of matching the hatch with relatively minor color changes.

Another interesting example occurred on the upper reaches of Silver Creek in Idaho, when a quiet morning suddenly came to life with a good hatch of sizable pale mayflies. The insects looked like our eastern *Stenonema* hatches that emerge in early summer, pale yellow and chalk-colored duns imitated by traditional patterns like the Light Cahill.

However, when I tried the pale ginger Cahill it was refused by the porpoising rainbows.

That's odd, I puzzled. *It sure looks like those flies coming down the currents.*

Fifteen minutes later I was finally convinced that my Light Cahill was a complete waste of time. Thirty-odd fish had rejected it after brief inspection rises. It was time to collect several of the naturals to determine the reasons behind my failure. The first little dun was a revelation. It was not straw-colored at all, but a faint shade of pale olive yellow, completely unlike the pale ginger hackles and woodduck wings of my Light Cahills. It had three tails, rather than the two tails usually associated with such pale hatches in the east.

It's an Ephemerella! I thought.

The olives in my box were too olive green for this hatch, and the trout refused my pale ginger dressings. My tying kit in the car had a pale olive gamecock neck that had taken the dye poorly, and was too pale for most olive mayfly imitations. It took twenty minutes to tie a pair of imitative patterns, but they took fish regularly that morning until two particularly large fish bolted into the moss and broke off. The hatch was over before I could tie another.

It was a satisfying and instructive morning.

There was a similar problem on two rivers in Wisconsin several years ago, when I was fishing with the late Art Besse. The late afternoon hatches on the Brule were good, and my last day there I sat waiting for the pale little duns. Upstream from my sitting place in the shadows, two raccoons foraged under the stones and logs for crayfish. Both raccoons were comical. Working a half-submerged log, they started at opposite ends and scuttled slowly toward each other, rooting underneath the trunk. The crayfish clambered backwards along the bottom until they were trapped between the raccoons; then they were quickly dispatched, dismembered and washed, and carefully eaten.

Shrimp cocktail! I laughed to myself.

The raccoons had fastidious table manners. They killed the crayfish, picked them apart like a skilled chef shelling a lobster, and washed each tidbit carefully before devouring it. It was fascinating, and I watched them capture six or eight crayfish before I realized a fly hatch was coming down and the fish had started to rise.

It was a hatch of Pale Sulphurs, with their faintly bluish wings and pale bodies flushed with orangish yellow. My tiny imitations were tied with pale blue hackle-point wings, and pale ginger hackles and tails. The bodies were white hackle quill lacquered with pale yellowish orange fuel-proof dope. It is a dressing originally worked out on Letort Spring Run, using the example of the Fox-type sulphurs, with their single turn of orange hackle mixed with the pale ginger. Pennsylvania fishermen on difficult limestone streams from Spruce Creek to the Little Lehigh swear by a touch of orange in their imitations of the sulphur hatch. The fish on the Brule those afternoons were busily working on these pale *Ephemerella* flies, and they accepted my imitations without hesitation. The hatch lasted several afternoons and evenings.

Before you drive back to Princeton, Besse suggested on his return to Ashland, *I want you to try the East Fork water.*

The East Fork? I asked.

It's a secret place of mine, Besse explained. *It's the East Fork of the Iron, and it's a helluva river!* He grinned conspiratorially.

What makes it so good? I pressed.

It's a limestone stream, Besse replied. *It comes out of some marl swamps southeast of the Brule.*

Try the East Fork tomorrow? I grinned.

Sure, Besse said.

It was hot that next day when we hiked downstream through the woods and fished back to the car. Later a filmy overcast muted the brightness, and a hatch of pale little duns started emerging from the swift runs along the willows.

Sulphurs again, I thought.

But that diagnosis was completely wrong. The imitative patterns that had proved so killing on the Brule failed miserably on these limestone brown trout. Fish after fish rejected my size sixteen sulphurs, until I stopped and waded upstream to find Besse. His flies were doing better, and he took several average-sized trout while I watched.

What are you using? I asked.

It's taken from your book, Besse laughed. *It's that pale little two-tailed subimago you described.*

But the usual imitations won't work!

The hatch is a little different on the East Fork, Besse continued. *It's got an olive-colored body.*

Pale olive gray? I asked.

Yes, he explained. *It's your Little Marryat with a faint olive dubbing mixed into the cream fox.*

They're that picky! I laughed in disbelief.

Try one, Besse suggested.

It seemed improbable that a faint olive cast added to the dubbing mix could make so much difference, but Besse was right. His dressing took fish readily, yet when I put my regular pattern back on the tippet, they refused it. It was clearly an example of subtle color preference, and I fished out the day using his olive-bodied flies.

Those fish are really tough! I said.

It's not such a problem. Besse had reached the highway and stopped. *The flies are in your book!*

Hate guys who read books! I laughed.

You should try it!

There was a similar experience on a smooth riffle on the Roaring Fork in Colorado, when a pale mayfly hatch started coming off just at twilight. The small hatchery rainbows took a sixteen Ginger Quill or Light Cahill readily enough, but there was a run tight against the willows where some bigger fish were rising. These fish refused such flies, and before it was dark I caught several specimens and put them in a killing jar.

That night in Basalt at the Frontier Lodge I examined the fresh specimens in their alcohol bottle. The preserving fluid had already turned their bodies a bright pink, and I wondered if the freshly hatched naturals also had a faint pinkish cast. Later I tied two or three Little Cahills with bodies of pink cellulite floss over a hook shank painted white. The pinkish cast was so faint that they looked like ordinary Light Cahills until you studied them carefully, and they darkened only slightly when wet. The following night I took four browns between twelve and eighteen inches along the willows, and only a faint pinkish color was the difference between the successful flies and the patterns that had failed before.

Several months ago, after a lecture in New York, a young man and his wife came up to the podium.

Pink-bodied Cahills! he shook hands enthusiastically. *We want to thank you for solving the problems of that hatch!*

Where did you fish it? I asked.

Wyoming! he was still bubbling. *We tried everything on the fish and nothing worked until we checked your books!*

And tied some pink-bodied flies! his wife added.

It has become a relatively common occurrence and one of the principal gratifications of writing a book like *Matching the Hatch*, since every fisherman has similar knotty problems of selectivity on his waters.

Perhaps the most unusual example of selectivity on mayflies and the sensitivity of the fish to color occurred a number of years ago on the Frying Pan in Colorado. We were fishing the Ruedi water from the ranch above the still water, a marvelous reach of river forever buried under the Frying Pan Reservoir ten years ago. Hatches were unusually mixed that week. The first evenings there were fine egg-laying flights, and we took a lot of fish with dark little sedge imitations. Later these Trichoptera became mixed with bigger mayflies that hatched just at twilight, and our caddis patterns stopped working. It was difficult to see the bigger flies on the swift currents of the footbridge pools above the ranch, and we first learned about the bigger flies through stomach autopsies of the fish.

The partially digested mayflies were still identifiable, and we started to take fish regularly again. We fished our little down-wing sedge flies from early evening until nightfall, switching to the bigger drakes after it got dark. Subsequent stomach autopsies and consistently good catches seemed to confirm our diagnosis, until one night the fish started feeding heavily, and our flies were systematically rejected.

What're they doing now? Frank Klune asked.

God knows! I answered.

Finally we caught one of the selective feeders when I started fishing a partridge-legged nymph in desperation, but it was the only fish that responded, and the feeding stopped with the hatch.

Autopsy time! We waded from the river.

We checked the stomach contents in a white dish back at the cabin once our Coleman lanterns were going. Deep in the entrails the digested insects were an undecipherable mass, but up toward the throat there were several sedge pupae. Adult sedges followed in good numbers, and finally there were a few big mayfly nymphs and several duns that we were not able to identify in those early years.

No wonder we couldn't get them, I said. *It was too late in the hatch for nymphs to work, and our dry fly patterns are completely wrong.*

They sure are, Klune agreed.

Earlier in the week, the twilight hatch of mayflies had dark lead-colored wings and bodies ringed with rich reddish brown. There were three heavily mottled tails and grayish mottled legs, but our mystery hatch was completely different.

It had grayish wings with faint mottlings, although the wings were so fragmented or wrapped around the bodies and themselves that it was difficult to tell exactly. It also had three tails, but they were speckled like the 'fibers from a darkly-barred flank feather of woodduck. The legs were dark amber, marked with brownish mottlings, and the thorax and abdomen were amber ringed with brown. Some specimens had a hint of orangey red in their body markings, and the flies were big enough that their wings measured as much as three-quarters of an inch in length. Except for the number of tails they looked familiar.

They're a little like our eastern March Browns, I said.

Let's tie some! Klune suggested.

The March Brown pattern was tried, with the addition of a dubbing spun on dark-orange silk ribbing a cream-fox body. The woodduck wings and mixed brown and grizzly hackles worked perfectly, and for several days we matched three hatches in sequence each evening. The sedges were still hatching in late afternoon and early evening, and we fished imitations effectively until the lead-winged duns started coming off the water. These flies were effective until the larger brownish drakes started coming off just before nightfall.

However, it was not this serial problem in matching the hatch that proved most instructive. It was the remarkable selectivity to color in the dark that intrigued me. Both imitative patterns were dressed on size ten, and had precisely the same materials, configuration, and silhouette. The woodduck wings were identical, and both bodies were dubbed and ribbed with fur spun on silk. Hackle color varied between dark bronze-blue dun and brown gamecock mixed with grizzly. Body color was different, too. Those still-water brown trout consistently rejected the March Brown pattern while feeding on the big *Ephemerellas,* and they refused the bluish gray dressings when the mottled brownish drakes started hatching at nightfall.

They're even selective after dark! Frank Klune laughed.

It was a remarkable lesson in both selectivity and color sense, and I shall never forget it. It has proved valuable on selective trout from California to Austria, clearly proving that no trout fisherman should ever underestimate the color sense of his quarry.

Serial problems in matching the hatch are not limited to overlapping emergence of several insects; they also lie within the spectrum of a single insect species. Mayflies are quite typical of such behavior. The nymphs of each species progress through a series of instars, or physical stages of growth, between hatching from the eggs to full nymphal maturity before emergence. This means that each species reaches a number of intermediate growth stages, and that a nymphal imitation that suggests pre-hatch maturity in size twelve is also useful in the smaller sizes from fourteen to twenty-two, simulating earlier stages of development. Each pattern is useful in a number of sizes.

Behavior is another factor in matching the hatch, particularly in the nymphal stages, although the fluttering behavior of some adult insects is important as well. Such tactics are explored extensively in *Fishing the Dry Fly as a Living Insect*, which Leonard Wright first published in 1972. My subsequent book *Nymphs* makes the point that effective nymph fishing is as dependent upon presentation and manipulation of fly speed and motion as on the fly pattern itself.

Burrowing mayfly nymphs are as agile as baitfish when swimming toward the surface to hatch. Other swimming nymphal forms do not bury themselves in silt and detritus, but forage freely among the stones and current-rich weeds, darting swiftly from place to place. Clambering nymphs range about clumsily in various types of water and are best imitated with nymphs fished deep with a slow, deliberate retrieve. Tiny swimming nymphs are agile, but their agility is barely perceptible except in slow-moving rhythms in the rubble and weeds. Clinging nymphs of swift water and the crawling nymphs, as well as sedge larvae and other similar diet forms, are virtually helpless when caught in faster currents. Their imitations should be fished deep and deaddrift. Stoneflies typically clamber and cling along the bottom, and imitations of their nymphal forms should also be fished deaddrift.

Hatching behavior is equally important. The larger swimming nymphs, and clambering ecotypes like the stoneflies, migrate into shallow water and cling to fallen logs and stones to split their nymphal skins and hatch. Many large nymphs hatch in the surface film, experience considerable difficulty in escaping their nymphal skins, and ride the shucks before flying off. Other species actually hatch into the winged stages while their nymphs still cling to the bottom. Many hatches begin to escape their nymphal forms well below the surface film, wriggling along for several feet before actually breaking through as winged insects. These patterns of behavior suggest varying approaches to imitation: different types of hooks, weighting of the flies with lead, tying the patterns with different winging styles from minimal development to the fully winged state, and manipulation of fly speed and retrieve.

The cycle of mayfly hatching also suggests a number of phases in matching the hatch during a single emergence cycle. Nymphs along the bottom mean heavy-wire hooks, possible weighting of the flies, and a sinking-line presentation. Partially developed wings should be included for species that actually hatch along the bottom. Hatching mayflies at intermediate depths are often wriggling and struggling clumsily, both to escape their nymphal skins and reach the surface. Some nymphs split their thoracic cases before reaching the meniscus, and their wings begin to unfold underwater. Others emerge using the tensile force of the surface film, their wings unfolding clumsily and partially awash. Nymphs that escape their nymphal skins slowly often ride them in the surface film for as much as sixty to a hundred feet. Such imitations should be dressed with emerging-type wings, while a fully hatched dun is best imitated with upright wings.

Mayfly spinners pose different problems. Many large species lay their eggs from two large sacs while actually riding the current. Several species leapfrog along the surface in a series of graceful parabolas, extruding a few eggs each time they touch the water. Others form their ova into fat little egg sacs, dropping them or washing them off in the river, and still others ride the current momentarily while extruding their eggs, flutter upward briefly, and settle again to lay more ova. Several minute species of mayflies and several sedges migrate underwater to oviposit their eggs.

Such behavior has interesting implications for fly making and matching the hatch. Windy weather can deposit any species of mayfly spinner into the river, and imitations with upright wings are useful as well as the typical spent-wing dressings. Since the eggs are extruded well before the flies are spent, egg-sac patterns are probably most useful with upright or divided-style wings. Many spinners fall into the current after mating and laying their eggs, their wings divided and faltering. Finally the wings lie spent in the surface film, and such spinners are virtually invisible drifting on the water.

Many spinners reach the streamside foliage after mating and expire slowly, dropping hours later into the river. Some fall spent immediately after oviposition, and a few species molt and lay their eggs shortly after hatching. Such spinner falls are difficult to diagnose and offer challenging sport on many streams.

Spinner falls usually occur immediately after a mating swarm is finished, and sometimes the spent flies are still available the following morning. Even the larger spinners are difficult to see drifting spent on a still flat, and with the smaller species it seems as if the fish are taking something invisible. Such spinners are often found in good numbers, and the fish take them with a quiet, methodical rhythm in which one rise form is scarcely finished before another insect is taken. Their steady feeding rhythms can be frustrating, particularly when an angler fails to diagnose feeding on spent spinners.

Some of the finest rises to a spinner fall occur on Idaho streams like the Henry's Fork of the Snake, and the famous Silver Creek in the Sun Valley country. Ruedi still water on the Frying Pan once provided marvelous fishing to spent mayflies in its tail shallows before it was inundated behind the Ruedi Reservoir, particularly during the fine *Leptophlebia* hatches in September.

There are also minute species like *Caenis* and *Tricorythodes* that hatch, form into mating swarms, oviposit, and fall spent almost immediately. Their duns and spinners are often virtually identical. Tiny no-hackle spentwings tied of polypropylene or fur dubbing are often effective imitations. Over the years I have fished some excellent twilight hatches of *Caenis* flies on both slow streams and low-altitude ponds, while the ubiquitous little *Tricorythodes* is typically a hatch of early and late morning. Such tiny flies are imitated with size twenty-four to twenty-eight hooks, yet they are present in such vast numbers that surprisingly big fish take them on the surface. It is interesting fishing.

This past summer on Silver Creek in Idaho I fished over some early *Tricorythodes* hatches, using tiny iron blue hackle nymphs when the hatch was starting, tiny white-winged uprights in the thorax-style during the hatch itself, and finished with spent no-hackle spinners. The big rainbows took the little nymphs on a simple downstream swing, teasing against the tension of the leader, and later sipped the hatching duns with audible sucking rises. They took the tiny spinners with gentle dimples and porpoising swirls as if they knew the spent flies were pinioned in the surface film and could not escape.

However, the spinner fall is not the only type of quiet feeding that occurs with nothing visible on the water. It often takes place when fish are concentrating on midge larvae and pupae, and sometimes it happens when midges are actually hatching.

Years ago I was fishing the South Platte in Eleven Mile Canyon when the fish began working steadily. The rises barely disturbed the surface. The feeding rhythm was so steady that the first gentle rise form had scarcely ebbed before a second had dimpled the surface. The fish seldom have such an abundance of food, and I started using a tiny parachute spinner, thinking it might be a fall of tiny spinners, but the trout consistently refused my imitation.

What are they doing? I wondered.

Flying ants sometimes trigger such regular feeding rhythms, but none were evident anywhere in the shallows. No other insects were visible on the surface, yet the fish were working steadily.

It's in the film, I thought, *and it's something small!* Several fish were dimpling in a deep run below some rocks.

Such feeding is sometimes focused on concentrations of midge larvae or pupae, which occur in several cycles during the season. These concentrations can occur virtually any time through the spectrum of the season, although on western rivers I have seen the largest numbers of such subaquatic Diptera from June through October. We were fishing the South Platte on the final day of the season, warm and perfectly still in the canyon above Deckers. Several mule deer drifted down through the stand of ponderosa and crossed the river below.

There were two men fishing salmon eggs illegally in a deep run among the boulders two hundred yards upstream. Since I had often experienced good fishing with a small Whitcraft or Adams, I started fishing these flies over the feeding trout. When they refused both of these patterns, I tried a size twenty Blue Quill, another pattern that has often proved its worth on the Platte. It was also systematically refused.

It must be midges, I thought finally.

There was nothing visible on the water, and I studied the current for several minutes without discovering anything. There were a number of tiny dubbing midge larvae in several colors in my fly books, and I selected a slender pattern which was nothing more than some dark olive dubbing delicately ribbed with condor quill and mixed with a few short guard hairs. It was lightly oiled with a film of silicone on my fingertips, and I clinch-knotted it to the 7X tippet. The fly worked a miracle.

These difficult browns were unusually wary, their senses honed in a season-long parade of fishermen from Denver and Colorado Springs. After refusing my conventional patterns, these same fish seemed as gullible as hatchery trout. The fish in the run above me were not large, although two went twelve or thirteen inches, and each took the tiny larva without hesitation.

The trout were almost totally browns, although Colorado stocks mostly rainbows. There were still a few rainbows left from the spring stocking programs, but most had either been caught or had migrated downstream by late October.

It is always satisfying to solve a difficult problem when the fish are dimpling everywhere in a smooth current. I caught and released fifteen or twenty good trout in the next one hundred yards. The two bait fishermen caught a sucker drifting their eggs on the bottom in the hole between the boulders. Their creels were still empty when I reached the smooth flat fifty yards below them.

Mister! they yelled. *You catching trout?*

The tiny midge imitations had produced about forty trout, and I had released them all. *Yes,* I replied.

You ain't keeping none? The question had a sullen tone.

No, I answered quietly.

There were ten or twelve fish dimpling between us, including a few rising less than twenty feet below the bait fishermen.

You using flies? they continued. *Catching all them fish?*

Yes, I said.

The fish between us still took my flies readily in the film, and I hooked and released a half dozen in the flat below them. They were not large trout, but they fought well on my delicate tackle, and I released them gently. There was a dark run along a fallen log in the shallows upstream, and a faint movement there seemed to disturb the current.

Was that a fish? I watched the log carefully.

The quiet disturbance came again, bulging slightly in the current against the deadfall, and the rise form died quickly. The fish rose again and again, barely showing itself. There was a swift current tongue between my position and the run along the tree, and I decided to get closer to the fish. It looked like a good trout and I approached on my knees in the shallows. The fish was only twenty-five feet away, and I dropped the little olive larva softly above its station. It was impossible to see the fly, and when there was a quick dimple I tightened gently. The shallows exploded.

Big fish! I thought wildly.

It was a fish of about three pounds, and it bolted upstream toward the bait fishermen, stripping line with a shrill chorus from the reel. It stripped more line in a second run and jumped just below their boulder hole, and both bait fishermen stood up angrily on the rocks.

Goddammit! one muttered, *I seen enough!*

They were already well up the trail above the river when the good brown finally turned weakly on its side and drifted head first into my waiting net.

Working the tiny hook free, I held it briefly in the shallows until it struggled out of my hands. The fat brown drifted off below my legs and held there, moving its gills steadily. The dubbing was thin and shredded, and I was replacing my fly when a gargantuan splash echoed in the canyon.

Sonofabitch! one of the men shouted. *You ain't catching them fish in our hole!* Another big stone whistled over my head, and fell heavily into their hole in the boulders.

Sonofabitch! The third stone made a huge splash.

Such episodes are mercifully rare, although impressive rises of trout are common on heavy concentrations of midge larvae and pupae. Fishermen on big water like the East Branch of the Delaware in New York, the famous Muskegon and Big Manistee in Michigan, and the Upper Yellowstone or Snake are familiar with the sight of hundreds of fish dimpling softly in the film.

The Au Sable in Michigan is another river, rich in alkalinity from its marl swamps and springs, with frequent concentrations of midge larvae and pupae. It is the origin of a fly dressing called Griffith's Gnat, which is often a surprisingly effective pattern when the midge pupae are actually hatching. It is a simple fly worked out by George Griffith, the founder of Trout Unlimited, who has a charming cabin on a high moraine above the Wakeley Bridge.

His original dressing was a peacock herl body, palmer-tied with a small grizzly hackle. Light-wire hooks from size sixteen to a tiny twenty-eight are typically used. Fished half-awash in the film, the pattern is an excellent imitation of a hatching midge still tangled in its tiny pupal skin. Other color combinations are effective too, and these little palmer-tied gnats have often produced well for me during midge-feeding activity when conventional flies failed to take fish. It undoubtedly provides a color mix, silhouette, and light pattern in the surface film not found with other midge imitations. Such differences are often important, and once made the difference on a huge flat in the Yellowstone.

Literally millions of midge pupae were drifting into the river from the marl-rich ecology of Yellowstone Lake, and its surface was covered for miles with the dimples of countless rising fish. It was one of the most impressive rises of trout I have ever seen, unrivalled except for the brief periods of heavy spinner-fall feeding on the Henry's Fork of the Snake.

The hatching midges were brownish gray, and their swarms filled the windless twilight. Many times with that particular *Chironomus* hatch I have taken some remarkable catches of fish, using either a tiny Adams or Whitcraft when the fish were taking the adult midges. Brownish midge larval and pupal imitations are also often effective when the fish decide to concentrate on the subaquatic stages. But this time these patterns failed utterly.

Standing waist-deep in the smooth flow of the Yellowstone flats, I placed cast after cast over the rising cutthroats. My flies dropped softly above each fish I tried. The fish invariably rose just before my flies reached them, and dimpled again just after my flies floated past. It was frustrating, and I tried pattern after pattern, over fish after fish. The exquisite torture lasted more than an hour.

Finally I tried a small Griffith's Gnat over them, half expecting it to float back unmolested, and I was surprised to see it disappear in a quiet dimple. The fish was a surprise too, since it bolted upstream along the bottom, taking all the fly line and about fifteen yards of backing. It was twenty minutes before I worked it back against the fragile nylon, and when it drifted close I gasped.

Six or seven pounds! I said breathlessly.

It was a huge female cutthroat. It circled weakly against my frail tippet for another ten or fifteen minutes, and when it finally surrendered, it disgorged a handful of half-emerged midge pupae. Most of these pupae washed free into the current, but many caught in the meshes of the net and the gills of the fish. The pupae had all been taken before they could fully escape their subaquatic skins, and were dark little silhouettes pinioned in a diaphanous shuck of half-transparent chitinous covering. Neither a conventional dry fly nor imitations of the subaquatic forms had worked, and a fly dressing that suggested a partially hatched midge still pinioned in the surface film was the solution that September twilight.

Steady feeding in hot windy weather is usually focused on terrestrial insects like ants and leafhoppers and beetles. It takes relatively warm weather to make these ecotypes active and venturesome enough to explore the bankside foliage and vegetation, together with gusts of wind to tumble them into the water.

Sometimes it happens unexpectedly.

Several years ago I was fishing the South Raritan one afternoon in early April. It was unmistakably Hendrickson time and there were a few mayflies hatching at two o'clock when I waded into a pool below Califon. The fish were already working steadily. It was warm and I expected a good mayfly hatch that afternoon, so I started fishing the rise forms with a Hendrickson nymph.

The fish kept rising along the willows, but nothing came to my carefully fished nymph except two small sunfish and a fat Warmouth bass. The selective fish among them were probably trout. It was almost hot at three-thirty, and a brisk April wind blew downstream. The temperature and the wind should have been the clue, but I missed its importance until later in the day.

The trout were working regularly now, their quiet rises barely dimpling the current. The rise forms should also have told me something, but I missed that clue as well. When a thick mayfly hatch started, I began fishing a dry-fly imitation. The fish refused it several times until a bluegill took it solidly when it started to drag. It had tiny ants in its small gasping mouth.

Damn! I thought in disgust. *You should have guessed as much!*

The rises were too quiet for the fluttering mayflies or their hatching nymphs. The temperatures meant that ants would be unseasonably active in the willows and trees, and the wind was getting them into the river in good numbers. It was then that I noticed the third clue I had missed. There was an obvious relationship between the wind and the rising trout: as the wind stirred through the willows the number of rises quickly increased.

The wind is blowing them onto the river, I thought.

It was easy after that, and a tiny seal-fur ant dressed on a size twenty hook took a dozen browns and rainbows before it finally grew cool and the trout stopped feeding. They were carefully released in gratitude for a fine day's sport.

Sometimes terrestrial feeding is a mixture of things, particularly in midsummer when several kinds of insects are in the trees and foliage. There was another hot windy day on the Beaverkill that season when I discovered twenty-odd fish in surprisingly shallow water. The fish were lying over a stony bottom in patchy sunlight, and I fortunately saw them before they spotted me. Some of these browns were lying together in groups of three and four, and others were lying alone. The fish were virtually resting on the bottom.

Wonder what they're doing? I said aloud.

The fish lay quietly until a strong gust of wind riffled the water, and suddenly there were rises everywhere. The fish were sipping and dimpling in the film, and when the wind dropped the trout were quiet again.

Ants, I thought.

It was a good choice, and I quickly took three fish with a tiny twenty-two ant, but a third trout inspected it and refused.

Wonder what he wants, I laughed to myself. *Cinnamon ant?*

The little cinnamon ant was rejected, too, and a twenty-two rusty ant with dun hackles was not even studied when it floated over the fish. It rose and took something tiny from the film, scarcely disturbing the surface. It quickly dimpled again.

Maybe they're taking leafhoppers along those willows, I thought.

The fourth trout took a small Jassid with delicate black hackles, but the fifth fish moved to intercept its float, studied it briefly, and returned to its lie over the gravel.

Try the ant again. I trimmed the Jassid off.

It worked and the fish threshed in surprise, while I coaxed it gently downstream away from the others. It was a good fish, brightly spotted and butter yellow along its belly, and it lay in the shallows after I released it, eyeing me balefully for disturbing its meal. Two more fish took the ant before another balked.

Another difficult gourmet? I wondered.

It was a fish of fifteen or sixteen inches, and it refused my Black Jassid as well. *Tiny beetle?* I thought.

There were several small green-feather beetles in my fly boxes, imitations dressed on delicate size-twenty hooks. Clinching one to the tippet, I made a short cast that dropped it softly above the fish. The tiny beetle lay flat in the surface film, and the big fish nosed it curiously before refusing.

Maybe the beetle's too big. The scissors on my fishing knife trimmed the feather wing until it was a tiny oval an eighth of an inch in length. *Maybe he'll take it when it looks a size smaller.*

It worked perfectly and the big trout inhaled it without a qualm, bolting angrily through the shallows when I tightened. The remaining fish scattered like frightened quail, fleeing past me downstream and leaving the shallows upstream. It was no longer necessary to stalk them on my knees, and I stood up to play the big fish that had taken the beetle. It writhed in the shallows and tried to foul my leader in some roots, and I parried it with measured pressure from the delicate straining of my Leonard. It scuttled sideways to work under a flat stone, but it was much too large, and the delicate tippet did not touch its rough edges. It came back stubbornly with the gentle tension of the rod tip, and then stripped line again, while my little Hardy played its ratchety melodies. It was stubborn with such a tiny hook and a spiderweb tippet, but it finally came to the waiting net, its gills and fins working weakly in the shallows.

It was finally over and I released the fat two-pound fish. It was a valuable lesson about selective trout and matching the hatch in the heat of midsummer.

Sometimes it gets complicated. I studied the beautiful fish that lay exhausted at my feet, its spotted gill covers slowly recovering their strength. *Sometimes you have to match the hatch on a fish-by-fish basis.*

It is a valuable axiom on hard-fished water.

12. Ethics, Manners, and Philosophy Astream

It has been more than twenty years since that first Colorado summer. The cutting in the hayfields was almost finished, but several rainy afternoons had made the irrigation bottoms too wet for mowing. The irrigation ditches were dry except for the rain. Their sluice gates were closed, and their flow had been returned to the little creek that tumbled down the northeast shoulder of Mount Massive. The creek had run milky for a day or two, and then the turbidity settled and cleared. Its currents were unseasonably high for late summer, but it was fishable.

The overcast obscured the mountains across the Arkansas bottoms, and the morning train climbed achingly up the long grade from Granite to the Malta Crossing. There were four engines pulling two miles of freight cars. The lead engine whistled, and the diesels strained slowly toward the Tennessee Pass and the Pacific watershed in the Pando bottoms beyond. The steady rain had stopped its drumfire rhythms on the roof just before daylight, and the radio promised better weather.

Hatches should be good, I thought.

There was no haying scheduled that morning, but I had chores in the horse barns. There was manure to clear and shovel out, and I worked slowly until the water ran swift and clean again in the stone gutters behind the stalls.

Finished, I announced back at the house.

You're off fishing again? my aunt asked. *Will you be back in time for lunch?* She was baking fresh bread.

I'll just take a sandwich, I said.

My tackle was in the bunkhouse. The rod hung on three finish nails in the wainscoting wall, and I shouldered into my waders and wading vest and

209

creel. It was a two-mile walk through the irrigation bottoms to the serpentine willows that marked the winding course of the creek.

Its currents begin in the snowfields below the three-part summit of Massive, tumbling through high meadows bright with tiny alpine flowers. There are curious quaking bogs far above timberline. It flows through a chain of tiny lakes and beaver ponds filled with small cutthroats and brook trout. There is one large beaver pond above the main ranch buildings, and sometimes I saddled a horse to fish it in the evenings. The creek below the big beaver pond held many brook trout and some rainbows, but there were also a few cutthroats and deep pockets that sheltered browns.

The creek tumbled wildly down its final boulder-strewn ravine to the valley floor, less than one hundred yards south of the ranch. It wound into the Arkansas bottoms through willow-lined channels, looping toward the river in the distance, and its lower mileage was brown-trout water.

Its deep meadow pools and cut-bank runs were typical of brown-trout fishing. It was water that often seemed empty, but the fish were always there. It was possible to fish for hours on most days without catching a brown. There were always a few rainbows and the odd brookie below the ranch buildings, but when a gentle rain misted down the valley and triggered a good hatch of flies, its seemingly barren water was suddenly alive with surface-feeding browns.

The creek joins the river in a long sweeping bend with deeply undercut banks. Its currents are soft and smooth over fine gravel. Coarse grass trails in the waist-deep water tight against the banks, and although it always seemed like a perfect pool, I had never seen a fish rising there.

The pool was strangely empty, and I thought about it sometimes in the last half-wakeful moments before sleep, hearing the glowing coals shifting in the pot-bellied stove and mice scuttling in the bunkhouse walls.

The solution to its riddles occurred to me that morning, while I was walking down through the hay meadows. My approach to those last fifty yards of the creek had always been from upstream, walking on the grassy path beside the pool. From the waist-deep grass that lined the path it was possible to see every pebble on the bottom, but it was also possible for every trout to observe an approaching fisherman.

Idiot! I thought angrily to myself. *Cross the creek and wade up from downstream!*

The opposite bank was thickly overgrown with willows and the driftwood tangles gathered during the spring snowmelt. It was difficult going and I fought through the thickets, carrying my rod high above the branches or butt-first in the brush. Half-wild cattle bellowed and crashed deeper into the willows like buffaloes, and I was soaked with perspiration when I finally escaped into the open river bottoms. It was almost noon and getting hot, and I washed my face in the water.

The creek joined the river fifty yards upstream, and I waded slowly toward the gravel bar and sat down to rest and cool off. It felt good to strip my waders off and shed my tackle vest. There were a few mayflies hatching. They were fairly large insects, fluttering down the smooth-flowing run. Their pale wings had a slight olive cast, and they looked like big Cahills rising off the current into the willows.

Since that summer I have learned that they were *Ephemerella inermis,* but that season such hatches only set me searching my fly boxes for pale imitations. There was a fresh Light Cahill in one compartment, its rolled woodduck wings and pale ginger hackles stiffly cocked and unsoiled. It was carefully knotted to my tippet, and I studied the dark-water run along the grass. The flies were still emerging sporadically, but no rises showed in the quiet currents. The pool flowed still and smooth.

Weather is capricious at 9,000 feet. Clouds gathered on the high saddle of Mount Massive, where they had been forming since midday, and a brief squall moved across the valley. The fine drizzle scarcely disturbed the stream, but it seemed to trigger a full-blown hatch of the tiny straw-colored mayflies.

It happened almost imperceptibly.

The flies emerged from the smooth current, fluttered awkwardly in the rain while their wings dried, and flew off haltingly into the willows. The pale duns went virtually unnoticed until a sudden splash engulfed a fluttering insect tight against the grass. The disturbance of the rise spread downstream on the current.

Big fish! I thought excitedly.

There was a second porpoiselike rise, showing a thick well-spotted bulk.

No wonder I've never seen other fish in this pool, I thought. *He's got the whole pool staked out!*

Working stealthily into position, I checked the leader for casting knots and frayed places while the big trout rose again and again. My cast dropped softly and cocked the fly above the fish, reached its feeding position, and disappeared into a bold swirl. There was nothing there when I tightened.

Damn! I muttered. *Missed him!*

The rises stopped, and for some reason I stood still in the current and waited. Just when I had decided it was hopeless, there was another impressive rise fifteen feet above the place where I had missed the first fish. It seemed unlikely that two fish that size might share such a minor pool, and I waited nervously while the big trout settled into a methodical feeding rhythm. It took a dozen fluttering duns before I tried a cast that fell perfectly, and the trout rose lazily and took my fly.

He's on! I yelled aloud.

The shrill reel protested and the delicate rod danced to the threnody of its writhing head-shaking fight. All the foot-long brown trout I had taken that summer were quickly forgotten, along with the sixteen-inch rainbow taken in the ranch-house pond. These runs stripped line from the reel, reaching high into the riffles above, and once the fish threatened to escape into the heavy river currents downstream. Several times it bored deep under the banks and trailing grasses, ticking the leader across the willow roots and sticks, but the tippet held safely.

The fish struggled desperately when it finally saw the waiting net, working its tail in tight circles, just out of reach. It was close several times, but each time it bolted off again until I worked it slowly back.

Finally it surrendered and came to the net, and it threshed and writhed deep in the meshes.

It's huge, I thought wildly and waded ashore. *It's better than twenty inches!*

It was the biggest trout I had ever seen, and I killed it eagerly with my priest, but in the weeks that followed I always passed that pool with a touch of sadness. Although there were other good hatches, I never saw another fish rising there, and I covered it often. There is nothing so empty as a pool without trout, particularly when the guilt is yours.

It is a lesson we learn too slowly.

The typical odyssey we travel in learning to fish is a gradual and satisfying journey. It is a slow evolution from beginner to expert, and it involves a subtle metamorphosis from fisherman into angler. However, it is not merely the refinements of fishing and our fish-catching skills that occupy this transformation. It is also a remarkable evolution in attitudes. The full metamorphosis is complete when a man realizes that his fishing skills have been so developed that he can deplete his own sport.

It is a singular milestone of self-knowledge.

Each trout fisherman experiences a similar development, usually under the tutelage of an older angler. His genesis often lies in fishing the live baits. My father guided me along that path toward the eventual role of fly-fishing, and I started toward that unseen goal with live grasshoppers on a small meadow stream in Michigan. Two things make the small stream a perfect classroom for the beginner: there is no better place to discover the hair-trigger wariness of a wild trout, and the splashy strike to a grasshopper is not unlike the rise to the dry fly.

Like all beginners with skilled tutors, I was taught to creep stealthily to a chosen pocket, peer cautiously through the leaves and grass, and lower my grasshopper gently above the trout. The fish were not large in that meadow creek, but they were wary enough to teach caution, and they responded with an eager splash that was an exciting preparation for the fly-fishing I finally began the following year.

The transition from grasshoppers to a rather simple and effective wet-fly method was relatively easy. From this basic foundation, I gradually branched out into the other methods, using dry flies and bucktails and streamers. It was a surprisingly productive season, and before it was ended, several limits of trout had fallen to my dry flies. As my skill increased, I passed into a stage that seems to afflict every fisherman during his early evolution: the desire to kill and bring in large numbers of fish to prove and demonstrate his prowess. It is a malady we all contract in our fishing careers, and some men never escape its ravages.

Three years after my start on that meadow brook in Michigan, I met a white-haired gentleman on the upper Pere Marquette who smilingly inquired about my luck. With the bursting pride of a ten-year-old, I raised the lid of my wicker creel to reveal fifteen trout from eight to eleven inches in length.

Female Beaverkill, I explained proudly.

His kindly expression soured, and the old man asked quietly why I had killed so many fish. The old man added that if every angler were so fortunate, there would soon be few fish left in our river. Flushed with hurt pride and anger, I testily dismissed his criticism as jealousy of my catch; but looking back I see a man mellowed with years of rich pleasure and skill on the river, and I am ashamed of my boyhood greed. Several times that summer I watched the same man fish difficult water on the Little South, and he caught trout almost at will every time he appeared along the river. It was obvious that he could kill the limit any time he wished, yet he released most of the trout he caught.

It was a puzzle half-understood for years, but finally on that meadow stream in Colorado, I understood after I had killed the big fish and later regretted its absence. The skilled angler does not need dead trout in his basket to feel satisfaction. His skills have long since demonstrated that he can catch trout, and he needs no proof for his companions. There is no need to fear the ridicule of others for his empty creel, and some anglers no longer bother to carry a creel on the stream. Limit catches are often easy to fill and carry no particular badge of excellence.

The sophisticated angler counts as his highest reward the number of fish released for another day. His basket may contain an occasional fish if someone has expressed a desire for trout, or a fish has been hurt taking the fly and cannot be released successfully. But the really skilled fisherman loves his sport far too much to spoil it with wanton killing.

Gerry Queen once told me the story of a great trout that lived in the pool just above their cabin on the Little South. Although their stretch of river was not posted, these men improved its pools unselfishly with deadfall deflectors and rock wing dams. The water bordered by their property soon became the finest on the river, and it was not long before big wild fish began appearing in their pools. One large trout settled in the deep, eddying pool below their fishing house, and it quickly became a favorite with this circle of anglers. All had raised it at least once, and two or three had hooked and lost the fish. One actually landed and released the fish during a Michigan mayfly hatch, and measured it at twenty-seven inches.

It became like an old and familiar friend.

And then an outsider armed with nightcrawlers and twenty-pound nylon wrestled the big trout from the river during a spate, and brutally killed it on the spot. It was unceremoniously gutted and its entrails were heaved into the stream for the crayfish. Without its magnificent eight-pound brown, the magic of the Cabin Pool was gone.

Finding such a trout is the greatest thrill, since it is an adversary truly worthy of our skills. We may work on it for days without success, and still return home satisfied and filled with thoughts of another day. One seldom remembers the hundreds of average fish encountered over the years, but those few trophy-size trout taken or lost under difficult conditions are long carried in our memories. Just the knowledge that such a big fish exists adds a delicious flavor of anticipation to each pool.

Nonfishermen seldom understand why we fish when we usually release our catch, and too many fishermen sadly share their myopia. They fail to grasp that the *live* trout, lying in its sun-dappled riffles, rising over its bright-gravel shallows, and fighting the delicate rod, gives our sport its entire meaning.

Dead trout are just so much meat, however deliciously they might be prepared for the table. Food cannot be the reason we fish for trout, since an equal amount of work would secure much more at the supermarket, and the fish counter is a cheaper place to obtain it. We cannot begrudge the local angler his occasional catch of trout, particularly if such fish supplement a meagre income, but the fly-fisherman who travels hundreds of miles to fish a stream is paying astonishing amounts of money in terms of each pound of fish. When we consider our motivation in economic terms, it becomes obvious that we fish for the sport of trout fishing and not for killing the fish we catch.

My good friend John Hemingway, whose famous father taught him to love trout fishing on the swift rivers of Idaho, is adamant about this subject.

These days no one really fishes for food, Hemingway insists. *It is not the business of our Fish and Game Commissions to supply protein!*

There is no pragmatic logic in our behavior, and fishing only to release the fish we catch unmistakably has the overtones of philosophy. Chinese history includes a philosopher who omitted both hook and bait from his tackle, since actually catching a fish interrupted the richly contemplative moods of his sport.

Our philosophy of trout fishing does not demand such ultimate asceticism, but catch-and-release fishing is itself an example of illogical and intriguing behavior. It carries obvious nuances of ritual hunting. The blood rhythms of fishing and hunting clearly demonstrate the fact that our civilized veneer remains surprisingly thin, and we still share the instincts of our primordial ancestors. Yet we have evolved to the point that the rhythms of the hunt are more exciting than the anticlimax of the kill.

Fly-fishing is the only field sport that provides an equilibrium between these points of view. It has all the blood rhythms of the hunt, particularly when we are working on a rising trout, but it does not demand the actual kill to complete its liturgies. Unlike bait or lure fishing, catching trout on flies seldom injures the fish. The captured trout can be safely released. Therefore, releasing a trout is a kind of ritual kill that satisfies both our primitive instincts, and our mixture of reverence and respect for the beauty and courage of the trout.

It also makes good economic sense.

Given our modern fishing pressure, it costs millions of dollars to stock our streams to provide put-and-take management. Yet less than half of the fish planted are actually recovered, and each bait-caught fish is enjoyed only once. Catch-and-release fishing not only provides multiple use of each fish stocked, but it also provides better sport. There are more fish of better-than-average size on such waters, and the fish that has been caught several times is unquestionably more wary. Our club water on the Brodheads in Pennsylvania is managed on a fly-only no-kill basis, and it is heavily fished by our members. Comparison of our fishing logs with the Henryville House register seventy-five years ago demonstrates that our fishing is fully equal to the sport of earlier years, except that we rarely kill a trout these days.

During our last spring outing, when the members and their families gathered for a picnic and annual meeting, more than three hundred trout averaging a pound were caught. None were killed in the weekend of fishing, and the best trout was an estimated four pounds. Public water downstream cannot provide such fishing, yet it is more heavily stocked over the season. The difference lies in the philosophy of stream management.

Any discussion about releasing trout always triggers a number of counter arguments against the practice. Most men contend that if they do not kill the fish, someone else will later. This is often true, but they still have enjoyed the sport of catching them, and two fishermen have utilized a single tax dollar.

There is no question that catching a trout adds to its shyness, provided we release the fish to benefit from the experience, and it may put a trout beyond the reach of men less skilled than the angler who first released it. Some fishermen will grant this point, but argue that it makes the trout too difficult to catch. It is a strange argument born of laziness rather than logic. Its emphasis is on easy fishing, rather than the challenging and difficult sport we all love, and any fisherman who really knows the bountiful cornucopia of wilderness fishing, as well as the sophistication of a selective trout on hard-fished waters, will invariably choose the satisfaction that comes with a measure of success on hard-fished waters.

The final argument against catch-and-release management is that the fish die anyway. Research has long since proved this argument false, and over the years I am fully satisfied that a fly-caught trout almost always survives when released properly.

Several studies of trout mortality under fishing pressure clearly demonstrate that the fish suffer a seventy percent mortality with natural baits, forty-five percent mortality with lures, and a two percent mortality with flies—without particular care in releasing them.

Many years ago I experimented with releasing trout on a small ranch pond in Colorado. It held about thirty trout from ten to twenty inches. Each fish surrendered a fragment of his dorsal, pectoral or caudal fin, and the exact nature of its surgery was recorded in a notebook. Each trout had its own page, complete with the data of its captures. No fish died from my handling, and many were taken several times a week. The fish were not handled with wet hands, contrary to the old wives' tale about dry hands damaging the protective slime covering their scales. The fish were also handled in a landing net, because its meshes give the fisherman a better grip on the fish with less squeezing. Dry hands help accomplish the same purpose, since a fish may be handled with less pressure than with wet hands. The threat of internal injuries is infinitely more serious than the risk of fungus from dry hands, and their possible damage to the protective slime of the fish.

Trout must be given time to fully recover. The fisherman must sometimes devote as much time to releasing his trout as he spends playing them. They must be held gently in the water, in a natural swimming position, until they wriggle free in their own time. This is the only way to release a fish, since a tired and frightened trout thrown back carelessly into the stream will seldom recover his equilibrium. Fish can be rocked forward and back, working the water through their gill structures when they are too weak to breathe themselves, in a form of artificial respiration. Stream trout should be held with their heads facing into the current while they recover. Gentle patience is the secret.

Some of the pond trout were caught almost forty times during the summer of my experiment, and the only brown trout in the pond was caught about once every two weeks. There was one brookie that succumbed three times in a single day's fishing. Catching and releasing these fish left occasional hook sores in their jaws, but their energy and fight were unimpaired; and the trout did indeed become increasingly difficult to catch.

The catch-and-release philosophy is sadly unpopular with a large majority of fishermen, even in regions that have outstanding examples of such management. The quality of the fishing on rivers like the Firehole and Madison in the Yellowstone, the Beaverkill and Amawalk in New York, the Bushkill and Young Woman's Creek in Pennsylvania, and the Au Sable in Michigan is a remarkable demonstration that no-kill and fly-only regulations can provide first-rate sport under the fishing pressures of present urban populations. The special management on the Henry's Fork of the Snake, which limits the killing of fish to only two fish per day and prohibits the killing of anything over fourteen inches, is a remarkable success. Its smooth currents literally boil with big, selective trout during a hatch.

Yet there are still local agitators in each of these states who want such special management streams opened to the bait and hardware fishing that would quickly ravage the fine trout populations that enlightened management has built up in recent years. It is tragic that some men cannot look down from a bridge and see trout without wanting to slaughter them. The frontier myth and the theology of endless abundance die slowly.

Such rapacity and greed are a legacy we can no longer afford in an America of more than two hundred million people. Yet I still see men who call themselves outdoorsmen point with pride to creelsful of small trout, even on big western rivers where the limit in pounds, if one wishes to kill his trout, is regularly possible in only three or four fish. It is surprising that seven- and eight-inch trout are large enough to satisfy the mindless greed and self-indulgence that seem to motivate those who must strive to kill baskets full of trout.

It is an attitude that must end.

Somehow our fishermen seem to think there is a relationship between fishing-license fees and the hatchery trout they should be permitted to catch and creel. Resident license fees are seldom more than five dollars, and tourist licenses are from ten to twenty dollars. Considering the fact that trout cost from two to three dollars for every pound of fish stocked, these greedy fishermen cannot help but see that the license costs cannot cover the propagation and stocking costs of hatchery trout. License fees will seldom cover a single day's limit of fish, and there is no extra money for enforcement and research and other costs. The fish-hog fisherman costs everyone money, ruining future sport for himself as well as others. Few things are as empty as trout streams without trout.

Our problems are unquestionably a matter of ethics and self-discipline. William Michael phrased it perfectly in *Dry-Fly Trout Fishing*, when he defined it as a matter of limiting our kill instead of killing our limit. Our country may have more than three hundred million people before the close of this century, and regulations restricting both our fishing attitudes and our catch are the only method we have to provide anything but echoes of past public fishing. Our tradition has always been one of public fishing, unlike the completely private trout streams of Europe, where fishing rights began as the prerogative of royalty and the nobility. It is the egalitarian tradition to which we all subscribe, but we must extend our fly-only no-kill philosophy to much of our remaining trout waters, if we are to preserve public fishing of any real quality.

Fishery management in our national parks clearly proves this argument. Their regulations are not warped by the myopic pressures of local know-nothing clubs and have long been designed to provide good fishing even under heavy vacationing pressure. Their success is obvious. Few rivers can boast that their present fishing is better than it was twenty-five years ago, yet this is true of virtually all fly-fishing-only water.

Opinions vary widely on what constitutes good trout fishing, and the polarity of these arguments lies between the meat-and-potatoes school that is fascinated with the huge catches possible on wilderness water and the classical school that seeks the difficult and intriguing sport of outwitting selective fish on streams not far from our cities.

Both modern stream management and experiments in habitat improvement have pointed the way to better trout fishing, but many of our rivers are almost past reclaiming. Pollution and fishing pressure, with crowds trampling the banks, littering the river, and slaughtering the trout, have all taken their tragic toll. More and more water is being posted, because of thoughtless fishermen and the impossibility of finding either solitude or decent sport on public water. We have no one to blame for the loss of such water except ourselves and our fish management.

Solitude may not be possible within easy reach of our major urban centers, and anything approaching real sport with crowds is at the mercy of regulations and manners. The success of private water is obvious. Our Brodheads mileage is fished by fifty members and totals less than five miles. Its pools are all taken on a crowded weekend, and the highly skilled membership could easily fish it out in a season. Unlike most private clubs, we stock few trout and kill less than one hundred fish per season, and only flies are legal. Stocking is limited to between 750 and 1,000 brown trout per season, yet we regularly catch as many as 6,000 to 8,000 fish. Improving habitat and catch-and-release fishing mean that we catch $6,000 to $8,000 worth of trout for $1,000 worth of annual stocking in costs. Given an average winterkill, we still have at least $500 worth of carry-over trout left the following spring. It is an equation that clearly works—and there is public water a few miles downstream that has been barren of fish for years. Philosophy is our secret, since the water chemistry of the Brodheads is practically identical on both stretches of the river.

Such regulations should not be applied in blanket terms to all trout waters. It is pointless to manage marginal trout habitat with fly-only no-kill regulations, since such regulations have been conceived to build a long-term sustaining population. Such marginal water does not support trout through an entire season, and should not be stocked with Salmonidae at all, except for perhaps a short-term harvest of hatchery trout with put-and-take regulations in early season. Fly-only and no-kill policy is best suited to quality streams with good sustaining populations and viable spawning, and streams having a character particularly suited to wading and fly-fishing. Bigger water might be open to other methods, except those rivers suited to float fishing and flies. Small brush-sheltered streams are often ideally suited to bait fishing or for children, unless they should be closed as primary spawning and nursery tributaries. Each river and its tributaries is a unique management problem, its singular rhythms suited to different species of trout and varied regulations. Trout lakes also have varied character, and only those with shallows rich in fly life are best suited for special regulations. Big reservoirs could provide open fishing with less restrictive management, and overpopulated back-country lakes could often actually improve with the killing of more trout, in an attempt to balance the stunted fish with the relative scarcity of food.

But enlightened management is only half the battle in providing good sport on many overcrowded rivers. Stream manners are becoming a critical problem with the coming of vast crowds to many public waters. Breaches of common courtesy are common on the stream these days, and courtesy is scarcely possible in the elbow-to-elbow crowds of the typical opening day. Stream etiquette in the past was always carefully taught to each succeeding generation, but such tutelage has too often been lost in the explosive postwar growth of fly-fishing.

The rules of fishing etiquette are logical and simple.

Elbow room is one of the basic principles of stream manners. Any pool or reasonably definable reach of water belongs to the first person fishing it, and if he is fishing upstream or down, it is inconsiderate to start fishing ahead of him. The distance between you and another fisherman varies with the size of the river, the character of adjacent pools or holding places, the quality of the fishing, and how well you may know him. One hundred feet is perhaps a minimal buffer zone.

The stationary or slow-moving fisherman has the right to remain where he chooses. You should carefully leave the river and walk around him, taking care not to wade noisily or pass too close to either the fisherman or his trout. You should never walk along a bank in plain view of his fish as I have seen too many fishermen do thoughtlessly. There is a fine pool on a famous eastern river not far from New York that has three separate holding zones in its one hundred-yard length. Its spreading tail shallows hold a good number of selective free-rising browns that are always challenging. The middle spine of the pool is a strong smooth-flowing run with fish lying between its deepest reaches and the shallows along the bankside path. The throat of the pool is a strong chute, and its fish are less selective. The fish in the lower reaches of the pool are so wary that they can often occupy a good fisherman for hours. Since the streamside path drops down to the middle of the pool, and borders most of the pool in plain view of the fish, it is a typical place for a second angler to walk toward the head of the pool without realizing that he has ruined the fishing in the tail shallows. The fish quickly bolt from the shallows along the path, scattering into the middle and tail of the pool, soon putting the others down.

Standing beside a pool in a white shirt or other reflective clothing is equally bad manners. Leaning over a bridge railing above an angler working a pool full of selective trout is thoughtless as well, as is walking past another fisherman in full silhouette against the sky, even some distance from the water he is fishing. Each of these mistakes can spoil the fishing for another angler.

Several years ago I was shooting a picture essay with *Life* magazine on a charming eastern trout stream. George Silk was the photographer, and he wanted a back-lit scene of a smooth pool at evening, with its far bank in shadows and the angler in the sun, all shot through the pale olive green lacework of early foliage. We located a deep smooth-flowing pool in later afternoon that gave us exactly the mood and setting he wanted. Two fish were rising steadily in its tail shallows.

The pool was at a ninety-degree bend in the river. The current riffled down a fifty-yard reach of fast water, turned against a bank of sheltering rhododendron, and shelved off into deeper water. The throat of the pool surged against the stones of the hillside, lost in dense shadows, and the hill itself was already in the shade, but the swift tail shallows were still in warm sunlight. The fish were both good browns, at least fifteen or sixteen inches, lying in plain view over the stony bottom. They were rising steadily.

Think you can fool one of them? Silk asked.

I can try, I laughed.

Okay, he said. *I'll shoot from here, directly into the light, and you stalk them on your knees from the tail shallows.*

Carefully, I worked infantry-style up the shallows until I was within easy range of the fish. From their porpoising rise forms, it looked like they were nymphing, but they soon proved selective. I tried several patterns without success.

I'd like to get slightly above you, Silk yelled. *Can I get across from the fish without scaring them?*

I think so, I answered. *Just stay behind that line of trees about thirty feet from the river and walk slowly past them.*

Okay, he agreed.

Silk shouldered into his camera gear and worked up through the trees in a half crouch. He was at least fifty feet from the two brown trout, and slightly above their feeding lies, when both fish bolted upstream into deeper water.

Where did they go? Silk asked when he peered through the bushes above the run. *Can't see the fish anymore.*

They left, I said.

You mean I scared them from there?

Something scared them! I laughed. *I'm going to wade up there and you walk back along those trees.*

I waded upstream to the shallow run where the fish had been lying, and kneeled down in the current with my chin almost touching the water. Silk walked downstream along the treeline, his dark clothing blending with the leaves perfectly until he crossed a thin patch of branches and was strongly silhouetted against the evening sky. The fish had apparently seen him then.

It's my fault, I yelled. *I never dreamed those fish could see you that far back from the river—but they did!*

Too bad, he shook his head.

It was a lesson never forgotten, and it should always be remembered along the stream: never circle out around another fisherman without giving him an exaggerated berth, since trout are always more wary than you think.

Several weeks ago a good friend was fishing a long waist-deep flat just at twilight. He was starting a strategy I have often used myself on that piece of water. Several trout are often smutting toward the tail shallows, and I often occupy myself with them early in the evening, leaving the upper part of the pool alone. It is a good system, since the shy fish toward the middle and head of the pool are often more easily taken after they've settled undisturbed into their evening feeding rhythms. My friend was saving the upper currents for later, while he toyed with the selective free-rising trout working just above him in the shallows.

I was fishing another pool one hundred yards downstream when I watched another fisherman and his entire family settle into the meadow just across from my friend for a supper picnic. It was far from a quiet scene. The children ran up and down the meadow without a trace of discipline, throwing rocks into the pool and even slapping the shallows with a dead branch. There was yelling and shouting and the inevitable banshee-wailing that accompanies a hurt elbow or battered knee, and the parents uttered no word of either guidance or reprimand. It was quite a carnival, considering that no one had asked my friend if they might intrude on both his solitude and his sport.

Miraculously, he had taken three or four of the selective trout working in the tail shallows some seventy feet away, and the trout in the upper reaches of the pool had also forgotten about the rock throwing before supper. Several fish were just beginning to rise regularly, and my friend was starting to wade quietly upstream toward the middle of the pool when the man collected his rod and waded out thirty-five feet above him.

Didn't you call him on it? I asked later.

Call him on what? my friend shook his head unhappily and laughed. *He broke so many rules of stream etiquette that I didn't know where to begin!*

It is a sad parable that does include several cardinal rules of trout-stream behavior. You never even watch a man fish a pool without asking if it disturbs him, let alone permit your family to conduct a free-for-all along the banks. You never get into a pool that is already being fished, even on the most crowded streams, without first asking the other fisherman's permission. You never get into the stream too near another fisherman, and you never get in ahead of him, no matter whether he is fishing upstream or down. You never hurry to get ahead of another angler, and try not to interfere with his sport in any way.

Noisy wading or wading into the principal holding lies of a pool is always poor manners, even when no one else is fishing there. It will disturb the trout more thoroughly than the normal passage of fishing the pool, which is thoughtless and unfair to the next angler, whoever he might be. Wading should always be patient and slow, both from consideration for others and because it will produce better results in your own fishing.

There are other similar transgressions of good streamside manners. Experienced anglers will often study a pool instead of fishing it blindly, and sometimes it is good practice to stop fishing and rest a pool for a few minutes. Such a fisherman has first priority on the pool he is studying or resting, and you should never start fishing without his permission. Most good anglers are courteous and generous toward others, and will even grant their permission to fish a pool they have been resting, if you have the good manners to stop where they are sitting and ask.

Traditionally, the dry-fly fisherman wading upstream has the right of way over a wet-fly man working down. It is a tradition that makes sense. Fishermen wading upstream are forced by the current to move slowly, cover far less water, and approach the trout from behind. Fish always face the currents and will see an angler fishing downstream more readily. His technique both covers and disturbs more water. The man working down with a wet fly or streamer should retire from the river and move unobtrusively around an angler fishing upstream.

Generosity along the stream extends itself to other things as well. There was a boyhood evening many years ago when I was casting over a big smooth-flowing reach of the Madison in the Yellowstone, and a man fishing across the river was catching fish regularly. There were a number of good fish working on my side of the river, but I had failed to touch them for more than an hour.

What're they taking? I finally asked in desperation.

Whitcraft! came the reply.

It was an unfamiliar fly pattern in those boyhood days, and when he caught two more fish I finally swallowed my pride.

What's a Whitcraft? I yelled back curiously.

Take it! The fisherman cast his fly past me and the leader drifted down against my legs.

I picked it up. *Can't do that*, I protested feebly.

Cut it off the tippet, he insisted. *Wouldn't have cast it over if I didn't mean for you to have it!*

Thanks! I clinched it to my tippet.

It was a fine evening, and we both took fish regularly in the one hundred yards of perfect dry-fly water. It was a lesson in generosity I have never forgotten, and I always try to give a taking fly to another fisherman if I have an extra pattern or two. Sometimes I have given my only taking fly to a stranger when I have already caught enough fish to satisfy me. It is a good rule to remember on any river.

Fishing together is often fine sport, but it has several basic rules of conduct. When you are invited to fish with someone, the invitation is limited to you alone, and you should not add anyone else to the party without his permission. Although fishing contests have become fashionable in recent years, particularly the famous salt-water tournaments and bass competitions, such a competitive spirit has absolutely no place in fly-fishing for trout. Our sport is not a contest between anglers, and status games over the biggest fish or the heaviest creel are totally outside a tradition of contemplative sport that traces its lineage to Father Walton.

The competition astream is not between fellow anglers, but between you and the most beautiful and difficult fish on earth; and its unique mixture of beauty and shyness and selectivity should be competition enough for any man.

Fishing invitations have another cardinal rule or two. Big water can permit two anglers to fish opposite sides of the river, while on small streams, a pair of fishermen can often fish alternate pools or holding places. There is something happy about fishing together with a really good friend, and an experienced angler takes as much pleasure in the success of his companion as he finds in his own luck. There is fine camaraderie in such fishing, comparing notes and solving problems together, although there is an opposite coin to such fellowship. The talkative fisherman who engages everybody along the stream in ill-timed monologues about tackle and experiences and theories is an unmitigated pest, interminably badgering friends and strangers alike.

Fishing talk is almost as much fun as fishing itself, but there are still many anglers who cherish solitude and silence on the river. Brief conversations with a fellow fly-fisherman are an obvious courtesy, but extended dialogues without invitation are another matter, and a stranger on the stream will soon let you know if he wants to debate your theories or would prefer fishing alone.

One unwritten rule lies in being taken to fish a new lake or reach of river by a friend. Such confidences are a sacred trust between fishing comrades, and it is a betrayal of that trust to show a secret place to another angler. Some old-time anglers valued such a confidence so highly that they would never fish a secret place again without the friend that first took them there. Although fewer and fewer such places exist, even in the high country of our western mountains, it is a spirit of courtesy that should prevail on all trout waters.

Similar respect should govern our attitude toward private water or public streams and lakes subject to special regulations such as fly-fishing only or no-kill water restricted to single-hook lures. Trespassing or violating the special-water regulations is unacceptable behavior among fly-fishermen, and such breaches of obvious courtesy utterly betray the ancient and honorable origins of our sport.

The courtesy of asking a landowner for permission to fish is usually observed and granted on most waters, sometimes with a small rod fee for a day's sport. We should always remember that private water is *not* stocked with fish raised in public hatcheries, and that taking a fish not paid for with public funds is not much different from stealing. Some fishermen poach private water with the mistaken belief that its fish are actually public property, often arguing that fishing from public road rights-of-way or bridges is legal. No state allows bridge or roadside fishing for reasons of traffic safety, but even if fishing from such public easements were legal, the fish themselves are still private property and not the natural spawn of the stream. Respect for private property includes other things too, like leaving both the banks and the stream itself free of litter, carefully closing all gates, particularly where there is livestock, being cautious with cookfires, and the ethic that always leaves a pool or campsite a little better than you found it.

There are some places where men must fish together in relatively close proximity. Pools on salmon rivers like the Narraguagus or the Miramichi, with their taking lies crowded when the fish are running, give a fisherman little chance of solitude. Similar crowds are found on steelhead rivers when the big sea-run rainbows are moving in, and several fishermen are often found on a single pool. The fly water on the Henry's Fork of the Snake is often crowded with men who like fishing over its frustratingly selective rainbows.

Let's leave, somebody groans in the gathering twilight. *Let's go find a few dumb fish someplace!*

The rules of etiquette in such fishing are geared to the techniques of covering the water. You cast quartering downstream across the current on steelhead and salmon, and work the fly around with a teasing rhythm through its fly swing. When a cast is fished out, the angler takes a step downstream and repeats it again, covering the entire pool with a series of concentric quarter-circles. Stream etiquette dictates that other anglers wait until the first man is about one hundred to two hundred feet down the pool, depending on its width and the average casting distance. The water is covered in a rotation system, with each angler fishing through in his turn.

There are some other unwritten rules about steelhead or salmon fishing. The man with a hooked fish has undisputed right-of-way, and his fellow anglers should stop fishing to give him all the room he needs.

The Henry's Fork is another problem. Its regulars stand patiently to fish in one place or cover surprisingly little water, since stealth and patience are its cardinal rules for success. Entering the river and wading to a fishing stand should be accomplished quietly, and your departure from the current should be equally circumspect, even when the selective rainbows have defeated you soundly.

There is also a code governing the final landing of a good fish. Spectators should keep well back and stay as motionless as possible to keep from frightening the hooked fish and prolonging its struggles. Several years ago I watched a good fly-fisherman playing a big brown in the straw-colored Nez Percé meadows of the Firehole. It was a fish of five or six pounds, hooked on a tiny dry fly with a cobweb-fine leader in a mirror-smooth flat. The fish had been patiently beaten, and it floundered weakly on the surface, but it still had enough strength to hang well out in the main current. The fisherman played it gingerly, managing his fragile tippet with cunning and skill, and the fish was about ready to surrender.

Best fish I've ever hooked, the fisherman said quietly when I stopped to watch. *It should go five or six pounds!*

Beautiful fish, I agreed.

Took a tiny twenty-two Adams, the man continued proudly. *Tied it myself over to Madison Campground last night!*

They like small flies on the Firehole, I said.

It's been some fight, the fisherman sighed happily. *It's only a 6X tippet and those weeds kept me worried!*

Pretty fine leader, I nodded in agreement.

The fish was finally coming now, circling weakly in the shallows, when a tourist car with Nebraska plates turned off the highway to the Fountain Freight Road in a cloud of dust and gravel. It roared off the road and rocked to a stop near the river, disgorging a man and a large covey of noisy children.

Look there! the man yelled. *He's got one!*

The grassy bank swarmed with children, and the big trout surged back toward midstream in terror. The fisherman looked at me and rolled his eyes in despair.

Hey mister! the father cackled with a false men's club friendliness. *What'd you use for bait?*

Dry fly, said the fisherman unhappily.

Big fish like that don't want no flies, the man laughed to his chattering children. *You need doughballs or nightwalkers.*

How 'bout cheese, screeched one of his older boys.

Good bait too! the man agreed.

It was a nightmare for the fisherman. His face was flushed with anger, but he said nothing and patiently worked the big fish back from the swift currents downstream. The children were throwing pebbles at each other now, racing around through the coarse-grass meadows, and a stone splashed into the shallows near the trout. It bolted back into the heavy currents at midstream. The angler groaned and patiently coaxed it into the shallows again.

Come on! I said to the tourists finally. *Corral your kids and keep them back from the bank!*

You own the river? the man said belligerently.

No, I said, *but all this yelling and running around isn't fair to this man—he could lose his big fish!*

The angler looked at me gratefully.

Hell! one of the children yelled at me, *that fish ain't big—you should see the carp we catch!*

Why don't you pull it in? the man asked.

The angler said nothing and worked the trout into the shallows along the bank. Its strength was spent now, and the fisherman was looking for a gravel bar to beach it when his nightmare reached its frustrating climax.

Here, mister! the man said helpfully and scuttled down the bank. *Let me give you a hand!*

Don't touch the leader! the angler screamed.

But the man ignored him and started hand-lining the fish toward the gravel. *You got him, daddy!* shrieked a pig-tailed little girl. *You got him!*

It was too much for the exhausted trout. It gathered its remaining strength into a final wrenching splash that sheared the fragile nylon like a cobweb and it was gone.

Hey mister, the girl said. *Your string broke!*

The helpless fisherman stared at her wordlessly, and finally he waded out of the shallows toward his car, shaking his head in despair as he passed me. His eyes were glazed with shock. The other man herded his children back into their car.

Can't catch fish with line that weak, I heard him tell his wife, who looked like a Martian with her hair full of plastic rollers.

It was an incident filled with almost bizarre exaggerations, but it has lessons for all anglers. You should never interfere with another fisherman who is into a fish, and you should never offer to net or gaff a fish for another angler unless he asks you. There is an unwritten rule among skilled fly-fishermen, particularly those who fish for trout and salmon, that landing a fish yourself is both the *moment critique* of our fishing and a gesture of homage to its beauty and sporting character. Helping net or gaff a fish for a stranger is always perilous, since the fish may escape in the final moments, and you will always be blamed, however wordlessly. Never assist another fisherman in landing his fish unless you are asked, and even if you are asked, decline unless you are really skilled and experienced. Remember that a fisherman who does not request your help is not necessarily selfish or unfriendly but playing a part in a tradition that believes a big trout or salmon is a quarry with almost mystical qualities, and deserves to meet its fate in a hand-to-hand struggle.

With the construction of many new reservoirs throughout the United States, the basic courtesies of trout fishing have become mixed with boating manners. It is poor form to crowd in close to a boat that is catching fish, just as it is bad manners to congregate along the river near a successful fisherman. Elbow room is part of common fishing courtesy on lakes and streams. It is also thoughtless to bang tackle boxes and bailing cans in the bottom of your boat, or row noisily with thumping or rattling oars, since these vibrations are transmitted directly into the water and can spoil the fishing for everyone. Throwing cans and bottles and aluminum can lids into a lake is unforgivable. The boat moving upwind has the right-of-way, and a stationary boat should always be passed slowly and given a minimum berth of two hundred feet. Since a stationary boat or fisherman on shore is disturbing far less water than a trolling boat, and its wake can disturb their fishing, the moving boat should circle out well around them or throttle back to pass. Anchors should be lowered and raised quietly in any fishable areas, both because it will mean better sport for your party, and because it is considerate of nearby boats. Such consideration also applies to arriving or leaving the fishing grounds. You should not come into a fishing area or leave it under rich-mixture throttle settings, or row noisily through productive water frightening the fish. These are simple things to remember along trout water, but it is surprising how often we forget them, and sometimes there are incidents that are unthinkable.

Several years ago I was fishing a small eastern stream in a lovely gorge of slate ledges. It was a sparkling morning in early summer, with the fresh new leaves moving against a cobalt sky. The phoebes were catching mayflies above a bright riffle that danced in the sunlight, and enough fish were rising to provide good sport. The fly hatch consisted of slate-colored *Paraleptophlebias*, and I was matching it with an eighteen Blue Quill dressed with sooty dun hackles. It was working consistently, and I had caught and released a dozen trout, working upstream slowly from the little clapboard hotel to the Footbridge Pool, where the trail into the gorge crossed the stream on a small suspension bridge.

There were several fish rising there, and I hooked and released a half dozen below the bridge. They were fat little browns not long from the hatchery truck, and they took the little dry fly eagerly. The cool wind eddied downstream, smelling of pine trees and laurel deep in the slate-walled gorge, and the solitude was pleasant.

Two boulders broke the smooth current below the cable-span, and I saw a fish rise softly in their current tongues.

That looks like a good fish, I thought happily.

The little Blue Quill was dried with a few quick false casts and I settled it along the eddying run. It danced down the current and disappeared in a quiet rise, and a twelve-inch brown bored upstream, stripping line noisily from the reel. It was a plucky fish and it fought stubbornly against the delicate leader tippet, and its struggle was resourceful, exploring and probing under the ledges upstream and searching out snags to foul the leader. Finally, it tired and I worked it downstream into the waiting net. It was a wild fish, fat and richly spotted above its pale orange belly. It struggled feebly while I freed it from the hook and lowered it gently into the current. It held in my fingers a moment and then splashed free.

The tiny fly was matted with slime, and I washed it carefully in the stream. Then I oiled it with silicone and let it dry a few moments before false casting it back into fishable condition. While it was darting lazily back and forth in the sunlight, I saw another good fish rise softly above the second boulder. The cast bellied out and dropped.

It rose and took without hesitation. *Pretty,* I thought.

The fish threshed in surprise when it felt the tiny hook, and it too bolted strongly upstream in the shadow of the ledge. It was heavier, and it was some time before I succeeded in working it back into the sun-dappled shallows. The fish surrendered stubbornly and I unhooked it carefully, holding it gently in the meshes.

Okay, mister! The voice was an angry explosion from the bushes above the bridge. *I've watched you let six or seven fish go since I've been standing here—and if you let that trout go too, you're in trouble!*

The man had startled me with his anger. *Why?* I stammered. *What's the matter with letting them go?*

Been fishing this creek since daylight! The man was huge and he came down to the stream, still shaking with agitation. *Ain't caught nothing all morning, and now when I'm walking down out of the valley, I have to watch you letting six or seven go!*

But I caught them, I protested, *and I can do whatever I want with the trout I catch. They're too beautiful to kill!*

Maybe, the man said sullenly, *but it's goddamn sure I don't have to watch you do it!* The fish was still in my net, and I lowered it carefully into the smooth current.

He's pretty tired, I said.

You ain't letting that fish go! The man came angrily into the stream. *You're giving it to me!*

No, I said quietly. *It's going back.*

The trout was frightened when the fisherman splashed toward me, and it fought free of my fingers. It held a moment below my waders and darted nervously upstream into the deep smooth-flowing throat of the pool where it was safe. The man stood in a rage, spluttering with anger and frustration. *Goddammit*, he shouted, *it ain't fair for you fancy-pants fly boys to fish and let your fish go—when a man like me ain't caught a trout all morning!*

I'm sorry about that, I said, *but a man has to catch his own trout—then you can decide to kill them or let them go.*

What's wrong with my gear? he asked.

It was a heavy spinning rod with a monofilament of about twenty-pound breaking strain on its reel. There were several split shot on the nylon, and a nightcrawler was laced on a big bait hook. It was pretty coarse tackle for hard-fished water.

The fish can see your nylon, I said, *and that's an awful lot of lead for a small stream like this one.*

You mean the trout are that smart?

Smart is the one thing trout really are, I smiled. *You have to sneak up on them like a deer or wild turkey.*

Well I'll be damned, he said.

You mean you haven't been concealing yourself from the fish? I asked. *You let them see you before you start fishing?*

Afraid so, he admitted.

Look, I said, *you get yourself some small hooks and a four-pound leader and use less split shot—sneak up on the pools and get your bait into the water quietly.*

You think that'll help catch fish? he asked.

It should. I nodded my head.

Thanks, the man extended his hand. *If it works out, I might even try some of them flies sometime.*

Good luck! I laughed.

It was an incredible episode, and there were moments when I thought I had a fight on my hands, but it codifies a whole galaxy of problems about trout fishing in our time. The streams and lakes and impoundments are being devoured these days by an explosion of people fishing for trout, without any background or understanding of either the character of the trout or the centuries of tradition surrounding the sport. Past experience with bass or walleyes or bluefish has not prepared them for the skittish behavior of a trout on hard-fished waters, and their experiences in fishing for other species provide no prologue to the poetry and ethic of trout fishing or its centuries of contemplative literature.

And these hordes will have no one to teach them its gentle truths in future years, no father or grandfather or uncle in baggy tweeds and worn sweater, with a closetful of exquisite split-cane rods and a library of well-thumbed fishing books. The world of primeval trees and crystalline little streams is dwindling, and our aspiring trout fishermen are condemned to finding riffles filled with bedsprings, beer cans, tires, milk bottles, golf clubs, bumper jacks, and other refuse. It is an unthinkable sickness of the mind that can push rusting farm machinery into a crystalline riffle, or jettison a half-dozen rotting truck tires into a beautiful pool. There was once a stretch of water on a famous eastern river we jokingly called the Plumbing Yard. It had a rusting bathtub, two shattered lavatories, an incredible palette of pipe fittings, and a broken water closet—once I even took a good brown trout that was nymphing in the concealment of its toilet seat. Somehow the dark currents along a mossy ledge or current-bleached deadfall would have provided a preferable setting.

The character of trout water is perhaps the most fascinating thing about our sport, and that character is always changing in the kaleidoscope of weather and the seasons.

The fish themselves hover in nervous flight above the intaglio of bright gravel and detritus and leaf drift that lies under a current as rich as a vintage chablis. Our hours along trout water are filled with streamside distractions, like a nervous phoebe catching mayflies in the April sunshine, or the deft scissor-swift patterns of swallows working on a hatch.

There are pelicans diving along the Yellowstone, primordial skeins of geese weaving north against a pale sky, scores of ducks feeding in a wilderness pond in the Jackson Hole country, and rutting elk bugling along the Firehole. The memory is rich with the river sounds, and the soft *pianissimo* sighing of the wind in the trees, and the melancholy calling of whippoorwills at twilight. The mind remembers the swift passage of a canoe among the cedar sweepers along the Au Sable, and the rhythmic music of oarlocks on the Madison and the MacKenzie. There was once a grizzly foraging among the watermelon rinds at a campground along the Gibbon, and an eagle circling lazily on the thermals, high above the wild rapids on the Middle Fork of the Salmon.

No sound is quite like the melodic cry of a loon on some mist-shrouded northern lake, and we all have heard the shrill cackle of a pheasant in a rich limestone valley, its brown trout porpoising lazily among smooth channels in the watercress and elodea. There are memories of flowering dogwoods along the Nantahala in the Smokies, and the strange intensity of the Wyoming sky on crisp September mornings above the New Fork and the Green. The gentleness of a doe and fawn wading a Boardman riffle at twilight in Michigan is mixed with memories of a great blue heron I startled from a swamp along the Namekagon, and the raccoons I watched catching crayfish along the Brule. There are sandhill cranes nesting along Silver Creek at Sun Valley, and ospreys still prey on small trout and fat dace on the Henry's Fork of the Snake. There was a mother bear with cubs crossing the swift Madison in Montana, and the memory of a three-pound brown on the Ausable is pleasantly mixed with the calling of warblers on Adirondack ridges. And a fishless evening in the Catskills was salvaged by the soft pine-sweet wind that came down the river just at dusk.

Each of these memories is as important as the fishing itself, and their enjoyment depends greatly on solitude and the consideration of others along the stream. Regard for the rights and enjoyment of fellow anglers is paramount, and the inconsiderate fisherman who shoulders in when you have taken a fish, wades rudely through a pool you are fishing, or tries for a trout you are resting is a thoughtless boor.

The skilled fly-fisherman does not hesitate to pack-saddle his part of the duffel or fill his time on a portage between lakes. Such anglers always dress their share of the trout, peel and slice the potatoes, or scour the dirty skillets in the sand. There are no secret fly patterns or tactics, and a true angler will always help a less-experienced fisherman in any way he can, with no jealousy of the competition that might result. Generosity and brotherhood are the hallmarks of fly-fishing, and many close friendships are made along trout water. There is no caste system along our lakes and tumbling trout-country streams. Given enough skill in the presentation, a selective fish will rise as unwittingly to the imitation clumsily dressed in some farmhouse along the river as it will roll to take the exquisite woodduck-winged pattern fished by the wealthy banker or stockbroker or chairman of the board.

Trout fishing at its best is a gentle art, both humbling and satisfying. Trout fishing demands far more than its sister sports that the angler escape the threnodic rhythms of his mind, and lose himself in its secret clues and rhythms like Adam and Eve returning to Eden. Many who pursue the sport never discover the riches of its subtle universe, but those who engage in its refinements and complexities are never without rich memories and the satisfactions that come with anything done well.

Walton observed more than three centuries ago that angling was a contemplative sport, best attuned to the poetic moods and pastoral rhythms of life. His classic *Compleat Angler* added that a man who would become a skillful angler must combine the qualities of searching intelligence and powers of observation, but also a good measure of curiosity and optimism and patience. It might be argued that patience itself is the single most important quality in the character of a fly-fisherman. It is equally true in our time of hard-fished waters and the cacophony of urban life. Our ethics and manners and philosophy play an increasingly critical role in the modern practice of our sport—and to Walton's historic prescription of hope and patience we must add the spice called charity.

Many people ask me why I fish, and beyond the obvious qualities of trout and trout country and enjoyment, it is a perplexing question. Haig-Brown put it perfectly in his conclusion of *A River Never Sleeps*, when he confessed that he did not know why he fished, or why others shared his passion, except that it made them think and feel.

Perhaps it is simply the beauty of fly-fishing. Such beauty is rare in the cacophony and ugliness that too often fill our lives, and trout fishing is often beautiful. Its skills are a perfect equilibrium between tradition, physical dexterity and grace, strength, logic, esthetics, our powers of observation, problem solving, perception, and the character of our experience and knowledge. It also combines the primordial rhythms of the stalk with the chesslike puzzles of fly-hatches and fishing, echoing the blood rituals of the hunt without demanding the kill. Its subtle mixture of these ancient echoes and our increasing reverence for life make it unique.

Fly-fishing is remarkably beautiful in a time when such beauty is becoming more and more precious, perhaps essential to both the quality of our lives and our survival itself.

Its beauty exists in a lexicon of peripheral riches: its overtones of history and tradition, several centuries of paintings and books, its patina of split-cane rods and reels and wicker creels, the obvious elegance of its fly-boxes and flies, the patient ballet of fly lines working in the rain, mornings and bright-skied afternoons and twilight, the symmetrical perfection of a blood knot, weather and wind, cottonwood leaves in the current, the rich palette of hackles and pheasant skins and tinsel on our fly-dressing tables, the choreography of barn swallows capturing a hatch of flies, the shrill music of the reel, the fish themselves, and their bulging rises over bright gravel.

Poets are the voices that best capture the rich character of trout and trout country, and our sport is worthy of their skills. The perspective of time teaches us that the essence of fly-fishing, and the lyric qualities of both rivers and their trout, are seldom found in books about fish and fishing techniques and fly-hatches. Fishing images are found in the work of such disparate poets as John Donne and William Butler Yeats and Ezra Pound, but the most evocative images perhaps lie in the little-known *Pied Beauty*, in the nineteenth-century work of Gerard Manley Hopkins:

> Glory be to God for dappled things—
>   For skies as couple-color as a brinded cow
> For rose-moles all in stipple
>   Upon trout that swim.

INDEX

233